D0848485

On the Trail of the Yorks

On the Trail of the Yorks

Kristie Dean

AMBERLEY

This book is dedicated to my husband and my family for always supporting me.

First published 2016

Amberley Publishing
The Hill, Stroud
Gloucestershire, GL5 4EP

www.amberley-books.com

Copyright © Kristie Dean, 2016

The right of Kristie Dean to be identified as the Author of this work has been asserted in accordance with the Copyrights, Designs and Patents Act 1988.

All rights reserved. No part of this book may be reprinted or reproduced or utilised in any form or by any electronic, mechanical or other means, now known or hereafter invented, including photocopying and recording, or in any information storage or retrieval system, without the permission in writing from the Publishers.

British Library Cataloguing in Publication Data.
A catalogue record for this book is available from the British Library.

ISBN 978 1 4456 4713 5 (hardback)
ISBN 978 1 4456 4714 2 (ebook)

Typesetting and Origination by Amberley Publishing.
Printed in the UK.

Contents

Acknowledgments

I would like to thank the following people for their contributions towards helping make this book a reality:

Amboise: Mark Métay, Executive Director

Berkhamsted Castle: Linda Rollitt, Berkhamsted Local History & Museum Society Former Archivist

Bewdley: Heather Flack, Historian

Calais: Christmas Gavignet, Service Manager Archive Service; Joseline Aubert, Benoit Diéval and François Lurette, Marketing

Cerne Abbey: Wayne Lewin, Clerk to Cerne Valley Parish Council; Fulford-Dobson Family

Collegiate Church of St Mary, Warwick: Glynis Nixon

Coventry: Richard Briggs, Continuum Attractions, Group Head of Development; Kathy Byrne, Team Leader, Priory Visitor Centre

Ewelme: Revd Jonathan Meyer, Priest in Charge – Ewelme Benefice; Carol Sawbridge, Ewelme Society, Village Historian

Grafton Regis: Judy Kendrick-Simonsen

Leicester Cathedral: Liz Hudson, Communications Director and Bishop's Press Officer; Keith Cousins, Media Officer

Little Malvern: The Rev'd Cannon Eric G. Knowles

Low Countries: Hans van Felius, Senior Archivist at the Noord-Hollands Archief, Haarlem, the Netherlands

Mechelen: Dieter Viaene, Archivist, City Archives of Mechelen; St Rombout's Cathedral: Bram van der Auwera

Montgomery Castle: Jeff Spencer, Historic Environment Record Officer

Palace of Sheen/Shene: Bev Kerr, Council for British Archaeology

Rouen Cathedral: Guillaume Gohon, Historics Furnitures of the Cathedral to the Archbishop of Rouen

Tutbury Castle: Judith Collision; Lesley Smith, Curator

Trim Castle: Tony Roche, Photographic Unit

Westminster Hall: Pooja S. Avlani, Media and Communication Assistance, House of Commons

Worcester Cathedral: Christopher Guy, Worcester Cathedral Archaeologist

Winchester Cathedral: Jo Bartholomew, Curator and Librarian

Wingfield Church: Revd Canon Andrew Vessey and Revd Michael Womack

I'd also like to once again express gratitude to those people who helped me with the initial research for locations and who were acknowledged in *The World of Richard III*. I would like to thank my husband, Jonathan, who allows my writing to dictate our schedule. I would also like to thank my parents, Gary and Dianah, for always supporting me, and my brother and sister-in-law, Matt and Kayla, for continuously allowing family conversations to centre on writing. I also appreciate my mother-in-law, Jo Ann, who always offers assistance, and my father-in-law, Alan, who always enquires on my progress. I would also like to express thanks to my aunt and uncle, Betty and Randall DeVault, for their support of my travels.

Thanks to Valerie Brook for her research assistance and to Autumn Speegle for patiently waiting while I would walk every inch of each location. James Spears, thank you for your photographic genius! I would also like to take this time to acknowledge Sharon Bennett Connolly (a wonderful translator) and Anne Marie Bouchard, co-administrators of my Facebook group, *Richard III and His World*, for their time and support. Wendy Dunn, Susan Higginbotham, Amy Licence, Geanine Teramani-Cruz, Diana Milne, Danny Newman and Lisl Zlitni, your help was invaluable! Elizabeth Milne of Lady White Art, thank you for your work on the maps. To all of my friends and family, thank you for everything. Finally, I would like to thank the team at Amberley for their support, especially my editor, Annie Campbell.

York Family Tree

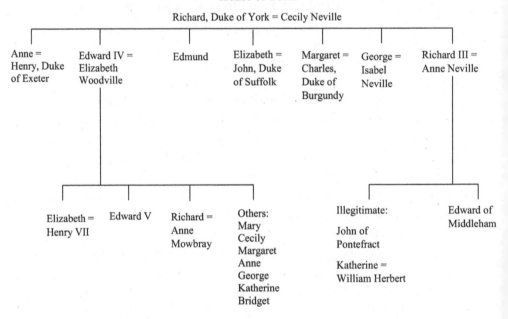

House of York

Richard, Duke of York = Cecily Neville

Anne =
Henry, Duke
of Exeter

Edward IV =
Elizabeth
Woodville

Edmund

Elizabeth =
John, Duke
of Suffolk

Margaret =
Charles,
Duke of
Burgundy

George =
Isabel
Neville

Richard III =
Anne Neville

Elizabeth =
Henry VII

Edward V

Richard =
Anne
Mowbray

Others:
Mary
Cecily
Margaret
Anne
George
Katherine
Bridget

Illegitimate:

John of
Pontefract

Katherine =
William Herbert

Edward of
Middleham

Note: While the Duke of York and
Cecily had several children, only those
who survived childhood are shown in
the table.

Map of England, Wales and Ireland

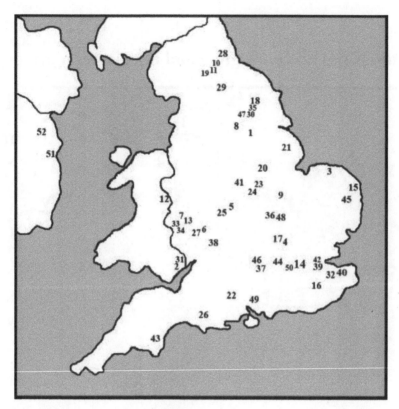

Map of France, Belgium and the Netherlands

Locations in France, Belgium and the Netherlands

1	Rouen, France	6	Damme, Belgium
2	Angers, France	7	Bruges, Belgium
3	Amboise, France	8	Brussels, Belgium
4	Calais, France	9	Ghent, Belgium
5	Sluis, the Netherlands	10	Mechelen, Belgium

Introduction

When I finished *The World of Richard III*, I was left with a nagging feeling that locations associated with Richard III's family also deserved exploration. Richard is a fascinating historic figure, but his family members are equally intriguing. I knew some sites would repeat from the first book because Richard and his family would have places in common. However, at each of these locations, Richard's family would have their individual histories to explore too. Many other sites presented themselves that were unique to certain family members.

Because I felt that most people purchasing a book on the York family would expect to see a chapter on arguably its most famous member, I decided to incorporate a section on Richard. While I knew it would be impossible to include every spot associated with all family members in one book, I have attempted to place the Yorks in locations that were important to them while trying to include as many extant sites as possible.

While I was researching the section on Elizabeth of York, I found evidence that caused me to agree with Alison Weir about the location of Elizabeth's body after her death. While many historians say that Elizabeth's body was taken to the Chapel of St John the Evangelist in the Tower, early sources say that her body was taken to the Tower's parish church, which would have been St Peter ad Vincula.

As with *The World of Richard III*, I have chosen not to use footnotes or endnotes due to the nature of the book. However, this does not indicate a lack of research. I have travelled to almost every site in the book, and I have talked with local historians, archivists, and authors to gather the necessary research. I have also extensively read both primary and secondary sources, both about the family member and each location.

Designed to bring the history of each setting alive, the goal of this book is to help both the armchair traveller and visitor alike place each location in the historical context of the York family. In addition, it will provide a backdrop of the site's history prior to their arrival.

I thoroughly enjoyed visiting the places associated with each family member, and I hope this excitement is evident in each section. For the extant locations, I tried to include relevant travel information, like phone numbers or websites. As always, phoning ahead or checking the website is advised since many of the sites may close at short notice. As you plan your travels, I wish you as much fun as I enjoyed exploring the world of the Yorks.

How to Use This Guidebook

The book has been organised with portions on each family member, with every section arranged in a loose chronological framework. Since several family members have associations with the same locations, I have endeavoured to place the site with the family member for whom it made the most sense. For example, the portion on Warwick falls under George, Duke of Clarence, even though Anne Neville was born there. However, the parish church in Warwick is found in the section on Anne. While I discussed Rouen in the portion on Richard, Duke of York, I placed the segment on Rouen Cathedral with Edmund. When this happens, I have noted it inside each section. When several family members have had an association with a site, I have included the history of all the family members in that location's section. So, even though Warwick is placed under Clarence, I discuss all the York family history with the castle. As Richard and Anne, Edward and Elizabeth, and Elizabeth of York all had coronations, I placed the coronation information with Elizabeth of York since she was the last of the family to experience the ceremony.

Each entry is meant to be able to stand alone as its own guide, as well as to be part of the greater whole. Readers can explore the various sections when they travel without losing the benefit of the entire book. This means that at certain times, historical facts may be repeated across sections if they relate to more than one family member or location. Buckingham's rebellion is one such fact.

I have tried to examine as many extant locations as possible, but felt that it was important to include locations that influenced each family member even if they no longer exist or are no longer accessible. To this end, I have included places that have no visible remains and locations that are now privately owned.

Contact information is given at the end of each section so that readers can easily locate current opening times, prices and directions. In some locations, I have also included any travel information I have felt might be pertinent, like ease in parking.

Part 1
Richard, Duke of York

Richard, 3rd Duke of York, was a powerful magnate and political force in the fifteenth century. Although one of the richest magnates in England, his political struggles against the Lancastrians are well documented. Unfortunately he would not live to see two of his sons crowned king, but it was through his granddaughter Elizabeth that the two rival parties would be joined together in marriage.

Conisbrough Castle, South Yorkshire

Perched on a hilltop beside the River Dun (Don), Conisbrough Castle is a sight to behold. Its importance in the history of the York family lies in its ties to the Duke of York through his father, Richard of Conisbrough.

This Richard was born here. The second son of Edmund of Langley and his wife, Isabella of Castile, Richard became Earl of Cambridge in 1414. He was knighted in 1406 in preparation for his trip to escort Princess Philippa to her marriage to Erik, King of Denmark. However, his influence in the government was slight because he had neither extensive lands nor power. A marriage to Anne Mortimer produced a son, also named Richard, who would become heir to both the York and Mortimer inheritances. Anne died soon after Richard's birth, and the Earl of Cambridge remarried, this time to Maud Clifford.

Perhaps driven by bitterness, Richard of Conisbrough instigated a plot against the king in 1415. Once the plot was exposed, he was beheaded. Luckily for his minor son, he was not attainted and the young Richard inherited. A few months later, Edward of York died, his titles and lands also passing to his young nephew.

Since his stepmother, Maud, used Conisbrough for one of her residences, York would have rarely stayed here. After her death, Conisbrough began its slow decline into ruin.

Conisbrough Castle History

A large curtain wall, approximately 7 feet thick and containing several towers, enclosed the castle, with a deep fosse adding an additional measure of security. On his visits, the Duke of York would have entered the inner bailey through a gatehouse. Once inside, he would have seen a hall constructed to the north-west about 60 feet from the keep. Nearly 70 feet long, it would have been impressive. When it was first built, the hall was heated by a central hearth, but later a fireplace was added for comfort. The hall abutted the grand chamber, which was the main apartment for the lord.

The keep was built in the twelfth century by Hamelin, half-brother to Henry II. Here on the site of the original earth-and-timber fortification, Hamelin constructed a cylindrical five-storey tower of dressed ashlar, rising 90 feet in the air and measuring more than 60 feet in diameter. Six wedge-shaped stone buttresses were added to ensure its stability.

Access to the keep was by a grand staircase of more than thirty steps on the south-west side. Once inside, a visitor would have seen a trapdoor which led to the well below. The chamber on the next floor was ornate, with an immense fireplace described by John Wainwright in the nineteenth century as 'ornamented by a low triple or clustered pillar on each side, with capitals of corresponding character, highly-finished; the mantel piece is twelve feet long'. The room also contained a latrine, which emptied outside the curtain wall.

A staircase wound its way up to the next floor, which was equally impressive. This floor contained a small chapel, built into the buttress. The chapel was approximately 13 feet long and vaulted with arches, crossed by zig-zag ribs resting on plain round pillars. The spiral staircase led on up to the battlements, which included a rooftop wall walk, with a commanding view of the countryside filled with rolling hills and valleys. According to English Heritage, in addition to the chapel, the other buttresses contained a pigeon loft, a cistern and an oven.

Visiting Conisbrough Castle Today

The castle, while ruined, is an excellent example of a cylindrical keep. The keep was reroofed in the late twentieth century with additional reconstruction done recently. Following the extensive refurbishment, the castle reopened in 2014. Visitors today are in for a treat because the keep now boasts a restored roof and floors. On each floor, the story of Hamelin and his wife, Isabel, is told through wall projections. A visitor centre is also available to help a visitor place the castle in its historical context.

Conisbrough is approximately five miles from Doncaster. If driving, the castle offers a small, free car park. The castle may be reached by bus or train, with a short walk from the town. For prices and opening times, visit the castle's website at http://www.english-heritage.org.uk/daysout/properties/conisbrough-castle/prices-and-opening-times. Postcode: DN12 3BU.

Usk Castle, Monmouthshire, Wales

Situated on the banks of the winding River Usk, the ruins of Usk Castle belie its great heritage. Only remnants are left today of the once great fortress in the heart of Monmouthshire. The stone castle was begun by Richard de Clare, and the Norman gatehouse was also likely his work. William Marshal, who today is known by the sobriquet 'the Greatest Knight', received the castle through his marriage to Isabel de Clare. According to the castle, he probably built the formidable Garrison Tower.

During the reign of Edward II, the castle came into the hands of the powerful Despenser family through the marriage of Eleanor de Clare, the king's niece, and Hugh Despenser the Younger. Following the downfall of the Despensers, the castle passed to Elizabeth de Burgh, and from her to another Elizabeth, who married Lionel, Duke of Clarence, the son of Edward III and Philippa of Hainault. The child of this union, Philippa, married Edmund Mortimer, 3rd Earl of March. It was from this marriage that the castle would eventually fall into the hands of York.

In the opening decade of the fifteenth century, Owain Glyn Dŵr (Owen Glendower) led a widespread rebellion against the English in Wales, and Usk Castle did not escape the violence. However, it is believed that the castle held out against the rebels, who lost the subsequent Battle of Usk. Glyn Dŵr was never captured but is believed to have died while hiding from the English.

Some writers in the nineteenth century mistakenly believed Usk Castle to be the birthplace not only of Edward IV but also Richard III. However, Edward was born in Rouen, while Richard was born at Fotheringhay.

York was at Usk in March 1434. On other occasions, he and Cecily would have stayed at Usk while visiting his holdings in Wales. While there is not much of the castle left today, its association with the Duke of York makes it worth a visit.

Visiting Today

The castle is usually open during daylight hours. From the fire station, take the lane opposite to the castle. To the right of the stone archway is a kiosk where you should be able to find a castle guide. For more information, call +44 (0) 1291 672563 or visit the website at http://www.uskcastle.com/Visiting-Landing. Usk Castle postcode: NP15 1SD.

Rouen, France

Settled initially by the Romans, the area was later inhabited by Germanic tribes. Soon, the abundant riches of the area attracted the eye of the Vikings, who made intermittent attacks before seizing the land, which became known as Normandy. After William the Conqueror invaded England the area was under English control until King John lost the city to the French in 1204. For the next century, Rouen was a French city until the Hundred Years War changed everything. Rouen surrendered in 1419 to Henry V and would remain under English control until 1449.

In June 1441, the Duke of York, accompanied by his wife, Cecily, arrived in Rouen. It was not York's first time in France, but this time his appointment as Lieutenant Governor was for five years. Cecily travelled with him, apparently not willing to be separated from her husband for an extended time.

As Richard and Cecily arrived at this city, resting on the banks of the Seine, which would serve as their home for the next several years, they would have known that this was an opportunity for Richard to prove himself. While they rode along Rouen's narrow streets, the recent death of their son Henry may have been fresh in their minds. Perhaps Richard saw this move as a new start for his family.

Rouen Castle

After he gained control of the city from the English in 1204, Philip Augustus (Philip II) set about consolidating his power base in the area. According to the Franco-British Cooperation Project, the site he chose for his castle was atop the remains of the Roman amphitheatre on Bouvreuil Hill, overlooking the city.

Richard and Cecily would have entered the castle via a bridge over the moat. Circular with ten towers, including a half tower and the donjon, which was built on the curtain wall, the castle was a formidable building, with thick, impregnable walls.

Soon after arriving in Rouen, Cecily became pregnant with the future Edward IV, who was born on 28 April 1442. Years later, controversy would surround Edward's legitimacy, but his birth was not controversial at the time. He was christened within one of the small chapels set within the castle. He may have been premature, which would explain why he did not have the same type of elaborate christening his brother Edmund received. Within the next two years, two additional children would be born to Richard and Cecily – Edmund, in May 1443, and Elizabeth, in April 1444.

During this time, decisions were being made back in England which would impact York's job on the Continent. John Beaufort, Duke of Somerset, was appointed to bring an army to help the commanders in Normandy. His expedition frustrated York because it diverted both funds and power away from him. The expedition was a failure, and the council was quick to try to mollify York.

Soon afterwards, negotiations were finalised for a match between Margaret of Anjou, a niece of Charles VII of France, and Henry VI. Around the same time, there was talk of a marriage between Charles VII's daughter and York's heir, Edward, but this never reached more than the discussion phase. In one particular letter to Charles VII, York discusses which daughter he thought most suited to Edward. Charles had suggested his daughter Magdalene (Madeleine), but York thought her too young and asked about the possibility of another daughter, Joanna.

In 1445, escorted by York, Margaret of Anjou stopped in Rouen on her way to England. Cecily, as the Lieutenant Governor's wife and the highest-ranking Englishwoman, would have received and entertained her. Although Margaret was supposed to enter Rouen in ceremonial splendour, she was too sick to do so. Margaret spent several days in Rouen before York accompanied her on the next stage of her journey.

Visiting Today
All that is left to visit is the La Tour Jeanne d'Arc, which was the donjon (keep) of the castle. The tower received its name because Joan of Arc was questioned here. Visitors can explore the keep, with its vaulted ceilings and its several exhibitions. Most are about Joan of Arc, but a replica of the castle and stained glass believed to be from its chapel are also on display. There is also a model of the city in the early fifteenth century which gives an idea of how it would have appeared to Richard and Cecily. Be sure to take time to walk around the keep to get an idea of its layout in the castle. For more information about visiting the tower, see the website at http://www.rouen.fr/tour-jeanne-darc. Postcode: 76000.

Rouen Cathedral will be discussed in the chapter on Edmund. One other interesting site that Richard and Cecily would have seen while in Rouen is the Grosse Horloge Clock. While the clock itself is from 1389, the facing is from a later period. The two fourteenth-century bells are known by the names La Rouvel and Cache Ribaut. There are two legends around the naming of La Rouvel. One is that it is known as the silver bell because silver coins were tossed into its mould. Another is that it has so much tin in it that it has a clear colour.

Trim Castle, Ireland

York was appointed to the lieutenancy of Ireland in 1447, but it would be two years before he landed on Ireland's shores. When he did land at Howth, he was greeted with 'great honour, and the earls of Ireland went into his house … and gave him as many beeves (beef) for the use of his kitchen as it pleased him to demand'. Hall says that Richard received 'such love and favour of the country and the inhabitants, that their sincere love and friendly affection could never be separated from him and his lineage'.

York spent much of his time at Dublin Castle. This castle will be explored in further detail in the section on George, Duke of Clarence, since it was his birthplace. However, York also spent quite a bit of time at Trim Castle in County Meath.

When Hugh de Lacy was granted the Liberty of Meath in the twelfth century, he built a wooden fortification here at Trim. Soon, a stone castle replaced the wooden one, and it was eventually surrounded by a curtain wall and enclosed by a moat.

As he approached the castle, York would have seen the River Boyne gently lapping at the side of the castle. The portcullis would have been raised so he could pass through the forward tower, cross over the drawbridge and enter through the arched gatehouse. The thick walls of the soaring keep, at 105 feet high, would have immediately caught his eye. If arriving by river, he would have docked near the River Gate and made his way via the stairs to the solar. According to the castle, several canals gave access for boats to get close to the castle and dock in its harbour.

Once inside the inner bailey, he would have turned left and made his way to the solar in the Magdalen Tower. This tower was built into the northern curtain wall and was one of the strongest towers in the castle. Its original use had been to defend the ford of the river before it was repurposed for chambers. A spiral staircase would have led to his chamber, where a roaring fire would have greeted him. He may have enjoyed his meal here or made his way to the Great Hall.

The Great Hall was built in the fourteenth century and was sumptuously decorated. York would have conducted state business while seated on a raised dais at one side of the hall. From here he could view the river and the harbour through one of the several large windows which flooded the room with light. Large pillars resting on stone bases supported the roof. The winter's chill would have been kept at bay by a central hearth, with smoke escaping through the louvre.

Visiting Today
I visited Trim on a bright, sunny day. The castle rests on the bank of the river and seems to have stepped right out of the medieval

period. It is no wonder why scenes from the movie *Braveheart* were filmed here. The atmosphere is magical, and even with so many people around the history of this place is palpable. While it is possible to wander the grounds on your own, the only way to get inside the keep is with a tour guide. Although the Yorks would not have stayed in the keep itself, it is still worth a visit. Models depicting the castle throughout its history are displayed within the keep and allow visitors to see the progression of its construction.

After finishing your tour of the keep, take time to wander around the entire complex, noting the layout. The castle's chapel was believed to be on the right wall (when you enter), but few ruins are extant today and certainly not enough to determine its layout. The chapel within the keep, however, still has an atmospheric quality.

Once your visit to the castle is complete, make your way outside and turn right. Cross the bridge across the river and make your way up the hill. If you time your visit just right, at the top you will see the Yellow Steeple glowing in the sunset. This is all that remains of the Priory of St Mary. Once the home of Augustinians, the priory was a place of pilgrimage. York probably made his way to the priory to see the 'Idol of Trim', a statue of the Blessed Virgin Mary that was known for miracles. Unfortunately, during the Reformation the statue was destroyed.

Trim has much to offer someone interested in medieval history. For more information on visiting the castle, see the Heritage Ireland website at www.heritageireland.ie/en/midlandseastcoast/TrimCastle/. The castle is easily reached by car, and it may also be reached by bus from Dublin. For more information, see http://www.buseireann.ie/. If arriving by bus, plan for a visit of at least four hours.

Our Lady of Walsingham, Norfolk

Situated in the Norfolk countryside, the shrine of Our Lady of Walsingham was reputed to be one of the richest shrines in England. As legend has it, the shrine was founded in 1061 by Richeldis de Faverches, who claimed she received a vision from the Virgin Mary while praying. Soon, two more visitations occurred of Joseph, Mary and Jesus, and de Faverches was instructed to build a replica of the home where Mary received news from the angel Gabriel that she was to bear the Messiah.

Geoffrey de Faverches, Richeldis's son, endowed the church with the intention that it be made a priory and granted it land from his manor. The priory was established in the mid-twelfth century, and Our Lady of Walsingham quickly became a place of pilgrimage, as popular, or even more popular than the later shrine of St Thomas of Canterbury. Pilgrims visited from as far away as the Continent, and the main road they are believed to have traversed wound through Newmarket and Fakenham and is still called the Palmers' Way.

Many notable foreign visitors arrived, including Desiderius Erasmus, who left an account of his visit. Royal visitors to the shrine were not uncommon and included Henry III and Edward I. Two of Henry VIII's wives visited Our Lady of Walsingham, and Katherine of Aragon left money to it in her will.

Evidence remains in other wills that the shrine was popular. In addition to the items left to the priory, several bequests were left for pilgrims to travel to Walsingham on behalf of the dead. In 1498, William Mauleverer left the priory 'a litell ring ... that king Richard gave me'. According to Jonathan Sumption in *Pilgrimage: An Image of Mediaeval Religion*, John Paston sent a wax model to the priory to commemorate his being cured. When he made his will before his execution, Anthony Woodville remembered the priory, granting it his trapper of black cloth of gold.

The 'holy house' of the shrine was described in 1847 as having a 'fine perpendicular east front' filled with niches along with two turrets dressed with flint and stone. Buttresses were connected 'by the arch and gable over the east window'. Although the east window was destroyed, the gable contained a 'small round window, with flowing tracery, set in the middle of a very thick wall'. It is more probable that the author was actually describing the ruins of the priory and not the holy house.

The priory church contained a nave with two side aisles, a choir, a chapel and a square middle tower. The chapter house was connected with the priory and the cloisters, while the 'holy house' was attached to the church on its north side. The pointed arches of the cloisters rested on octagonal columns, and a large stone wall surrounded the grounds.

After the Dissolution, the house was dissolved and the statue of the Virgin burned. The once opulent priory's treasures went to Henry VIII, and the priory fell to ruin.

The Medieval Period and the Priory

Erasmus's description of the priory says that pilgrims approached the shrine by way of a narrow gate. Upon entering, they would be taken to the first relic, where after paying they were able to kiss the finger bone of St Peter. They then were led to the wells, where they could take the waters. After this, they were finally taken to see the statue of the Virgin, which was the main attraction for the pilgrims.

The Duke of York visited the shrine after returning from Ireland. A pilgrim's final stop on the way to Walsingham was the fourteenth-century Chapel of St Catherine of Alexandria. Here York would have confessed his sins in the little chapel before removing his shoes to walk the last mile to the shrine barefoot. Once at the abbey, he would have entered its precincts through the gatehouse and porter's lodge on the high street.

Immediately upon entering the Chapel of the Virgin, he would have noticed the pervasive fragrance of incense. The chapel was dimly lit by long, slender candles, so he would have had to carefully make his way to the altar. To the right stood the statue of Our Lady, surrounded by the gold and jewels of the shrine. He would have knelt in prayer here before presenting an offering, which an awaiting priest would have immediately taken up.

He would have next made his way to the outer chapel, where he would have prostrated himself at the altar and once again prayed. The canon in attendance, attired with a surplice over his cassock and a richly ornamented stole with decorative trim around the neck, would also have prostrated himself on the ground in front of the altar and worshipped, before offering the Virgin's milk for the duke to kiss. Encased in crystal to protect it from contamination, the milk of the Virgin was set in a crucifix.

In addition to visiting the shrine, York had other ties to Walsingham. As the patron of the friars minor in Little Walsingham, he requested permission from the king to grant the priory a cottage, three acres of land and a garden.

Richard's sons would also come to Walsingham. Edward IV,

Richard, Elizabeth Woodville and several members of her family visited the shrine in 1469. The duke's granddaughter, Elizabeth of York, would also visit the shrine several times while queen.

Visiting Today

The first place to visit while in Walsingham is the slipper chapel of St Catherine of Alexandria. Today, the chapel is part of the Roman Catholic Shrine of Our Lady. Within the chapel is the beautiful Annunciation Window by Alfred Fisher, which was placed here in 1997. Once you leave the chapel, go into the adjacent room. The ambience from clusters of burning candles, serving as poignant reminders of the prayers left behind, is touching.

After visiting the chapel, take some time to wander within the shop or eat a small bite at the café. You may see modern-day pilgrims since many people still make pilgrimages here each year. Some may even walk the last mile to Walsingham barefoot.

The original shrine is gone; the statue of Our Lady of Walsingham was taken and burned during the Reformation. Today, there is a marker for it on the abbey grounds. The Anglican shrine, however, contains a replica of the holy house, which is lit by flickering flames from candles left by today's pilgrims. The shrine of Our Lady of Walsingham sits at the far end of the house. The Anglican shrine also contains an ancient well whose waters one can drink.

To visit the abbey ruins, head up the hill from the Anglican shrine to the Shirehall museum. Although very little is left today, the arch of the magnificent East Window can still be viewed, along with the marker showing the former location of the 'holy house'. The stones from the west tower are still extant, along with the crypt. Inside the crypt are several educational panels detailing the history of the surrounding region.

After visiting the picturesque ruins, make your way down the high street to the gatehouse and porter's lodge to see what used to be the main entrance of the Augustinian abbey. This gateway was where the Duke of York, and later his sons, would have entered following their visit to the slipper chapel. For more information about visiting times and prices, see the website: www.walsinghamabbey.com/ Home.html. The Anglican shrine postcode is NR22 6BP and the Roman Catholic shrine postcode is NR22 6EG.

St Albans, Hertfordshire

A settlement has been in this spot since the ancient Britons first came here. Later occupied by the Romans, it became one of the larger Roman settlements in England. Known by Verulamium, it was an important centre of government, commerce and trade for the area. During Boudicca's revolt, the town suffered widespread destruction and its inhabitants were massacred.

After this uprising, a large fosse was constructed around most of the town for further protection against future uprisings, but it did not protect it from the fire that would rage through the area. Under the leadership of the Romans, the town was prosperous. During the interval between the Roman departure and the Norman arrival, the people left Verulamium and settled around the abbey. The new town stood on a hill overlooking the plain surrounding it, with the River Ver flowing nearby.

St Albans continued to thrive when the power structure passed into Norman hands. Several members of the royal family visited the shrine and town. Eleanor, wife of Edward I, was here during her husband's reign. Her funeral procession also passed through St Albans on its way to London. For the York family, however, the town would be known mainly for the battles fought here.

The First Battle of St Albans

During the illness of Henry VI, York had been named Protector and had imprisoned the Duke of Somerset. After Henry recovered, he released the duke from the Tower and dismissed York as the Captain of Calais, restoring the post to Somerset. Still upset over losing his status as Protector, York retreated to Sandal Castle. Soon he was summoned to appear before a council in Leicester. His fear was that Somerset and his allies were trying to force him into another humiliating oath of submission. Despite his oath at St Paul's that he would 'never hereafter presume to gather a body of men or assemble your people without your command', he gathered his allies together and began marching towards the king and his lords. The two armies met at St Albans, with the king's forces inside the town and York's men in Key Field nearby.

Letters were sent from York to the king declaring his loyalty and promising that he had only gathered forces for protection from those who were his enemies. One account has Somerset preventing the king from seeing York's letters. According to the *Dijon Relation*, Henry sent a messenger to York asking why he had come with so many people, and York replied that he 'had by no means come against the king and was always ready to do obedience, but he intended in all ways to have the traitors who were with the king so that they could be punished'. The king's reply was that the only traitor he was aware of was York. With this, York realised his only hope was through decisive action.

Once the Yorkists decided to engage, they found that the king's forces had barred the main roads. The Earl of Warwick found another way in, leading his men up through the garden side along Holywell Street. They broke through and once they were in the town they began blowing trumpets and shouting 'A Warwick! A Warwick!' as fighting broke out in the streets of the city.

The *Dijon Relation* says Somerset took refuge in a house but was seen by the Duke of York's men and killed. Also killed were the Earl of Northumberland and Lord Clifford. The king was said to have been slightly injured. After the battle, York, Salisbury and Warwick approached Henry and reassured him they had not intended to hurt him. Henry VI was taken to the cathedral and treated with all respect, but was now under Yorkist control. Many of the fallen were interred in St Peter's church, but most of the nobles were buried at St Albans in the chapel of the Virgin.

When Parliament met on 9 July 1455, Henry issued a declaration in Parliament proclaiming that Richard and all those that helped him at St Albans were true liegemen and pardoned them. Following this, on 24 July, the lords temporal and spiritual gave an oath to Henry that they would keep their allegiance to him.

The Second Battle of St Albans

This battle took place after the death of York at Wakefield. Although he was obviously not present at the second battle in St Albans, it was an important event in his family's history.

Following the Battle of Northampton, Warwick had captured Henry VI and returned to London. Learning of the disastrous defeat and death of his father and York at Wakefield, he began taking steps to create a larger Yorkist army. Soon he left London and headed towards St Albans to block the roads that Queen Margaret would take on her march towards London. He stationed his men both on St Peter's Street to protect against a surprise attack and nearby at Dunstable. A spy in his ranks sent information to Margaret, and her army was able to surround the men at Dunstable, making sure to count them so no one escaped to warn Warwick.

Warwick was defeated, with several of his men switching sides in the middle of battle. However, he managed to escape and meet up with the Earl of March. Henry was found by a tree and rejoined his wife and son, spending the night at St Albans Abbey. He was implored by Abbot Whethamstede to forbid plundering, but the soldiers sacked the town taking anything they could find, which did little to endear the king's party to the citizens.

One death that day would have a profound impact on British history. Sir John Grey, the husband of Elizabeth Woodville, was killed during the battle, after having been knighted just the day before. This made Elizabeth a widow and freed her to later marry Edward IV.

Edward IV's son, Edward V, would pass through St Albans for a night on his way to London. In the company of his uncle, the future Richard III, the young king would spend the night as the abbey's guest. Elizabeth of York and Henry VII also visited the church for the feast of All Hallows on their way to London prior to Elizabeth's coronation.

Church of St Peter

Originally built in the tenth century, the church needed to be rebuilt by the end of the fifteenth. Mainly Perpendicular in style, the church has a clerestory on each side of the nave. The south aisle is fifteenth century, but much of the rest of the church has been altered throughout the years. The tower was not extant in the medieval period.

In the north aisle a window contains the remains of fourteenth-century glass that has the arms of Edward III's son, Edmund. The Duke of York and his children were descended in the male line from Edmund and in the female line from Edward III's third son, Lionel. It was through Lionel that both York and Edward IV based their claim to the crown.

Following the thick of the fighting of the First Battle of St Albans, the church saw many of those that fell that day buried in its graveyard. While it is doubtful that York or his sons ever set foot within the church, it played an important role in the engagement.

The church is open during daylight hours, but you should check before visiting to confirm. For more information about visiting the church, see its website at http://www.stpeterschurch.uk.com/en-us/home.aspx.

Clock Tower

The clock tower at St Albans was built in the early part of the fifteenth century and is the only surviving example of a medieval clock tower in England. From this large square tower, bells would issue both curfews and alarms for the citizens. During the First Battle of St Albans, this tower's bells would have raised the alarm. Located in the centre of the city, the Tower is sometimes open for visitors. For more information, check its website at http://www.stalbansmuseums.org.uk/Your-Visit/Clock-Tower/Visitor-Information.

St Albans Cathedral

During the battles of St Albans, the cathedral was still an abbey, since the town did not receive its city charter until 1877. The abbey was named after a soldier named Albanus, who gave shelter to a Christian named Amphibalus. This was a dangerous time for Christians due to Roman persecution. After listening to Amphibalus's teachings on Christ, Albanus converted to Christianity. The Romans were searching for Amphibalus, and Albanus made the ultimate sacrifice – he traded clothes with him and was executed in his place.

First a basilica and later a Benedictine monastery stood on the spot where Albanus had been martyred for his faith. The present church replaced the earlier Benedictine one and was begun in 1077 by the Normans. Since ready materials were easily available from the old Roman city, the church was built quickly. Soon, the abbey became wealthy and powerful, and men like Matthew Paris were monks here.

Today, the monastic buildings that housed Henry VI, Edward V, Richard III and later Elizabeth and Henry VII were destroyed. The chapter house, the cloisters, the abbot's lodge and other buildings that were part of the monastery stood on the south side of the church. After the Dissolution, the layout of the church changed dramatically. A street even cut through the church at one point, separating it from the Lady Chapel, which had been converted into a school. It is not surprising that the memorials and tombs within the Lady Chapel were lost.

In the nineteenth century, the cathedral underwent massive renovation and much of its appearance was altered. The Duke of York's first view of the abbey would have been the tower with its embattled parapet topped with a spire, resting on a stone base covered with decorative mouldings. He would have seen a whitewashed church with a lead roof and large Perpendicular window filled with medieval stained glass when he accompanied Henry to the cathedral.

Visiting today, you no longer see the Norman arches and embellishments on the western porches, since the renovations changed the entire look of the building. On the south side, instead of buttresses, York would have seen a cloister walk with delicate arcading. He would not have seen the porch over the abbot's door because it was part of the later reconstruction.

Although the interior of the church has changed over the centuries, some of it would still be familiar to York. The plain Norman and Early English piers are the same. Despite having been renovated several times, the rood screen behind the altar with its two fourteenth-century doors would be recognisable. He would also know the delicate tracery inside the Lady Chapel.

Remnants of gorgeous medieval paintings were uncovered in the nineteenth century, including a set of crucifixions. The apsidal chapels of the transepts, along with the Norman gables, were removed during the sixteenth century. Also lost to history are the twenty-six altars that were located in the nave.

It is possible York visited the Shrine of St Alban while at the church. Pilgrims came from far away to worship here. They would enter the church, buy their beeswax candle and proceed to the shrine. Chamomile would be underfoot on feast days to keep a clean scent in the air. The layout of the church was such that pilgrims could experience its grandeur even though they could not visit every area of the building.

It is only through hard work that we are able to have an idea of the shrine's original appearance. It was found in more than 2,000 fragments and was painstakingly recreated using paintings and drawings of other shrines. The Purbeck stone of the shrine is topped by a bright red canopy and still retains some of its monuments. Pilgrims would place injured body parts into its recesses as they prayed for healing.

Perhaps York paused in the south aisle of the saint's chapel to visit a monument to a former friend, Humphrey, Duke of Gloucester. Humphrey was the youngest son of Henry IV and was protector of England during the minority of Henry VI. Eventually, Humphrey was arrested at Bury St Edmunds, and following what appeared to have been a stroke he died. York had not been present in Bury for the arrest but had arrived later. Humphrey's arrest had taught York a valuable lesson about trusting the king.

Duke Humphrey's tomb is in the saint's chapel near the shrine. While his coffin is in an underground burial chamber, a visitor may still catch a glimpse of it through the grate on the floor. The chapel is open on the side of the shrine, but is separated from the south aisle by an iron grille. Traces of red and blue paint remain, making one think it might have been painted to match the nearby shrine, which also contains these colours. Duke Humphrey's coat of arms, along with one of his badges, can be seen on the chantry. Each side of the chantry's canopy contain seventeen niches for statues. The north-side niches have been emptied, but the south side is filled with statues of kings.

According to Jane Kelsall, author of *Humphrey Duke of Gloucester: 1391–1447*, although monuments typically contain an effigy, there is no record of any figure of Humphrey being made. It is possible one was made but destroyed during the Dissolution.

After leaving the shrine and Duke Humphrey's tomb, make your way to the Lady Chapel where some of the Lancastrian dead were buried. Unfortunately, these tombs and memorials were destroyed years later.

Before you leave the church, ask the verger to remove the carpet in front of the altar. Here, a floor brass commemorates Sir Anthony Grey, the son of Edmund, Lord Grey of Ruthin, whose switching of sides helped lead to a Yorkist victory in the Battle at Northampton.

The massive structure of the Great Gate is all that remains of the prosperous abbey's gates. Built in the fourteenth century, it was the principal entrance to the abbey and was obviously built to impress guests. Standing in front of the gate, it is easy to see how wealthy the abbey once was. After the Dissolution, the gate served both as a gaol and a school.

Visiting St Albans Today

St Albans is a history lover's paradise. From Roman times to modern day, there is something for everyone. The cathedral is open daily, unless a special event has been planned. Before driving or travelling long distances, it is best to check ahead.

As you walk through the town, be aware that some of the battle took place along its streets. The Lancastrians were based in the marketplace and along other streets, like Cock Lane. A plaque on Victoria Street marks the area as the site of the Castle Inn, where tradition holds that Edmund Beaufort, Duke of Somerset, was slain. A legend grew that Somerset was terrified when he read the name of the inn, because a soothsayer had told him that he would die in a castle. While interesting, one chronicler records that Somerset reportedly killed four men before being mortally wounded himself, which does not sound like a man frozen in terror.

St Albans is a great day trip from London since it is only twenty minutes from the St Pancras International station by rail. You can check the timetables at the First Capital Connect website: www.firstcapitalconnect.co.uk/plan-your-journey/timetables/show-all/.

The city is a short stop from the M1 at Junction 6, and from the A1 (M) and the M25 at Junctions 21A and 22. There are plenty of car parks scattered throughout the city. Upon arrival, I recommend heading straight to the tourist information centre located in the town hall, which is open every day except Sunday. Before heading off to see the sites, take some time to learn more about the history of the town at the Museum of St Albans. Other sites of interest nearby include the Verulamium Museum and the Hypocaust and Roman mosaic. St Albans postcode: AL3 5DJ.

Old St Paul's Cathedral, London

Situated on Ludgate Hill in London, the earliest church on this spot is attributed to St Mellitus and St Erkenwald. Construction of a cathedral that is today commonly called 'Old St Paul's' was begun by Bishop Maurice in 1087. Materials from Caen and from the

Palatine Tower in London were used in its construction. Building commenced, but a fire in the twelfth century destroyed much of the work. The choir was completed in the mid-twelfth century, so by then people were worshipping here.

The cathedral's precincts were completely surrounded by a wall built in the early twelfth century and strengthened in the later part of the thirteenth. There were six gates into the churchyard, which were opened every morning and closed at night. The western gate on Ludgate Hill spanned the street.

The spire of the cathedral, which rested on the central tower, was between 460 and 489 feet high. It dominated the city as a landmark for all Londoners. It was a wealthy church, containing treasures like sixteen chalices – five of gold and eleven of silver gilt, along with silver dishes. The interior of the church was also filled with richly decorated chantry chapels, such as the one for John of Gaunt.

The Duke of York and St Paul's Cathedral

After the debacle at Dartford, the Duke of York was forced into giving an oath to Henry, which was to be delivered at St Paul's Cathedral. As York entered into the cathedral, he would have seen a packed room. Many had turned out to see the duke pay his obeisance to Henry. Entering the nave, with its beautifully groined ceiling, he walked through the crowd towards the high altar.

Passing by the great Gothic choir screen at the crossing, he slowly ascended the steps and made his way to the high altar. Here, in front of the tablet engraved with enamel decorations and encrusted with jewels, he made his oath to Henry on the sacrament and then received the sacrament. Next, he touched the cross and put his hands on the Holy Gospels. The beautiful painting of St Paul to the right of the high altar was witness to the entire scene. York's oath was later delivered in writing to Henry.

A few years later, the cathedral would also be the location for one of the more curious events in the Wars of the Roses. On 25 March 1458, an unusual procession headed towards St Paul's Cathedral. This 'loveday' was a simplistic solution to a complex problem. While an outward show of peace was evident, the inner struggles had not been resolved. In the procession, Salisbury and Somerset walked together, then Exeter and Warwick, all ahead of a crowned

Henry. Behind him followed York and Queen Margaret, hand in hand. The group entered the nave with its twelve bays and vaulted ceilings. The great Rose Window spilled light into the church as the group made its way to hear Mass. After Mass, the group left in procession, all semblance of peace restored. However, it would not be long before the quasi-peace would be broken.

In his visits to London, it is probable that the Duke of York entered St Paul's on other, happier, occasions. Perhaps while here he visited the shrine of St Erkenwald, since it was a popular pilgrimage destination. York would have seen the shrine of wood, surrounded by its iron gate, covered with plates of silver, precious stones and images. J. Saunders, writing in *London: Volume 4*, in the nineteenth century, described the shrine, saying that it

> appears a lofty, pyramidal, Gothic structure, in the purest and most exquisitely decorated style; the outlines formed by pinnacles rising one above another towards a single pinnacle in the centre at the top, and the central portion consisting of three slender windows side by side, and an exceedingly elegant one filling the triangular space above.

Making his way out of the cathedral, he may have passed the chantry chapel of John of Gaunt on the north side of the choir. The canopied tomb contained full-size effigies of Gaunt and his first wife, Blanche. Hanging from the monument was a tilting lance shield and a cap of estate. Angels supported the couple's heads while a lion rested at their feet.

St Paul's would play host to several 'crown-wearing' exhibitions of Henry VI when he was under Yorkist control. After Edward IV returned from exile, he went to St Paul's to make an offering and to secure Henry, who had been staying at the Bishop's Palace. Soon afterwards, Edward would have Henry's body brought here to be put on display, with face uncovered. Some chroniclers record that Henry's body bled onto the marble pavement while at St Paul's, before it was removed to Chertsey Abbey.

Richard III and St Paul's Cathedral
During Richard's reign, the door of St Paul's Cathedral was used by a man from Wiltshire, William Collingbourne, to pin up his derisive

poem about Richard. The lyrics 'the Catte, the Ratte and Lovell our dogge rulyth all Englande under a hogge' referenced Richard (the hog), Sir William Catesby (the cat), Sir Richard Ratcliffe (the rat) and Viscount Francis Lovell (the dog). As his loyal friends, these men had been placed in positions of power by Richard soon after he took the throne, which bred resentment among some members of the nobility.

Collingbourne was not just trying to publish his poetry; he was trying to incite a rebellion and bring Henry Tudor to England. Richard decided that harsh action needed to be taken and ordered him executed. In December 1484, Collingbourne was hanged, drawn and quartered.

Elizabeth of York and St Paul's

Elizabeth and Henry were at St Paul's in 1488 for the ceremonial presentation of a sword and cap sent from the Pope to Henry. The couple had travelled from Westminster that morning in 'so great a mist' that no one could say 'in what place in Thames the King was'. Attending the ceremony were ambassadors from several countries, including France and Spain, as well as 'divers other strangers, as Scots, Easterlings and others'. The cap was carried in procession on the 'pomel of the swerde' by the Pope's chamberlain to the high altar where it sat throughout Mass. After Mass, Archbishop Morton girded the sword around the king before placing the cap on his head. Afterwards a large feast was held to celebrate the occasion.

On Sunday 14 November 1501, Elizabeth and Henry watched their son Arthur wed Katherine of Aragon. So that all eyes would be on the couple, the king and queen secreted themselves in a closet above the consistory. The wedding was a lavish affair, with a platform constructed so that all the guests could see the young couple.

Visiting Today

Unfortunately there is nothing left of this masterpiece of architecture, so any visit will have to be through imagination. Thanks to the work of William Dugdale, we have an idea of how the old cathedral looked before the Great Fire of 1666 destroyed it and Christopher Wren rebuilt it. While built on the same grounds, it was not built to the same exact pattern. Where the cloisters once stood is an area that shows the layout of the old cathedral compared to the new. The best way to get a sense of the atmosphere is to just wander around outside, tracing the original outline. Of course, Wren's St Paul's Cathedral is well worth a visit.

Paul's Cross, where the children of Edward IV would be declared illegitimate to the citizens of London, is within the grounds of the church, but it, too, is not the original. The original cross was an open-air pulpit which was rebuilt in the fifteenth century by Bishop Thomas Kempe. It was a hexagonal building made of timber and covered with lead, with a stone staircase leading to the pulpit, which culminated in a cross. It would accommodate about three or four people. Here, Londoners would gather to hear the latest news, proclamations and explanations of policies. The cross stood in the north-east corner of the Old St Paul's Cathedral churchyard. Paul's Cross was torn down during the Reformation. Today, a new cross stands in St Paul's churchyard, but it does not resemble the original. A marker commemorates where the old cross once stood.

Coventry, West Midlands

The area was settled for years prior to the Normans. The Earl of Mercia and his legendary wife, Godiva (Godgifu), founded and richly endowed a Benedictine monastery here that became one of the wealthiest establishments in England. The priory was built into the slope of a hill and its buildings sat between the banks of the Sherbourne and the cathedral.

The fourteenth century saw massive, reddish-hued walls begin to surround the city, with opulent gates to admit visitors. Around its circumference were embattled towers which offered the inhabitants further protection against attacks. Leland, writing in the sixteenth century, said that the towers were not only defensive but also fair. Coventry was described by Michael Drayton in *Poly-Olbion*: 'Her walls in good repair, her ports so bravely built, Her halls in good estate, her cross so richly gilt, As scorning all the Towns that stand within her view.' Perhaps Coventry, along with its opulent priory, was trying to showcase its wealth.

Coventry in the Wars of the Roses

In February of 1456, York was removed from the protectorship by the king in Parliament. Later that year, the king and the court moved to Coventry. As the region enjoyed strong Lancastrian support, Margaret of Anjou and those loyal to Henry probably felt safer in the area. During the next few years several councils met in Coventry, including one in June of 1456, which the Duke of York attended. Soon afterward, Thomas Bourchier's position as Chancellor of England was given to William Waynflete. York and his allies were becoming increasingly marginalised, while Margaret of Anjou was playing a much larger role in the government.

Margaret's increasing prominence is indicated by her reception into the city. When Margaret and Henry arrived in Coventry in 1456, prominent citizens provided them with a ceremonial entrance. The *Coventry Leet Book* gives a detailed description of the ceremony. Brightly dressed citizens were placed in the streets to speak words of welcome to the king and queen. As Margaret entered through the Bablake gate (Spon gate) she was met with pageants, honouring her and her son. In the second pageant, a man representing the prophet Jeremiah spoke, saying, 'Empress, queen, princess excellent, in one person all three.'

At the Smithford Street Conduit, she was treated to the pageant of the Four Cardinal Virtues. Pageants of St John the Evangelist and St Edward the Confessor were placed throughout the town. The pageant of the Nine Conquerors was performed for her at Cheaping with speeches heard from men representing Hector, Alexander, David, Arthur and others. The final pageant would have appealed to Margaret since it featured St Margaret slaying a ferocious dragon.

Another indication of Margaret's prominence was evident when she left the city. On her departure, the mayor rode before her with his mace in hand, while the sheriffs with their white rods rode before him. Prior to her visit, this honour had been reserved for the king. In Coventry, Margaret seemed to feel assured of her power.

In June of 1459, a great council was called to meet in Coventry, which excluded Richard as well as Salisbury, Warwick and other close allies of York. Sensing a legitimate threat, the men met in Ludlow to determine their next course of action. After the rout of Ludford Bridge, the men fled into exile. Richard and his son

Edmund, Earl of Rutland, headed towards Ireland, while the others, including Edward, Earl of March, went to Calais.

Following the sack of Ludlow, a parliament was called to meet in Coventry. The parliament was a punitive one, earning it the moniker Parliament of Devils. William Waynflete opened the parliament in the priory's chapter house. Securing the attainder of York and his allies was a top priority. According to Charles Ross in his book *Edward IV*, only six peers were attainted: York, Edward and Edmund, the earls of Salisbury and Warwick, and John, Lord Clinton. Kinsmen of peers were attainted, along with knights and esquires. Most of the men who were attainted had already fled, and Henry VI offered others clemency for submission. Cecily seems also to have appeared before the king. Although Henry was not cruel to her, he did place Cecily and her younger children in the custody of her sister, the Duchess of Buckingham.

Coventry and Edward IV

Years later, Coventry would play a further role in the history of the York family. It was the scene of a conflict between King Edward IV and the Earl of Warwick, both of whom had been attainted here at the Parliament of Devils. The roots of the conflict lay in the fact that Edward blocked a marriage between Isabel, Warwick's daughter, and George, Edward's brother. Undeterred, George and Warwick began conspiring to gain a dispensation from the Pope for the marriage.

Warwick wrote to his followers in Coventry to announce the upcoming marriage, which took place in Calais on 11 July 1469. The defiance of Warwick and George did not stop with just the marriage. From Calais, the men issued a manifesto setting forth their complaints, which included grievances against Earl Rivers and other Woodvilles. The ensuing conflict resulted in the murder of Earl Rivers and his son near Coventry. According to the *Coventry Leet Book*, this occurred on Gosforth Green.

After a period of uneasy peace, conflict raised its ugly head, and once again, the Earl of Warwick was at the heart of it. Edward had fled to the Low Countries in the aftermath of an uprising led by Warwick and George. Once Edward returned, he headed towards Coventry, gathering followers as he went. Once he reached Coventry, where the Earl of Warwick was awaiting reinforcements from George, Edward boldly offered the earl a choice between a pardon and a battle. Short on men, Warwick chose neither option, instead choosing to stay within the relative safety of Coventry's walls.

Shortly afterward, Edward IV, with his brother Richard by his side, reconciled with George outside Windsor. Knowing that Warwick's necessary reinforcements were now out of reach, Edward marched back to Coventry and offered Warwick the same terms. Once again the earl refused, and Edward headed on to London to see his wife and his family, which now included a son he had never seen.

Edward had a long-term memory for slights, and although he sometimes forgave these, Coventry would not receive such clemency for sheltering Warwick. Edward removed the city's liberties as a punishment, forcing it to purchase them back.

Over the next few years, Coventry worked hard to regain Edward's trust. When his son, Edward, Prince of Wales, visited the city a few years later, they held huge pageants for him and gave him fine gifts. The mayor, garbed in green and blue finery, presented him with a gilded cup. Edward entered though the Bablake gate, where he would have seen the highly embellished gatehouse of reddish hued stone with its two embattled towers. Here a pageant was held in his honour, with Richard II honouring the young Prince of Wales as the rightful heir to the kingdom. After seeing the pageant, he would have passed the collegiate church dedicated to St John and made his way along the paved streets of Coventry. Edward then watched the other pageants in his honour. One of the largest pageants was the pageant of St George at the conduit of the Cheaping, with the saint armed, and with 'a kynges daughter knelyng a fore hym with a lambe, and the father & the moder beyng in a toure a boven, beholdyng Seint George savyng their daughter from the dragon'.

While the Prince of Wales was here, the mayor and other leading citizens swore an oath to him to accept him for their sovereign lord and to be his true and faithful subjects.

Richard III and Coventry

Richard visited Coventry while on his first progress. As most royal visitors to Coventry stayed in the priory, he almost certainly made his way there. As the priory's guest, he observed Mass in its cathedral, since the Feast of the Assumption of the Blessed Virgin Mary coincided with his visit. At more than 400 feet long, the cathedral was an immense structure, with large pillars supporting its roof.

Richard also visited Coventry on at least two other occasions. On one visit, he was moving to put down Buckingham's rebellion, so he did not stay long. However, in June of 1485, Richard came to Coventry to experience the city's famous Corpus Christi pageants. People came from all over to see the famous mystery plays, and scaffolds were set up for the spectators.

The procession of the guilds took place early in the morning before the mystery plays. Behind the guilds were the priests of the Trinity Guild carrying the Host, with a canopy of rich material above it. After the procession, the pageants followed, setting out the scenes of the life of the Virgin, who wore an expensive crown.

The pageants themselves were performed on two-storey scaffolds. A lower storey allowed the performers to change their costumes, while the upper level was for the performance itself. The pageants began at the priory gate, winding their way toward the mayor, who was stationed at Cross Cheaping.

One of the most elaborate of the pageants was put on by the Smiths guild. It was a representation of the trial, condemnation and crucifixion of Christ. It required, among other items, a gilded cross with a rope to draw it up and a curtain to hang before it; a red standard; gowns and hoods for the tormentors and a painted red cloth with silk fringe. The drapers' pageant included an apparatus for simulating an earthquake. As these are just two of the several pageants held that day, it is clear how impressive each pageant would have been. This was the last time that one of the sons of York would visit the city, since Richard would soon face Henry Tudor at Bosworth.

St Mary's Priory and Cathedral

Given its wealth, it is no surprise that St Mary's Priory and Cathedral did not survive the Dissolution. Frustratingly, we cannot know for sure what the cathedral church looked like because little remains of the once huge edifice, including descriptions. What we can be sure of is that the priory was opulent, with ornate decorations. Even though one can no longer visit the church, it is possible to see the ruins. Portions of its west front and remnants of its columns' bases still exist in the priory gardens.

After wandering through the beauty of the gardens, be sure to visit the excellent display at the priory visitor centre. The visitor centre contains a plan of the priory, including the location of the cloisters and chapter house in relation to other buildings. Fragments of once exquisite medieval tiles, ornate bosses, and figures from the cathedral, chapter house and other buildings of the priory are displayed, each one containing a detailed description helping the visitor recreate the building in his or her mind. The chapter house's painting of the Apocalypse is vividly described in one of the centre's displays.

Tickets are available for tours of the undercroft, which was discovered during excavation work and offers a tantalising glimpse into the priory. For more information, see the visitor centre website at www.prioryvisitorcentre.org/. Priory Visitor Centre postcode: CV1 5EX.

St Mary's Hall, Coventry

Another building the Yorks would have seen and maybe even visited is the Guildhall. St Mary's Hall is an impressive building chock-full of history. Although built in the early part of the fourteenth century, additions were made to the building throughout the following years until it reached its present size in the fifteenth century. The hall often received royal visitors, including Henry VI and Henry VII. It is not outside the realm of possibility that the Duke of York, Richard III or the future Edward V visited the building.

For medieval enthusiasts, the best portion of the visit is the large tapestry in the Great Hall. Believed to have been commissioned during the reign of Henry VII, the intricately woven tapestry is the *Glorification of the Virgin*. The king represented in the tapestry is thought to be Henry VI. According to the Guildhall, Richard III and several of his family members are portrayed. It takes some time to find each figure represented, but a close look will uncover Richard as well as the Duke of Gloucester, George, Isabel and Anne Neville.

Damaged by fire in the Second World War, the roof of the hall had to be largely restored, but many of the building's medieval carvings survived and were incorporated into the restored roof. Some of the carved stone corbels in the hall may have come from the priory since signs of weathering have been detected.

The pieces of medieval stained glass in the old council chamber used to be part of the hall's east window. The glass, which dates from the fifteenth century, would have been in the east window when Richard III was in Coventry. While in the chamber, look at the great chair in the room. The ornately carved chair dates from at least the fifteenth century, and may have even been the bishop's chair in the priory. If so, many members of the York family, including Richard III, would have seen it in its original location.

In the treasury room, intricate oak carvings on the wall once appeared in the priory's guest house. Richard III and other members of his family may have seen this representation of God, the Virgin and Child, and several saints and evangelists while staying at the guesthouse.

Admission to the guildhall is free, although donations are welcome. For more information about opening times, visit the website at www.stmarysguildhall.co.uk/info/4/visit/ or call +44 (0) 24 7683 3328. The hall is located on Bayley Lane, across from the ruins of St Michael's Cathedral. St Mary's Hall postcode: CV1 5RN.

St Michael's Cathedral

After the destruction of the priory church, the city was without a cathedral until 1918 when the medieval parish church of St Michael was consecrated as a cathedral. While it is doubtful any of the Yorks visited the parish church, they certainly would have seen it. Shortly after its consecration, German bombs decimated the gorgeous red sandstone church. A decision was made to leave the church in ruins for a memorial, with a new cathedral to be built nearby. The ruins are still lovely and are a moving reminder of the destruction of war. Remnants of the medieval church can still be seen among the ruins. The south porch, the oldest surviving part of the medieval structure, still stands facing St Mary's Hall.

While travelling through the city, Richard III would have seen the tall spire of the parish church. Although it has been restored today, the spire was completed by the time Richard visited Coventry. Even before it was finished the tower began sinking, and a full restoration had to be completed in the nineteenth century.

For more information about opening times, see the cathedral website at www.coventrycathedral.org.uk/. This website also has information about the ruins. The cathedral suggests that visitors arriving by car should park in the Pool Meadow car park. The car park's postcode is CV1 5EX. The cathedral's ruins are only a short walk from the Priory Visitor Centre.

Visiting Coventry Today

Coventry has much to offer a tourist and a visit could take several days. However, it is possible for an organised visitor to see all the sites related to the York family in just one day. If you decide to do a day trip, a good option is to depart by train from London. For information about tickets, see www.nationalrail.co.uk/. Trains leave from Euston station, and, depending on which train you take, the journey can be made in one hour.

Another option is to drive. Coventry has a good park-and-ride program. For more information on the park-and-ride scheme, see the webpage at www.networkwestmidlands.com/parkandride/indexparkandride.aspx. Postcode: CV3 6PT.

Worcester, Worcestershire

The Romans were the earliest known residents of this area, and after their departure the city floundered and was abandoned. Since this was a fording spot for the Severn, a Saxon settlement once again began to grow up near the river and a church and monastery dedicated to St Peter was constructed in the seventh century. This church was replaced by one built by Oswald in the tenth century, dedicated to the Virgin Mary and home to a Benedictine monastery.

With the coming of the Normans, the old church was torn down and a new one built in its place. Wulfstan, the Bishop of Worcester, served as a bridge for the church between the last two Saxon kings and the first two Norman kings and began the work of constructing a new cathedral in the eleventh century.

The city grew and prospered and soon stone walls surrounded it, adding an extra layer of fortification. Unfortunately, the wall did not protect against fire, and in the twelfth century the town burned four times. Like a phoenix, the cathedral rose from the ashes in time to house the body of King John.

York and Worcester

Crossing over the Severn, York would have seen the bridge constructed in the fourteenth century, with its six great arches of stone, and crossed through the gatehouse set in the middle. While in Worcester, he, along with the Nevilles, took an oath before the high altar of the cathedral pledging that they were acting for the king's 'high estate'. P. A. Johnson, in *Duke Richard of York: 1411–1460*, says that the men 'justified their assumption of arms with a plea of self-defence against those lords about the king'. Neither the oath nor their justification moved the king and soon the men left Worcester. According to Johnson, the route they took first headed south, but, finding the way blocked, they retreated to the York stronghold of Ludlow.

Worcester Cathedral

Dedicated to Christ and the Virgin Mary, a church has stood in this area for centuries. Throughout the years it has seen several rebuilding phases so that little remains of the cathedral Wulfstan built, with its mixture of green sandstone and golden oolitic stone, other than the Norman crypt with its four aisles. The cathedral was largely renovated prior to King John's burial in front of the high altar and is a mixture of several styles, including Norman, Early English, Decorated and Perpendicular.

On their way to kneel at the high altar, York and the Nevilles would have passed King John's tomb. Perhaps they took strength from remembering another time when a king had been forced to do something by his lords. It might also have been a sobering reminder of the ultimate fate of Simon de Montfort. Although the beautiful reredos seen today would not have been the ones that York and the Nevilles would have viewed, there would have been reredos in this spot in the fifteenth century.

Worcester Cathedral was a place of pilgrimage in the medieval period. Pilgrims came to Worcester to visit the shrines of St Oswald and the recently canonised St Wulfstan. Wulfstan's shrine had escaped several fires, furthering his reputation for the miraculous. England's kings and queens were frequent visitors to the shrine, with Edward I having a special preference for St Wulfstan's shrine. He sent the shrine an offering of two gold cloths and visited it frequently. As both these shrines lay near the high altar, perhaps the men sought solace here before leaving Worcester.

Standing in the nave, the scene is easy to picture – the men, kneeling before the high altar, making their oaths while flickering light from the tapers surrounding the nearby shrine cast shadows across them. All three men probably knew the oath would not sway the king.

One thing the men would not have seen is the chantry chapel for Prince Arthur. The son of Henry VII and Elizabeth of York, Arthur died while at Ludlow and his body was buried here. His chantry chapel sits to the right of the high altar.

Visiting Today

Once inside the nave, pause to examine the massive columns, with their slender shafts and capitals. Most of the nave is in the Decorated style. From here, make your way to the high altar where the men made their futile oath.

Worcester Cathedral is open daily for visitors with no admission price, although a donation is requested. For more information about opening times, visit the cathedral website at http://www. worcestercathedral.co.uk/Visiting.php/ or call +44 (0) 1905 732 900. If you have time, make prior arrangements to visit Worcester's library. Many medieval manuscripts are on display. Be sure to ask to see one with drawings in the margins. In addition, the guided tours at Worcester are excellent; I thoroughly enjoyed a tour I took a few years ago. While not York-focused, I learned a great deal about the cathedral from my tour guide, Ian.

Ludlow Castle, Shropshire

Viewed from across the glittering waters of the River Teme, Ludlow Castle is an imposing building, rising above the banks of the river, surrounded by tangled knots of green vines and tree limbs. Somehow it manages to look both formidable and romantic all at once. The poet Richard Wyke captured this feeling in his poem 'Lines on Ludlow Castle':

> There's not, in England's isle, a lovelier vale,
> Than that wherein the waters of the Teme,
> And Corve, unite; then wend their way through meads
>
> …

In this sweet vale, a rocky height ascends,
On which proud Dinan's ruin'd castle stands;
Whose moss-grown stones, and high embattl'd walls,
Have brav'd the cruel hand of ruthless Time...

Ludlow was one of the properties that came to the Duke of York through his Mortimer inheritance. Throughout the years, Ludlow Castle became both a stronghold and a much-loved family home. It was here that the Duke of York set up a separate household for his two elder sons, Edward and Edmund. Despite the fact that the boys were in their own household, the duke stayed in close contact with them. Sir Clements Markham's *Richard III: His Life and Character* includes a copy of a letter the boys wrote to York, excerpted below. The boys did not like their tutor, and after thanking their father for his gift of green gowns, wrote,

> Over this, right noble lord and father, please it your highness to wit that we have charged your servant, William Smyth, bearer of these, for to declare unto your nobility certain things on our behalf, namely concerning and touching the odious rule and demeaning of Richard Croft and of his brother. Wherefore we beseech your gracious lordship and full noble fatherhood to hear him in exposition of the same, and to his relation to give full faith and credence.

In 1459, an event occurred near Ludlow that would have lasting ramifications for the duke and his family. Tensions had been increasing within the court, and when a council excluding York and his allies was called to meet at Coventry, the men were suspicious. Was the king preparing to pass an Act of Attainder against them? The men decided to meet at Ludlow.

As Salisbury marched south from Middleham with his men, he was intercepted at Blore Heath by a royalist force under Lord Audley. In the battle, Audley was killed. Salisbury's sons were captured, but he managed to join the Duke of York.

Soon royalist troops advanced on the Yorkist position. On 12 October, royalist banners could be seen near Ludford. During the night, the Calais garrison, under command of Andrew, Lord Trollope, defected to the king. The dwindling number of his men against the large number of royal troops may have panicked York. The duke fled to Ireland with his second son, Edmund, while his older son, Edward, went with the Nevilles to Calais. The rout at Ludford Bridge was a tremendous setback for the Yorks.

Duchess Cecily is thought to have remained behind at the castle with her younger children. Although *Gregory's Chronicle* reports of the victors, 'and thenn they robbyd the towne, and bare a-waye beddynge, clothe, and othyr stuffe, and defoulyd many wymmen', it is unlikely Cecily would have been mistreated, given her status. A romantic myth has taken root about the 'rout of Ludford' where Cecily is portrayed heroically protecting her young sons at the town's market cross. While this makes for interesting novels, it is doubtful that she would have left the safety of the castle to stand within the city amid soldiers who may not have recognised her. Fabyan says that the king sent Cecily to her sister, Anne, who had married a Lancastrian and was now the Duchess of Buckingham.

Following the Battle of Northampton, the Duke of York returned from Ireland. A letter from a servant of John Paston says that 'my Lord [Duke of York] sent for hir that sche shuld come to hym to Harford [Hereford] and theder sche is gone'. Cecily immediately made plans to depart London, leaving her children there. The same letter reports that York had commissions from the king to 'sitte in dyvers townys coming homward; that is for to sey, in Ludlow, Schrrofysbury [Shrewsbury], Herford, Leycetre [Leicester], Coventre'. According to Caroline Halsted, York and Cecily reunited in Ludlow. However, since the letter says Cecily was to meet him at Hereford, and York went to Hereford after leaving Ludlow, it seems more reasonable that they reunited there.

Years later, the Duke of York's castle at Ludlow would become the residence of his grandson, the future Edward V. Edward's household was set up here much like his father's had been before him. Edward IV took great care to establish his son's household, including creating a series of regulations for its governance.

One regulation dictated his son's morning. Prince Edward was to arise at an hour convenient to his age, and no one was allowed to enter his chamber until he was ready, 'except our right trustye and well beloved the Earle Ryvers, his Chamberlayne, and his chapleynes'. After the chaplains had said matins, the prince was to go to Mass in the chapel. Afterwards he was to go to breakfast. Further regulations prescribed the rest of Edward's day.

Edward V and Anthony Woodville were at Ludlow when they learned of King Edward's death, which made Prince Edward the King of England. Plans were made for the young king to make his way to London, and his coronation date was set for 4 May 1483. As Edward left Ludlow, he had no idea it would be the last time he would see the castle that had been his home.

Ludlow was also the principal residence for Elizabeth of York's son, Arthur. Following his wedding to Katherine of Aragon, he and the young princess lived here for a few months until tragedy struck. Arthur fell sick and died. Elizabeth's grief over the loss of her son was great, but she realised her responsibility to protect the young widow and soon sent to Ludlow for her daughter-in-law to join her.

Visiting Today

Although Ludlow Castle is a ruin, enough remains to give visitors an idea of both its layout and its size. Visitors today enter the castle through the outer gatehouse, which was the main entrance from the town. The stables and porter's lodge were built in the 1500s and would not have existed in the Duke of York's time.

Stand with your back to the gatehouse and look across the outer bailey. On the far left you can see the remains of St Peter's Chapel, which was built by Roger Mortimer in the fourteenth century. While renovations occurred throughout the following centuries, traces of the original chapel can still be detected. Mortimer's Tower, which was constructed in the thirteenth century, is close by. According to the castle's guidebook, tradition holds that the Duke of York and his eldest sons escaped the Lancastrian forces through this tower.

From St Peter's Chapel, turn and face the keep. Originally a gatehouse, this tall Norman tower was added to in stages. The tower with its four square turrets can be entered once inside the inner bailey. One legend surrounding the tower claims that a lion was once kept in an area of the keep, where it served as the castle's executioner. Even though the atmosphere at the base of the keep is gloomy, this legend has no basis in fact.

To reach the inner bailey, enter through the arched doorway to the right of the keep. The buildings directly in front of you make up the north range, where the Duke of York would have spent most of his time when at Ludlow. The Great Hall's entrance would have been reached by a substantial staircase leading to the richly ornamented pointed archway. Visitors to the castle while York was in residence would have walked up the staircase, through the archway and into the Great Hall, where Richard and Cecily would have sat upon the dais at the upper end. While the room contained no fireplace at this time, an open hearth would have supplied heat for the inhabitants of the large room while they had their meal.

The solar wing and the chamber block are on either side of the hall. York and his family would have spent most of their time in their apartments. Unfortunately, the apartments are no longer extant.

Leaving the hall, make your way back into the inner bailey; here is one of the most interesting parts of the castle. The round chapel of St Mary Magdalene, built to imitate the Church of the Holy Sepulchre in Jerusalem, was an important part of the castle. While at Ludlow the family would have heard Mass in the church's round nave.

Before you leave the castle, be sure to climb to the top of the keep for some beautiful views of the countryside. It is a steep climb, but the sights are worth it. From here you can look down on the river winding its way toward Dinham Bridge, or see the hills in the distance. Turning towards town, you can see the spires of St Laurence's church. If you look down you can also get a bird's-eye view of the castle's layout.

For more information on visiting the castle, see the castle website at www.ludlowcastle.com. If driving, take advantage of the city's park-and-ride scheme. For more information, visit www. travelshropshire.co.uk/bus/park-and-ride/ludlow-park-and-ride. aspx. The postcode for the park and ride is SY8 1ES. Ludlow Castle postcode is SY8 1AY.

The Parish Church of St Laurence, Ludlow

While there is no evidence to suggest that the Duke of York and his family attended services here, the church's close proximity to the castle makes it a possibility. The duke certainly would be familiar with the church, which was built in the shape of a cross. Much of what is seen today was built in the fifteenth century, although portions date from the twelfth. The church has been witness to many of the historical events in Ludlow, including the sack of the town by Lancastrian forces after the flight of the Duke of York and his allies.

The church's Perpendicular architecture makes it easy to see why it is called the 'Cathedral of the Marches'. Today the nave is divided from the side aisles by pointed arches, but in the fifteenth century it would have held many side chantries. The roof would also have been brightly painted. Carved angels watch from the chancel, which was enlarged in the fifteenth century. In the west end of the chancel, look up to see if you can find the bosses of the white rose of York and the falcon and fetterlock. Take time to admire the misericords under the choir stalls. Some of them are unusual, while others are simply humorous. A moment is also necessary to appreciate the exquisitely carved bench ends in the chancel stalls. While in the church also look for the marker showing where Arthur Tudor's heart was buried.

Take a moment to view the beautiful nineteenth-century stained-glass windows. For our purposes, there are three fascinating panels in the elaborate West Window. Here you will find depictions of three generations of Yorks: Richard, Duke of York; Edward IV; and his son, Edward V. Now is the time to pull out binoculars if you have a set.

One of the oldest items in the church is the font. At least 1,000 years old, the font would have graced the church during the York family's tenancy at Ludlow. Take time to admire its simple elegance before leaving the building.

For the church's opening times visit its website. For the armchair traveller, the church provides a pictorial tour on its website, www.stlaurences.org.uk/history-and-virtual-tour/a-virtual-tour-st-laurences. Parish church of St Laurence postcode: SY8 1AN.

Before you leave Ludlow, stroll along the Breadwalk to get an idea of the landscape around the area. To reach the Breadwalk, turn right out of the castle, go down the hill and cross Dinham Bridge. At the end of the bridge, turn left and stay to the signposted path. The walk leads you along the riverbank and presents great views of the castle. Bring a picnic lunch and eat at one of the benches that line the path. At the other end of the walk, you will cross Ludford Bridge.

Sandal Castle, West Yorkshire

Following the claim of York to be the rightful heir to the throne, Parliament enacted an agreement whereby York and his sons would be heirs to the throne but Henry VI would remain king. It is easy to imagine the reaction of Margaret of Anjou to the news that her son had been effectively disinherited. Her support in the north began to grow, as men from the area who heard that York had been made the king's heir found the 'decree of Parliament ... detestable' and joined her faction.

York decided it was necessary to deal with Lancastrian movements and to secure the country from a possible invasion from Scotland. He, accompanied by his son Edmund, marched north with the Earl of Salisbury. When their forces reached Sandal on 21 December 1460, the castle was not ready for their arrival so it is possible food supplies would have been short. Christmas festivities at the castle were tense, since the men were aware how close the Lancastrians were.

Sandal held a strong defensive position above the River Calder, dominating the surrounding Calder Valley. Located about two miles from Wakefield, the castle was built by William de Warenne in the early twelfth century. Originally a motte-and-bailey castle, it was later rebuilt in stone. A deep moat surrounded the castle, with the dirt from the moat used to build the 50 feet high mound. From atop the mound, the castle commanded a view of the surrounding area.

By the thirteenth century, the castle contained a large deer park, two mills, a grange, a garden and a small pool containing fish. Using surveys of the time, it is possible to determine the castle's layout. It had a courtyard and a circular stone keep with several turreted towers. The kitchen and other domestic buildings lay to the east of the castle. An embattled curtain wall enclosed the outer ward of the keep, with a circular barbican tower of ashlar facing connected to the bailey by a drawbridge. From a drawing of Sandal Castle in 1562, it appears that the barbican tower was castellated. A steep, walled entranceway led to the castle.

J. W. Walker, a writer in the late nineteenth century, based his descriptions on surveys of the castle. He said that the entrance to the castle was by an external stone staircase of ten steps which opened onto a porch supported by pillars. The porch gave access both to the hall and long gallery, adjoined to the hall on its southern end. At the south end of the hall was a screen; at the north end was a dais. Directly behind the dais was a door which opened to the withdrawing room. Round-headed windows lit the room, while a fireplace in the outer wall would have provided warmth for York and his men.

The Lancastrians attacked on 30 December. While it is hard to know exactly what occurred, one theory suggests that some of the duke's men were out foraging for food when the Lancastrians appeared. Instead of staying within the safety of the castle, the other men joined the battle. The Lancastrians waited until the Yorkists were on level ground before attacking with their full forces.

Depending on the source, York was either slain in the battle or taken alive, belittled and then beheaded. Given the nature of the fight, he probably died in battle. Lord Clifford was said to have killed Edmund, Earl of Rutland, in cold blood, and Salisbury was captured and executed the next day at nearby Pontefract. The news of this tragedy soon would reach Cecily and her children, prompting her to send her two youngest boys, Richard and George, to the Low Countries. Her oldest son, Edward, Earl of March, would continue the fight his father had begun and would eventually be named king.

Edward IV and Richard III at Sandal

In 1470, Edward fled to the Low Countries to escape the Earl of Warwick. Richard joined Edward there and, after several months of exile, they headed back to England in March 1471. At Kingston-upon-Hull Edward and his men were denied entry, so he made straight for York. Despite initial misgivings from the citizens of the city, Edward and Richard, along with a few of their men, were allowed within the city walls. Leaving York, they made their way south to Sandal and on to face Warwick.

As their forces made their way to the castle, the battle at Wakefield may have been on the brothers' minds. Once again, a large Lancastrian force was nearby, and they may have wondered if another defeat for the House of York would occur here. This time, however, there was no battle, and the men soon left the castle, gaining supporters and making their way towards London.

Richard III would make Sandal one of the meeting places for his Council of the North, giving it the name King's Household in the North. It was from here that the council would dispense justice and hear disputes. During his reign, Richard ordered improvements to the castle, and it appears that some were carried out before Bosworth. However, by Elizabeth I's reign the castle was already showing signs of neglect. Besieged twice by Parliamentary forces during the Civil War, the castle was stripped of its defences.

Visiting Sandal Castle Today

Sandal Castle is a short drive from nearby Wakefield. The castle has a car park and visitor's centre. There is no admission charge so you can freely wander through the scant remains of this former stronghold of the Duke of York. Take time to visit the mound because the views of the surrounding area are outstanding.

A short walk from the castle leads you to the monument for Richard, Duke of York, which supposedly marks the spot where he was slain. Unfortunately it takes the place of an earlier monument destroyed during the Civil War, which was not on the same spot. However, it serves a memorial to York, making it worth a visit.

At the time of this publication, the castle offered 2 p.m. tours Wednesday through Sundays. It is advisable to call ahead, though, to avoid disappointment. The castle has a website: www.wakefield.gov.uk/residents/events-and-culture/castles/sandalcastle. Castle postcode: WF2 7DS.

Church of St Mary the Virgin and All Saints, Fotheringhay, Northamptonshire

The octagonal lantern tower of the Church of St Mary the Virgin and All Saints rises high above the surrounding landscape. Beautiful at a distance, the church is even more impressive up close. Originally a collegiate church, it was founded by Edward, Duke of York, in the fifteenth century. He established the college in 1411 beside the original parish church, which was incorporated into the design. A master, twelve chaplains, eight clerks and thirteen choristers made up the college, founded for the purpose of praying for the royal family.

Edward's untimely death at Agincourt prevented him from

accomplishing his entire vision, but enough was finished for him to be buried there. Richard, Duke of York, fulfilled his wishes and signed a contract with the freemason William Horwood to complete the church. Once Richard died at Wakefield, it would be some years before work would commence again. Richard's son Edward IV refounded the college once he felt that his reign was secure. Years later, Henry VIII would cause the college to surrender its liberties, and under Edward VI it was granted to the Duke of Northumberland, John Dudley.

Historians disagree regarding the level of destruction to the collegiate church that can be placed at Dudley's feet. Whether or not Dudley completely removed the roof from the choir and demolished some of the buildings is not completely clear. Regardless, the church did fall into ruin and many of the buildings surrounding it were destroyed.

One of the biggest events in the history of the church with regards to the York family was the reinterment of Richard and his son, Edmund. This momentous occasion was a proud day for the House of York. In July 1476, the bodies of the Duke of York and Edmund of Rutland were placed in the hearses built in the priory of St John at Pontefract. According to Anne Sutton and Livia Visser-Fuchs in their work *The Reburial of Richard Duke of York, 21–30 July 1476*, the coffin of the Duke of York, covered with his heraldic symbols, was placed in the centre of his hearse. A lifelike effigy inside the hearse was dressed in dark blue, wearing a purple cap. An angel was behind him, holding a crown of gold over his head. The royal trappings were possibly used to strengthen the claim of the dynasty of the House of York. The crown behind his head demonstrated that he was a king uncrowned – a king by right.

Bishops, including those of Durham, Chester, Hereford and Bangor, and other priests and abbots were present for the exhumation. After a requiem Mass the following morning, the coffins were placed in a funeral carriage. The Duke of York's son, Richard, was chief mourner and would have followed behind the carriage while it moved towards its final destination of Fotheringhay. He and the other mourners, including several of the leading nobles of the realm, would have been dressed in mourning habits.

As with other funeral processions, at each stop along the way religious ceremonies were held where the bodies lay in the church. According to Sutton and Visser-Fuchs, at every church a new hearse awaited. This was necessary because after a requiem Mass the old structure, with its valuable and decorative features, such as candles and valances, was left at the church for alms.

King Edward, dressed in the royal mourning colour of dark blue, met the procession when it arrived in Fotheringhay on 29 July. Carried by twelve men, the coffin and effigy were taken into the church and placed in the elaborate hearse. Sutton and Visser-Fuchs believe that the hearse used for the final ceremony at Fotheringhay was the same one used for the obit of 1463. If so, it would have been elaborately decorated with fifty-one wax images of kings, 420 wax angels and sprinkled with silver roses. Escutcheons of arms covered both the hearse and the valence. Edward IV's emblem of the sun would also have adorned the structure.

Edmund's coffin was carried to its waiting hearse in the Lady Chapel. The king and other nobles, including Clarence and Gloucester, accompanied the bodies into the church. Following the service, the king and queen gave an offering of yards of cloth of gold, which was draped in the shape of a cross over the coffin.

The official funeral and reburial occurred the next day. Three services were held, led by the Bishop of Lincoln. After the ceremonies, alms were distributed to the poor and then a large feast was held both outside and inside the castle. Tents and tables had to be constructed in order to seat everyone. Like with most large medieval feasts, there was plenty to choose from, as ale and wine flowed, while fish, rabbits, partridges, chickens and honey, along with other dishes, were brought out to the waiting guests.

Unfortunately, there is no extant description of the duke's tomb, and the original tombs were destroyed. York's uncle Edward's tomb was described by Leland as being a flat marble stone with an image flat in brass. Since Edward IV was implying that his father was a 'king by right' he would have commissioned a more elaborate tomb, one fit for a king.

Queen Elizabeth I visited Fotheringhay and was appalled at how dilapidated her ancestors' tombs were. The tombs currently in the church are the replacements she commissioned. A legend says that when Cecily Neville's body was unearthed, a ribbon with a papal indulgence was found tied around her neck and the ink appeared fresh. Today, the tombs bear the York badge of a falcon and fetterlock.

Visiting Today

Fotheringhay celebrates its ties to the Yorks, and the church contains several exhibits related to them. The York Window was erected by the Richard III Society and features shields to commemorate the family. One interesting display is William Dugdale's 1669 copy of the original 1434 contract for the building of the church.

The beautifully decorated pulpit, now painted to resemble how it might have appeared in the fifteenth century, is believed to have been given to the church by Edward IV. Be sure to look up at the falcon and fetterlock emblem while in the church. Before leaving the area, walk outside to the east side of the church. On this side you can see evidence of the arches where the choir of the collegiate church was once separated from the parish nave. Church of St Mary the Virgin and All Saints, Fotheringhay postcode: PE8 5HZ.

Part 2
Cecily Neville

As the great-granddaughter of Edward III, the wife of a powerful magnate, the mother of two kings and the grandmother of both another king and a queen consort, Cecily Neville had an adventurous life filled with hardship and joy. From the death of her husband and son on a battlefield near Wakefield to the coronation of her eldest son as king, she saw great fluctuations in the wheel of fortune. Her strength in times of crisis helped her family deal with its changing roles in the fifteenth century. She and her husband, Richard, seemed to have a successful marriage by both modern and medieval standards. They had several surviving children, and, since Cecily often travelled to be with her husband, seem to have enjoyed a loving relationship. In the middle of the nineteenth century, poet John Crawford penned the following lines:

> Fair Rose of Raby! I would weep with thee
> O'er all the horrors that oppress thine heart.
> Mother of Kings! the goodly parent-tree
> Of fruit, that deals thee sorrow's keenest smart.

While she was not called the 'Rose of Raby' by contemporaries, this seems a fitting tribute to this courageous woman.

Raby Castle, Durham

On a spring day in early May 1415, at Raby Castle, the Countess of Westmorland safely delivered a baby girl, whom she and her husband named Cecily. Tradition holds that Cecily was born here, at one of her father's many holdings.

Cecily was born into a large family, since both of her parents had been married previously. Her father, Ralph Neville, first married Margaret Stafford and had eight children. Cecily's mother, Joan Beaufort, was a granddaughter of Edward III, and the daughter of John of Gaunt by his mistress, Katherine Swynford. Joan had first married Sir Robert Ferrers, having two children by him before he died in 1395/6. In early 1396, Joan's parents married, and within the year she had been legitimised by a papal bull. Now a legitimate child of the Duke and Duchess of Lancaster, Joan's marriage prospects broadened. By November 1396, she had married Ralph Neville, then 6th Baron Neville of Raby.

For his loyalty to the king, Neville was created 1st Earl of Westmorland in 1397. The loyalty would not stand the test of time, however. In 1399 Neville supported his brother-in-law, Henry Bolingbroke, when he made his invasion of England. For this support he would receive many rewards. Many of his grants, like that at Penrith, came to him jointly through his wife, the half-sister of the king. In 1423, he purchased the wardship of Richard, Duke of York, who joined the household at Raby.

When John Leland visited the castle in the sixteenth century, he remarked, 'Raby is the largest cartel of Logginges in al the North Cuntery, and is of a strong Building, but not set other on Hil or very strong Ground.' Meant more to be a fortified manor house than a fortification, Raby Castle, as we know it today, was begun by John Neville. Since Raby was within the Palatinate of Durham, Neville received a licence to crenellate from the Bishop of Durham in 1398. He probably was making changes to an existing building, because parts of the castle date from an earlier time. Raby was soon surrounded by an embattled wall and a moat.

When returning to Raby from her family's other homes, Cecily would have entered through the ribbed vault of the Neville gateway. As she neared the four-storey machicolated gatehouse, she would have seen the shields of John Neville, his second wife Elizabeth Latimer, and St George and the Garter. Later, Cecily would be given the moniker 'Proud Cis' – perhaps she felt pride when she looked upon the magnificent building her ancestors had created.

On special occasions, her large family would use the Great Hall, commonly called the Barons' Hall, for their meals. In the nineteenth century, John Timbs described the Great Hall. Long, narrow windows lit the room on the east and west, while large windows with exquisite tracery dominated the north and south walls. A large stone music gallery sat at the north end, and an oak roof rested on cambered beams overlooking the room. Laughter and conversation would have filled the room when the family visited.

On two occasions, both before Cecily was born, the chapel at Raby was used for marriage ceremonies for two of her elder sisters. Katherine married John Mowbray and Eleanor married Richard, Lord Despenser. The chapel appears to have once been on the same level with the Great Hall, with a short passageway leading from one room to the other. Following the ceremonies, the hall would have been used for the wedding feast. Since we do not know where Cecily's wedding ceremonies were held, it is possible that she and York also married here at Raby.

The chapel would be familiar to Cecily since it was the centre of family worship. J. P. Pritchett carried out an investigation of the chapel in 1901. From his work and the work of Reverend J. H. Hodgson, it is possible to get an idea of the chapel as Cecily knew it. When entering the chapel, Cecily would have seen a six-lighted window which Pritchett believes was placed there to allow members of the household to see the service. A piscina would have either been on the south or east walls. On the south side were the sedilia and a narrow entranceway into a chamber, which was probably a priest's room.

Raby Castle would stay in the hands of the Neville family until the sixteenth century, when the family property was forfeited to the crown after the Earl of Westmorland took part in the Rising of the North. In the seventeenth century, Sir Henry Vane purchased Raby from the Crown, and his descendants still own Raby today.

Visiting Today

Raby has been through many restorations, renovations and rebuilding projects so most of its interior has changed a great deal. In the eighteenth century, the barbican was destroyed and the chapel and Great Hall drastically changed in order for a carriageway to be built through the home so visitors could escape the cold. The Duchess of Cleveland, writing years later, said, 'It is no doubt a novel and startling experience on a cold wet night to see the great gates fly open and to drive into a hall blazing with light between two roaring fires.' Unfortunately, the renovation means that Cecily would little recognise either the chapel or the Barons' Hall.

Although the exterior has changed, with some towers being torn down and at least one added, Cecily would recognise many of the towers we see today. Joan's Tower was named after her mother and was originally only three storeys tall. When Cecily was in residence at Raby, the pentagonal Bulmer's Tower was not connected to the rest of the castle. It was not until the eighteenth century that it was connected to the Chapel Tower.

Today, the castle grounds are entered from the A688. After paying at the kiosk, park in the car park and then walk past the gardens and tea rooms on your right and the cricket pitch on your left to make your way to the castle entrance. The best way to see Raby Castle is through a guided tour. Unfortunately the area where Cecily is believed to have been born is not open to visitors, but you may still visit the chapel and the Barons' Hall. Although the rest of the interior is largely altered, you are still within the same walls where Cecily spent much of her early years.

The Barons' Hall has changed so much that Cecily would recognise very little. The original hammer-beam roof was replaced by the roof you see today. According to the castle guide, only the windows on the west side and those above the minstrels' gallery remain from her time period. The gallery itself has also been changed to allow for the insertion of a doorway.

The chapel that you see today is much different than that which Cecily would have seen. The floor of the chapel was raised to allow for the construction of the carriageway. Since the original window traceries had decayed, replicas were installed. As part of restoration work in 1901, the arcade was uncovered and portraits of people associated with Raby were subsequently commissioned. Cecily is featured on the far right. This arcade is the screen that Pritchett believes once opened into the Barons' Hall.

The room that has changed the least since Cecily's time is the kitchen. The large room has passageways set within its walls for servants to make their way to the Barons' Hall. While in the kitchen, be sure to look at the medieval floor tiles. Since they are believed to have been taken from the Entrance Hall during one of the renovations, Cecily likely walked across them.

Once you exit the castle itself, walk back to the gardens. A garden would have featured at the castle during medieval times, but would have been mainly a herb garden. This walled garden was designed in the nineteenth century. Nearby are the gift shop and carriageway museum, both worth a visit. If you feel hungry, a tea room is usually open during the castle's opening times. Before you leave the area, be sure to visit the deer park. It is also worthwhile to drive towards Staindrop. At the lay-by, pull over for a view of the castle. Many times the deer are roaming in the park in front of the castle, making for a picturesque photograph.

The castle is open to visitors during the summer. The best way to get to Raby Castle is by car. For more information on visiting the castle, see its website at www.rabycastle.com. Postcode: DL2 3AH.

St Mary's Church, Staindrop, Durham

Within a mile of Raby lies the village of Staindrop. A church has existed here at least since Saxon times. Before the Normans came, Staindrop was granted to the monastery at Durham by Canute. Once the Nevilles built Raby Castle, the church, at that time dedicated to St Gregory, benefited from their largesse. In 1343, Ralph Neville received a licence to found and endow three chantries in the church. It was at this time that the south aisle and transept were rebuilt to make room for the chantries.

Ralph and Joan founded a college here dedicated to the Virgin Mary in 1408, and soon afterward began adding on to the church. The couple added the chancel choir pews with their misericords and raised the roof line, adding a clerestory. The tower also reached its current height in this period. The college was a large one, providing for a master, chaplains and clerks, poor gentlemen and other poor persons. At the Dissolution, its value was recorded at more than £126.

Cecily's first experience at St Mary's was her christening. While she may have been christened in the chapel in Raby Castle, it is more likely she was christened here. Through her childhood, she may also have observed Mass in the parish church.

While the church has received several additions, Cecily would still recognise many of its features today. She certainly would recognise the large alabaster tomb of her father, built using stone quarried from John of Gaunt's quarry in Tutbury. The effigies of his two wives, Margaret Stafford and Joan Beaufort, rest on either side of him, although Joan was buried at Lincoln Cathedral. Hutchinson, writing in the early nineteenth century, described the tomb:

> The effigy of the Earl represents him in complete armour, except the helmet, on which the head is rested, bearing the crest – a Bull's head; the Scullcap, which is much broken, has on the front I. H. S. in the old character; the hands are elevated in gauntlets; on the breast the Cross; the legs are extended, spurs on the heels, and the feet resting on a lion. The ladies heads are rested on cushions, supported by cherubs, and at the feet of each figure is a desk with two kneeling clerks. Around the Tomb are niches, ornamented with tabernacle work; but no inscription.

Unfortunately, the niches stand empty today, as the tomb suffered some destruction during subsequent centuries, but it is still an interesting monument to the 1st Earl of Westmorland and his two wives. According to Leland, the tomb used to stand in the choir. The vicar of Staindrop, Harry Lipscomb, writing in the late nineteenth century, says that the tomb was moved in order to make the family vault for the Earl of Darlington. When it was moved, the skeleton of the earl was found and was of 'uncommon large bones, and appeared to have been a very tall man'.

Lipscomb also quotes the Reverend H. J. Swallow, giving further description of Joan Beaufort's effigy being 'habited in a mantle, kirtle, and surcote, all richly edged and faced; her hair braided and coomed ... on her head, which rests on two cushions, the undermost tasselled, supported by three angels, is a coronet ... at the feet of each of the ladies are two dogs collared, peeping out from under their robes'. Today the effigy is surrounded by a fence, making it difficult to observe the rich details closely.

Visiting Today

There are many items of interest in the church, and a visit can take an hour or more. However, our tour focuses on areas related to Cecily and her Neville ancestors. Stand outside the entrance for a moment. The South-West Porch in front of you was built in the fourteenth century. As you enter the church, pass the oak tomb of

Henry, 5th Earl of Westmorland, and stop at the alabaster tomb of Ralph Neville. After examining the tomb for a while, imagining it gilded and brightly painted, turn and face the altar. The pews in front of you would not have been here in Cecily's time, but the wooden screen is one of the finest surviving examples of a medieval screen.

Walk up the south aisle which was enlarged to make room for the chantry chapels. The effigy of Euphemia de Clavering rests under a finely detailed canopy. Both the effigy and canopy originally would have been painted with bright colours, but this has faded over time. Other Neville ladies also lie here. Take some time to marvel at the intricate stonework of each effigy before heading to the choir. Most of the choir pews are believed to have been built soon after the college was founded, although some may date from a slightly later period. On the east side of the chancel is the sedilia. The hermit's window nearby allowed him to look at the altar without being seen.

Much of the roof is medieval, having been covered with lead during the renovations. Above the altar is a portion of roof which would have been brightly coloured and contained the heraldic symbols of the Nevilles.

The church does a good job of explaining its history with placards. At the time of publication, the church displayed models showing its appearance throughout its history. The church is open during daylight hours, but it is always wise to check its website at http://www.stmarysstaindrop.org.uk/Staindrop/St_Marys_Staindrop.html. Coming from Raby Castle, the church will be on your right hand side right before the A688 takes a sharp right curve. According to its website, while the church does not have a postcode, DL2 3NJ will get you to the church. Be aware that parking is limited.

Montgomery Castle, Powys, Wales

On 12 May 1432, York was granted livery of his estates. The following May he was ordered to pay Katherine (Catherine de Valois), the king's mother, £53 6s 8d every year and the arrears for the lordship and castle of Montgomery. As part of her dower, Katherine had been assigned the fee farm of the lordship and castle of Montgomery. In 1422, Edmund, then Earl of March, had been told to pay the same.

Richard and Cecily would have spent time examining each of York's properties, and, given its location, Montgomery Castle was probably their base in Wales. Perched high above the town on a rocky promontory, the castle was built in the reign of Henry III to replace the motte-and-bailey castle constructed a short distance away in the eleventh century by Roger de Montgomery. This motte-and-bailey castle, known as Hen Domen, was closer to the Severn.

Conflicts with Lylwelyn ap Iorwerth in the thirteenth century convinced the king that a new castle was needed. Matthew Paris says that the hill above the Severn was deemed a 'suitable spot for the erection of an impregnable castle' and work quickly commenced on a timber castle. This castle was later rebuilt in stone, and in early 1228 Henry granted it to Hubert de Burgh for life. Later that year, Lylwelyn attacked the unfinished castle. Luckily for de Burgh, the king's army saved it. Afterwards, the king granted de Burgh funds to enclose the castle. When Lylwelyn attacked in 1231 he burnt the town, but seems to have left the castle alone. Following this, the castle reverted to the Crown.

A fanciful mind can picture Cecily staring down into the same valley before you, enjoying the play of light on the hills in the distance. Perhaps she watched from here for her husband to return from visiting his other holdings.

Visiting Today
Only ruins remain of the large edifice overlooking the valley of the River Camlad. The scope of the castle, though, is easy to see, both from below looking up and from the site itself. Upon arrival you can either park in the town and walk up or park closer to the castle. The site itself will take about thirty minutes to an hour to visit, depending on how enamoured one becomes with the views from the area. Before visiting the castle, visit the Old Bell museum located on Arthur Street to see a model of the castle and pick up a guidebook. The museum is only open from April to September, but a castle guidebook is also available at the Post Office. For more information about the museum, see its website http://www.oldbellmuseum.org.uk/museum.htm. Montgomery postcode: SY15 6RA.

Bewdley Manor, Worcestershire

Also called Tickenhill and Tickhill, Bewdley Manor sits above the town of Bewdley. Situated at the edge of the Forest of Wyre, Bewdley rests on the Severn River. The manor home had been in the hands of the Mortimers, eventually passing down to York following the death of his aunt Anne. While some historians believe that Tickenhill and Bewdley were separate manor homes, evidence suggests they were actually the same manor, just called by different names through time. By the fourteenth century, the building was often called 'Beaulieu' manor. The manor overlooked the town, which according to Leland was beautiful: 'The Towne self of Beaudley is sett on the side of an Hill, soe comely, a man cannot wish to see a Towne better. It riseth from Severne banke by East upon the hill by west...'

York's itinerary has him in Bewdley in October 1446. According to local histories, he is credited with having done a great deal towards making the area prosperous, perhaps even contributing to the bridge built in 1447. The manor itself had fallen into disrepair by the fourteenth century, so York had to do some building works, although no direct evidence of such has been found.

Cecily would have been with York at Bewdley, and according to author Amy Licence, quite possibly became pregnant while here. She stayed here for a few weeks, and during that time would have seen the park overlooking the town. Perhaps she even participated in a hunt in the large park, which was described in 1612 as having 3,500 large oak trees and 180 head of deer.

When York was attainted, the manor passed to Edward, Prince of Wales. The stone bridge was torn down by the Lancastrians and its stone given to Worcester. The men of the town rebuilt a bridge with timber, which lasted until Richard III's reign.

After Edward IV took the throne, he granted that the town with its precincts may be a free borough. He also enlarged and renovated the manor at Bewdley, building a large hall, 100 feet long, which included chambers both below and above it. These rooms would have been plastered and hung with ornate tapestries. The manor itself was built of timber, with a large court and outbuildings. Some sources say it occupied two acres – a large manor – complete with a garden. Leland calls it 'a fayre manor place by the west of the Towne standing in a goodly Parke well wooded, on the very Knappe of an hill that the Towne standeth on. This place is called Tickenhill.'

When Richard III became king, he gave twenty marks for the completion of a new bridge at Bewdley. This timber bridge had five arches, and on the third pier was a timbered gate house. According to Bewdley historian John Burton, portions of this bridge lasted until the late eighteenth century.

Henry VII also made his mark upon the manor, largely redoing portions of it for Prince Arthur, his son by Elizabeth of York. On 19 May 1499, Arthur married Katherine of Aragon (by proxy) in the manor's chapel. Arthur made Bewdley and Ludlow his main residences, and his parents visited here on at least one occasion in 1495.

Following Arthur's death at Ludlow, his body rested briefly in Bewdley, before going on to Worcester Cathedral. John Burton quotes a description of the event:

> The Corpse was removed on St. Mark's day (Ap. 25) from Ludlow to Beaudeley: it was the foulist could windy & rayney day, & the worst way. Yea in some places fayne to take oxen to drawe the chare so ill was the way. And as soon as he was in the Chapell of Beaudley there, and set in the Quire, therewith such lights as might be for that room the Dirige began. That don the Lords & others went to their Dyner, for it was a fasting day. On the morning the Earl of Surry officiated at the Masse of requiem. A Noble in manner as before at which Mass season there was a general Dole of Pens, of two Pens to every poor Man & Woman. From Beaudley Sir Richard Croft & Sir William Overdale, Steward & Controller of the Prince's Horse, rode before to Worcester.

Following Arthur's death, the manor eventually was restored for Henry VIII's daughter Mary. Portions of it were still standing until 1738, when the old house was pulled down. Interestingly enough, parts of the walls must have been incorporated into the new building because in 1880 a shoe from the Tudor era was found when a wall was repaired.

Visiting Today

Today, the area where Bewdley Manor once rested is a private residence. It is possible to get a view of what would have been some of the manor land, however. If you arrive by car, turn left after the bridge into Gardner's Meadow car park. This is the easiest place to park to get a full view of the town. Walk back towards town along the River Severn, admiring Telford's bridge, which replaced the old bridge. Turn left into town, walk up the hill past the church, and then turn left up Park Lane. Find the public footpath. This is roughly the area where the manor park would have been, and it is possible to get an idea of the commanding view of the countryside that Cecily would have seen.

Walking back down into town, take some time to visit the parish church. The church as it is now dates from the Georgian period. However, a timber church, built during the reign of Henry VI, once stood in its location. In the early seventeenth century, there was stained glass in the church depicting the arms of Richard, Duke of York, Edward IV, and Elizabeth Woodville. Some sources claim that it was within this chapel that Arthur's body rested.

For more information about visiting Bewdley, see http://www. visitwyreforest.co.uk/explore-the-area/bewdley.aspx. Bewdley postcode: DY12 2AE.

La Neyte, London

The country grange of the Abbot of Westminster, La Neyte was located about a mile from Westminster Abbey. By the time of Edward III, the home was used mainly for pleasure and for the abbot's important guests.

Cecily stayed here as a guest of the abbot. Whether she arrived at the large house by river or road is unknown, since both methods of travel were used to reach the manor. To enter, she would have crossed over the moat and into the abbot's palatial country home. By the time of Cecily's visit, the crenellated manor was already ancient. According to author Charles T. Gatty, repairs were made in the early part of the fourteenth century, with glass windows being put into the lord's chambers. The manor must have had a large garden because at one point it took twelve men two days to weed it.

According to Caroline Halsted, it was here at La Neyte on 7 November 1448 that Cecily delivered a son, John, who did not live long. It was not the first child that Cecily and York had lost, and York probably took time away to visit Cecily here at the manor to commiserate over the loss of their son.

Following the Reformation, the area became a tea garden and a public recreation area. Samuel Pepys visited here and wrote about it in his diary. In 1679, Nell Gwynn's mother drowned in a pond on the property.

It is impossible today to catch a glimpse of the manor as it was. Concrete covers what used to be meadow, and the once impressive manor home is no longer extant. However, walking the streets, you can imagine Cecily arriving here as a guest of Abbot Edmund Kyrton.

Visiting Today

The manor home is long gone, and today houses and streets mask what used to be the abbot's manor. From Victoria bus station, head west on Terminus Place toward Buckingham Palace Road. Turn left on Buckingham Palace Road and cross Ebury Bridge. To your left is Warwick Way. Do not turn left here, but keep the location in mind as you walk straight ahead for a short distance. To your left, you will see Sutherland Row. The Manor House was located in this area, between Warwick Way and Sutherland Row, not far from the Thames.

Caister Castle, Norfolk

A short distance from the grey North Sea, Caister Castle was a palatial home built by Sir John Fastolf during the 1430s and 1440s on the grounds of his family's existing manor home. Fastolf, known for his role in the Hundred Years War, built his home over a period of several years. Looking at the ruins, it is obvious that he built a home that would impress his neighbours. Among its more impressive features was a stew, or bathing room, in Fastolf's chambers.

Even though Fastolf wanted the best of comforts in his home, he did not overlook defensive features. Machicolated towers equipped with arrow slits and gun ports protected the area, and the drawbridges which lay over the wet moat could easily be raised.

The castle certainly made a lasting impression on Cecily, since she and York pressured Fastolf to sell her the grand residence following her visit in 1456. She stayed here for some time, far removed from court. A plan of the castle from the eighteenth century shows an inner and outer court, separated by the moat. The inner court included the Great Hall, chapel and chamber towers. The castle guidebook speculates that there may have been another courtyard to the west with other buildings, but acknowledges this is not proven.

If Cecily approached the castle from Fastolf's barge from the River Bure, she would have ridden along a canal connecting the castle to the river before disembarking at the barge house. This is also how the Caen stone and other building materials for the residence had arrived.

Caister had two impressive towers for chambers. A smaller one stood at the corner of the western court. However, it was probably in its richest chambers that Cecily was housed. This tower stood in the southern area of the court. Her chamber would have been sumptuously decorated with tapestries and intricate cloths of arras. Several of the rooms in the castle were plastered and covered with murals, and it is within the realm of possibility that Cecily's chamber contained such a mural. Richly coloured furniture would have been placed in the chamber for her use. Alastair Hawkyard says that Fastolf had a bed in his chamber that had an arras cover with the pictorial design of a lady in a chair of estate. Perhaps he moved the cover to Cecily's bedchamber during her visit.

After the turbulence of the past few years, Cecily probably enjoyed the peace and tranquillity that Caister offered. As she walked to the chapel through the open cloisters that linked the buildings of the inner court together, Cecily could admire the rich brickwork and the turrets of the nine towers of the inner court. Later, when she made her way through the enclosed gallery above the cloisters, she could gaze out the glazed windows into the inner courtyard where servants of the household moved to and fro carrying on with their daily work. Fastolf would have provided entertainment for Cecily within the Great Hall, with its large oriel window.

Cecily would have spent some time resting in Caister's elaborate gardens, watching the clouds play across the broad Norfolk sky. Here, in this tranquil setting, Cecily had time to process the events that had transpired over the past years. Spending her time walking through the garden and watching the ducks swim in the pond probably soothed her while she worried about her family's future.

Visiting Today

Sadly, most of the structure that so enamoured Cecily is gone today. Enough remains, however, to give visitors a sense of its grandeur. After crossing the moat and entering through a picturesque archway, visitors can climb the 90 feet tower for views across the Norfolk countryside. According to the castle, the west wall was once the exterior wall of the Great Hall, and the chapel sat adjoining the entrance of the north-west tower. The wall where visitors enter today would have been a minor postern gate.

Today, those who want to see the grand castle ruins must purchase a combined ticket good for both the castle and Caister's vintage car museum. According to the castle website, the museum boasts the largest private collection of vintage cars in the country. On my visit, I spent my time in the castle ruins, but many people were purchasing tickets and heading to the car museum first. For more information about opening times and admission costs, visit the castle website at http://www.caistercastle.co.uk/ or phone +(44) 01664 567707. Caister Castle postcode: NR30 5SN.

Tonbridge Castle, Kent

Following the debacle at Ludford Bridge, Cecily was placed in the custody of her sister, Anne, Duchess of Buckingham. Anne's husband, Humphrey Stafford, was a devoted Lancastrian. In fact, it was Stafford who, shortly after Henry's son Edward's birth, had presented the prince to the king. Henry VI would have felt assured that Cecily would be in safe hands.

While there are no records detailing where Cecily stayed during this time, Cecily's biographer Amy Licence believes a letter written from William Botoner to John Berney in early 1460 gives a clue. Botoner says, 'My lady duchesse ys stille ayen rec'ved yn Kent.' Tonbridge Castle was part of the Duke of Buckingham's holdings in Kent, so presumably she stayed there.

It is hard to resist the impulse to wonder what Cecily was thinking when she first caught a glimpse of the market town with its fortified walls. Her husband and two eldest sons had fled England while she had been compelled to travel to Coventry to seek out the king. Now, she was in the custody of her sister with only 1,000 marks out of the Duke of York's estates to support her and her children.

Crossing over the great Burgh Dyke and through the North Gate, Cecily would have eventually seen the castle. Passing the barbican and crossing over the drawbridge, she would have reached its gatehouse, which had been built in the thirteenth century. The four-storey gatehouse, with its four circular towers, wide arch and sandstone-ashlar facing was an impressive sight. The curtain wall was also made of sandstone facing and in some points was almost 10 feet thick. Arriving through the arched entrance, Cecily would have made her way to the oval keep, which stood high above the bailey.

One chronicler suggests that the Duke of Buckingham treated Cecily harshly, with 'many a grete rebuke'. Perhaps this lasted her entire visit, or possibly sisterly bonds eventually prevailed. Whatever the case, Cecily was given a nice chamber from which she would have been able to look out across the bailey to the Stafford Tower and the Water Tower, both built in the fourteenth century.

For the next few months, Cecily's movements would have depended upon her sister. Anne would have continued to direct her busy household, perhaps with Cecily's assistance. As Cecily was a pious woman, she would have heard Mass at the chapel within the castle walls.

Cecily remained with her sister until after Northampton. As they waited impatiently for news, the two women may have been at odds, due to the circumstances. As news of the battle was delivered, Cecily probably tried to offer comfort to Anne, who lost her husband in the fray. As no records remain of their exchange, we will never know exactly what occurred. Perhaps Anne wanted Cecily gone from the castle or maybe she helped her escape. Whatever the events surrounding her departure, Cecily and her children were soon on their way to London.

Tonbridge History

The market town of Tonbridge was probably built upon a late Saxon settlement. Located in the heart of the Weald of Kent, the town was built along the banks of the River Medway. According to the Archaeology Data Service, the town's name is derived from Old English and means the bridge at the manor (or settlement). By the thirteenth century Tonbridge was surrounded by a wide ditch, built around the north, west and east of the town. Large walls were also built, and a licence to crenellate was granted by Henry III.

The castle was first mentioned in the late eleventh century after a motte-and -bailey was built here by Richard Fitzgilbert, whose family name would become de Clare due to their holdings in Clare. In the revolt of 1088, the de Clares chose to back the wrong brother and the town and castle were besieged and burned by William Rufus. Eventually rebuilt in stone, the circular keep, with its stone buttresses, stood high above the bailey.

The gatehouse was built in the thirteenth century. In the sixteenth century, the gatehouse was described as 'a strong fortress as few be in England'. It had a passage which led to the other towers, and its first floor consisted of two chambers and the portcullis room. Above the chambers was a room that ran the length of the gatehouse.

Visiting Today

Today, as with many sites, there is little left of the Tonbridge Castle that Cecily would have known. In 1999 a major renovation of the gatehouse was initiated, replacing missing floors and repairing the spiral staircase in the East Tower. This allows visitors to tour the gatehouse, although the rooms do not appear exactly as they were in the fifteenth century. The castle also offers an hour-long audio tour explaining life here in the thirteenth century.

Only a few masonry fragments remain of the keep where Cecily would have spent most of her time. However, visitors can still climb to the top of the mound and see the magnificent views of the surrounding countryside. From here it is easy to see why the Tudor Survey said that 'this castle was the strongest fortress and most like unto a castle'.

The best way to get an idea of the scope of the castle is to walk around the exterior where the moat would have been. From here, the motte soars high and it becomes easy to picture the grand keep above, where Cecily would have been housed in great comfort.

While visits to the inner bailey and motte are free, the audio tour of the gatehouse is fairly expensive. I felt it was worth the cost, but be aware that it does not address Cecily nor her time here.

Limited parking is available near the entrance of the castle, but further public parking is nearby at the swimming pool. From here a short, well-marked trail leads you up to the gatehouse entrance. For more information about visiting Tonbridge, see its website at http://www.tonbridgecastle.org/. Tonbridge Castle postcode: TN9 1BG.

Baynard's Castle, London

Towering over the Thames, Baynard's Castle was built to impress. Humphrey, Duke of Gloucester, had rebuilt the residence after there was 'a grette fyre at Baynardeys Castelle, the whyche fyre dyde moche harme'. The home he built was just west of Paul's Wharf. In the poem *The Lament of the Duchess of Gloucester*, his wife, Duchess Eleanor, bids the mansion goodbye after her trial, saying, 'Farewelle, fayer places on Temmys syde.' Eventually, the Duke of York came into possession of the residence.

After returning from Ireland, the Duke of York sent for Cecily to meet him. Stopping in several towns along the way, the couple finally entered London, and on 10 October 1460, the duke and duchess were reunited with the rest of their family at Baynard's Castle. It was one of their last times together as a family, since York would soon leave to go north.

Baynard's Castle continued to be a favoured residence of Cecily's for many years. Most likely it was here where Cecily learned of her husband's death at the Battle of Wakefield. Filled with grief and understandably frightened for her younger sons' security, she sent Richard and George abroad to the relative safety of the Low Countries, while she and Margaret stayed at Baynard's Castle. Here she awaited news of her eldest son, Edward, then Earl of March. Edward, while young, had a commanding presence and a good military eye. He soundly defeated the Lancastrian forces at Mortimer's Cross. This news would have pleased Cecily, ensconced in Baynard's Castle.

Cecily may have feared an approach by the royalist troops to London. Although the queen had once been a friend, it was doubtful she would be lenient to Cecily now. The citizens of London, hearing of the destruction caused by the royalist troops, were frightened and sent a delegation to the queen to express their concerns. Apparently deciding she would not be able to enter London, the queen retreated northward.

The citizens of London opened the doors willingly to Edward and Warwick. In St John's Fields, George Neville presented both the case against Henry VI and the case for Edward to be king. Edward was readily acclaimed by the populace. One chronicler has the people declaring 'yea' when asked if they accepted Edward as their king. How proud Cecily must have been when a great council met at Baynard's Castle to ask her son to be King of England. The next few days would have passed in a whirlwind of bittersweet excitement mixed with fear for Edward's safety. Soon, Edward would leave again to fight for his crown, leaving Cecily and Margaret in London.

The Bishop of Elphin was with Cecily when she heard news of the Battle of Towton. He wrote to the Bishop of Terni explaining how he 'was present in the house of the Duchess of York' when news of the battle was delivered to Cecily. After she heard the news, she, along with the bishop and two chaplains, climbed the broad staircase and returned to the chapel to say *Te Deum*. When Edward returned triumphantly to the city, Cecily attended his coronation.

While Edward IV allowed his mother use of the property, he also stayed here at times. Following his return from exile, he spent his first night in London reuniting with his wife and family here. Arriving by boat from Westminster, Edward and his family would have caught sight of the octagonal towers on either side of the huge building, which included four wings built in sandstone enclosing a square courtyard. Perhaps Cecily was watching from one of the windows, placed in pairs with one above another. Seeing her son and his family coming, she hurried down the staircase and to the right tower where a bridge with broad stairs led down to the Thames. Making their way from the dock to the heavy wooden doors of the residence, Edward's family would have entered the building, walking across the brightly coloured Norman tiles, decorated with birds facing back-to-back, and along the glossy, marbled tile into the Great Hall.

The hall would have been filled with joy that night while the family, including Richard and the Duchess of York, celebrated the men's safe return. As the servants milled about bringing food, and as warm fires blazed in the fireplaces, Edward and Richard would have regaled the others with stories of their time in the Low Countries, temporarily distracting themselves from the battles yet to come.

Richard III and Baynard's Castle

In June 1483, Richard was staying at Baynard's Castle instead of his residence of Crosby Place. After Buckingham had presented the case for Richard to be king, certain lords decided a petition should be drawn up proclaiming Richard the rightful heir to the throne. In Baynard's audience chamber, Richard agreed that on the next day he would accept the crown.

Shortly after Richard ascended to the throne, a meeting was held in the chapel of Baynard's Castle. In attendance were Richard, several bishops, the Duke of Buckingham, Thomas Stanley and John Gunthorpe. During this meeting, Richard presented the Bishop of Lincoln with a white leather bag containing his great seal. Perhaps Richard held other meetings within the large palatial residence on the bank of the Thames. It would not be long before Baynard's Castle would pass to the Tudors, but this home on the banks of the Thames had served the York family well.

Elizabeth of York and Baynard's Castle

Henry VII enlarged Baynard's Castle, adding three new brick wings towards the west and inserting a large octagonal tower in the centre. The side fronting the river was refaced in stone, with gable projections added. He used the palatial residence as a showcase for state purposes.

Elizabeth of York would have stayed at the castle often during her marriage. Perhaps it brought back bittersweet memories of time with her parents; but she now had her own children to help make new memories. Elizabeth, Henry VII and Arthur spent the night at Baynard's on the eve of Arthur's wedding to Katherine of Aragon.

During the reign of Elizabeth's other son, Henry VIII, Baynard's became a centre for great feasts and entertainment. Katherine of Aragon, Anne Boleyn and Anne of Cleves all resided here at some point while married to Henry.

Other royals used Baynard's Castle, too. Just a few short days after Jane Grey had been proclaimed queen, the council departed from here to proclaim Mary Tudor as queen. When Elizabeth of York's other granddaughter, Elizabeth, was queen, the castle belonged to the Earl of Pembroke, who treated Queen Elizabeth I to an extravagant display of fireworks from the castle.

Visiting Today

Sadly, all that remains of this opulent residence is a plaque showing where it once stood. The Great Fire of 1666 destroyed most of the castle and the surrounding houses, although at least one of its towers remained standing for several more years. To reach the plaque from St Paul's Cathedral, walk down Peter's Hill heading towards Millennium Bridge. Turn right on Queen Victoria Street and then left on White Lion Hill. The large grey building is Baynard House and it stands on the former site of the residence. Castle Baynard Street is also nearby, but is not equipped for pedestrian traffic.

Berkhamsted Castle, Hertfordshire

Berkhamsted Castle has a long association with royalty. William the Conqueror made his way here shortly after the Battle of Hastings to receive the submission of a deputation of men, including the Archbishop of York and the bishops of Hereford and Worcester. Shortly afterwards he granted Berkhamsted to his half-brother, Robert, the Count of Mortain, who quickly set about building a motte-and-bailey timber castle, which was later replaced by stone.

The ownership of the castle became complicated after Robert's son, William, was implicated in a rebellion against Henry I. It passed in and out of various hands, always reverting back to the crown. In 1155, Thomas Becket was granted the honour of Berkhamsted by King Henry II. He made various improvements to the castle, probably building the huge stone curtain wall with its ten turrets, before being accused of embezzlement by the king.

The keep, 60 feet in diameter, with walls almost 8 feet in width, rested on a 40-foot-high motte. The complex had both an inner and outer bailey, and the entire castle was surrounded by a double ditch. Strongly fortified, its defences were put to the test early in the thirteenth century, when in December 1216 it was besieged by Louis, King of France. Large earthworks in the outer ditch are believed to date from this time. After two weeks, the castle surrendered.

Richard, Earl of Cornwall, was granted the castle in 1227 and is believed to have built the three-storey tower during his tenure. The castle came to Edward, the Black Prince, as part of the duchy of Cornwall. During his tenure, another King of France, King John, came to Berkhamsted, but this time as a prisoner. Eventually, the castle passed to Margaret of Anjou. In 1469, Edward IV granted Berkhamsted, among other lands, to Cecily, in recompense for her surrender of Fotheringhay.

Cecily at Berkhamsted

Berkhamsted Castle did not immediately become Cecily's main residence. She was in London at Baynard's Castle following Edward's return from exile, and she travelled between her various holdings for several years. By the time Richard came to the throne, however, she was often at Berkhamsted. On 9 February 1484, Richard confirmed his brother's grant of Berkhamsted to his mother. While Berkhamsted was not at the centre of court life, it was not altogether off the beaten path, since it was situated near the main road from London to Aylesbury. Cecily would still have kept apprised of events in London.

Richard penned a letter while at Pontefract Castle to his mother at Berkhamsted. Whether or not Cecily had agreed with his taking the throne, this letter shows the depth of feeling that he possessed for her:

Madam, I recommend myself to you as heartily as is possible to me; beseeching you in my most humble and affectionate manner of your daily blessing to my especial comfort and defence in my need. And, Madam, I heartily beseech you that I may often hear from you to my comfort. And such news as there is here my servant Thomas Bryan, this bearer, shall show you; to whom may it please you to give credence ... And I pray God send you the accomplishment of your noble desires. Written at Pontefract, the 3rd day of June, with the hand of Your most humble son, Ricardus Rex.

Whether Cecily shared in his feelings is unclear, but Richard visited her at Berkhamsted shortly before his death. What they said to each other during this visit, the last time they would see each other, is not known. Whatever her feelings, Cecily would have seen that Richard and his retinue received the best in comfort. The evening meal was served in the Great Hall, with fires blazing to protect against the early spring chill. As king, Richard would have spent the night in the Painted Chamber of the castle, with light from the fire dancing across the bright, vivid paintings on its walls – much like those in the Painted Chamber in his palace at Westminster. Richard joined his mother the next morning for Mass, either in the Great Chapel of the castle or in one of the smaller chapels adjacent to his chamber. Soon he would leave with his retinue, crossing the inner bailey and then out the Great Gate and across the drawbridge. Despite any anger she may have felt towards Richard, she knew the threat from the Earl of Richmond was real, and, once again, worry for one of her sons probably consumed her.

After Richard's death, Cecily did not completely retire into obscurity. She petitioned Henry VII to allow her to ship her wool free of duties, and according to the Close Rolls of 20 June 1486, 'since the said duchess showed to the present king that payment of these sums out of the customs would be prejudicial to her, King Henry granted her the above said right to ship 250 sacks of wool annually free of all duties to him'. Other grants to her appear in the same year, when Henry ordered the bailiffs of Cicestre (Chichester) to pay Cecily out of the fee farm and all arrears since Henry had confirmed her jointure. Similar orders went to others, including the Sheriff of York.

We know quite a bit of Cecily's daily life at Berkhamsted because she governed her life by a set of ordinances. She rose every morning at seven, then her chaplain said matins with her; after she was fully dressed she heard low Mass in her chamber. Leaving her chamber, she went to divine service in the Great Chapel, followed by two low Masses. At eleven, Cecily had her meal and listened to a lecture 'of holy matter'. After this, she spent an hour giving audience to any person with a matter to bring before her. A short nap of fifteen minutes followed, and then she continued in prayer until evensong. If she desired, she would drink either wine or ale before going to the chapel for evensong. At 5 p.m. she enjoyed supper, and all who were with her listened to her recite the lecture from earlier in the day. A time for pleasant conversation with her ladies followed the meal; shortly before she went to bed, she retired into her private closet for prayer. By eight, her day had ended.

Cecily made her will while at Berkhamsted shortly before her death. She was buried beside her husband at Fotheringhay, according to her wishes.

Visiting Berkhamsted Today

In the mid-nineteenth century, poet John Crawford wrote a poem about Berkhamsted in which he lyrically described the castle's current state:

> The Castle's old magnificence is gone,
> Yet comely Grace is blended with decay:
> Green Ivy crowns each rugged mass of stone,
> And verdant shrubs bedeck the ruins grey.

His poem is as appropriate now as it was when it was first written. Today, crumbled bits of masonry stand forlornly in the castle bailey where they once stood as part of the immense fortification that graced the area. Flowers now bloom where regal chambers once stood. Still it is impossible to stand in the castle bailey and not feel a connection to the history of the place.

Entrance to the castle today is through what was once the south gate. The lodge near the entrance was not built until the nineteenth century and during the summer it serves as a visitor's room. Walk around the east portion of the bailey until you reach the motte in the north-east corner, where part of the wall which used to form the inner bailey still stands. Climbing up the modern stairs to the top of the motte provides an excellent view of both the bailey and the earthworks near the ditch. To the north-west is where the castle's deer park once stood.

Facing the bailey, the area to the right formed the chamber block where Cecily would have spent most of her time. Before walking down into the bailey, make sure to see the well which provided the keep with a water supply, especially needed when the castle was besieged. Now walk to the western portion of the castle. Here are believed to be the remains of the chapel and undercroft of a chamber. Take time to walk around the rest of the castle, enjoying the informative placards.

Berkhamsted is approximately thirty miles from London and can be reached by car along the A251. Be aware that parking is in short supply close to the castle, and you may need to use the paid parking at the rail station nearby. Trains to Berkhamsted depart from London Euston for a journey of about thirty minutes. For more information about visiting the castle, visit its website at https://www.english-heritage.org.uk/daysout/properties/berkhamsted-castle/. Berkhamsted Castle postcode: HP4 1HD.

Part 3

Richard, Duke of Gloucester and King of England

Richard was the eleventh child of his parents, born at the brink of civil war. At his birth, no one expected him to become King of England. The events surrounding his rise to the throne are prone to controversy, and throughout the centuries these very controversies have kept him in the forefront of history. The locations explored in this section are some of the places which helped shape him into the man he became.

Fotheringhay Castle, Northamptonshire

A grassy mound in Northamptonshire stands witness to the great castle that once graced its surface. The Norman Earl of Northampton and Huntingdon built a motte-and-bailey castle on this site around AD 1100. His widow, Maud, married King David of Scotland, and for a time Fotheringhay became a possession of the Scots. Eventually the castle passed to Edward III and he granted it to his son Edmund of Langley, who began a building programme to enlarge it. Edmund's son Edward inherited Fotheringhay, but he died at Agincourt. His heir was his nephew, Richard, who became the 3rd Duke of York. Richard was married to Cecily Neville and the couple often spent time at the castle, since it was a principal seat for the House of York.

On 2 October 1452, Cecily delivered a son in the keep of Fotheringhay. The boy, her eleventh child, was named Richard. Here, on the banks of the River Nene, Richard spent his early years with his two siblings closest in age, Margaret and George, in the charge of a nurse.

The castle that Richard knew was surrounded by a moat, with the entrance through an impressive gatehouse. The great stone keep sat atop the mound, surrounded by a wall, and was accessible only through a staircase from the inner bailey. In the fourteenth century the castle had a large hall, two chambers, two chapels, a kitchen, a bake house and a porter's lodge; Edmund of Langley had enlarged the structure by the fifteenth century. It would have been a busy place, especially when the duke and duchess were in residence.

Years later, in 1469, Richard and Edward returned to Fotheringhay while making their way north to deal with an uprising. Earlier that year, a small uprising led by a man calling himself Robin of Redesdale had been stopped by John Neville; another group quickly rose up in rebellion but was also stopped. Shortly, Robin of Redesdale resurfaced in Lancashire. The king, who had been on a pilgrimage to the shrines of St Edmund and to Our Lady of Walsingham, left and made his way to Norwich. From here Edward sent letters to his supporters telling them to assemble their forces. Eventually he made his way to Fotheringhay.

In 1476, the Duke of York and the Earl of Rutland were reinterred in Fotheringhay. Following the ceremony, a large feast was held both inside and outside of the castle. Records show that tents and tables were constructed in order to provide seating for the attendees. As with most large medieval feasts, there was plenty to choose from, as ale and wine flowed, and fish, pheasants, chickens, partridges and honey, along with other dishes, were brought out to the waiting guests.

Fotheringhay would be the scene of an important meeting, when in 1482, Richard and Edward would revisit the location with Alexander, Duke of Albany, to discuss the terms of England's support for Albany's seizure of the Scottish throne. Albany would be recognised by England as the lawful King of Scotland in exchange for certain land concessions to the English. Ultimately little of value came of the meeting, since Albany chose not to take the throne.

Fotheringhay and Elizabeth of York

After he won the Battle of Bosworth and became king, Henry VII married Edward IV's daughter, Elizabeth of York, and granted

Fotheringhay to her. Edward IV had enlarged the castle, and according to *The History of the King's Works*, had begun chambers, a gallery, latrines and turrets, among other improvements. In Elizabeth's time, the castle was a grand one. While visiting, she would have walked through the 'little park' that her father had enclosed with a 'garden and spinney'. The antiquarian John Leland visited Fotheringhay and marvelled at its 'Kepe very auncient and strong. There be very fair Lodgyns in the Castel.'

Mary, Queen of Scots, was executed at Fotheringhay in 1587; afterwards the castle was rarely used. Within a century there would be little left to remind visitors of its importance as both the birthplace of a king and the execution site of a queen.

Visiting Today
The first thing to do when arriving at Fotheringhay is to go to its church (see its section under 'Richard, Duke of York'). After visiting the tombs of the York family, walk back to the street and turn right. At the curve of the road is a sign that says, 'To the castle'. Follow the curving lane back towards the river and farm nearby. An informative placard depicts the former layout of the castle. From here you can see the canal boats making their way up the slow-moving waters of the Nene. Next to the river is a slab of fenced-in masonry and two memorials. One was erected by the Richard III Society to honour Richard III, while the other is for Mary, Queen of Scots. There is no admission fee to enter the grounds of the castle. Fotheringhay Castle postcode: PE8 5HZ.

York, Yorkshire

During its history, York passed through many hands. From its days as Eboracum, a Roman town, to the Vikings and the Danelaw, it has seen many rulers come and go. After the arrival of the Normans, two castles were built to fortify the unruly city. York became a self-governing city during the reign of King John, reserving the right to elect its own mayor. By the time of Richard's rule, the city was in the midst of an economic downturn.

It is obvious that Richard developed affection for the city of York since he often mediated for its citizens. When Edward IV threatened to revoke the city's liberties, Richard pled its case. The affection was returned by York's citizens, who appreciated the fact that Richard did not try to interfere with its mayoral elections.

Richard visited the city often. Each time he arrived, he would have seen the steeples of the parish churches rising high above the large stone walls surrounding the city. Entering through one of York's four main gates, he would have seen timber-framed buildings resting next to crowded, narrow lanes.

Micklegate Bar

Richard's earliest association with the city would have been Micklegate Bar, which has guarded York for more than 800 years. Although Richard would not have seen it, his father's severed head once rested on this very gate. On Richard's visits, he passed through Micklegate; that thought may have haunted him.

On Richard's visit in 1476, the council presented him with six swans and six pikes upon his arrival. When Richard and the Duke of Albany stopped on their way to Scotland, the aldermen dressed in scarlet and the chamberlains in crimson greeted them here. In March of 1483, the aldermen dressed in violet and the chamberlains dressed in blue to meet Richard to present him with gifts of fine wine, bread, pikes and lampreys, among other gifts.

When Richard and Anne reached York later that year, the mayor and city fathers met them at Brekles Mills and escorted them to the city through the Micklegate. As they rode with the aldermen, clad in scarlet, and the chamberlains, robed in red, Richard and Anne were met with a series of pageants which culminated in the mayor's presentation of gifts of marks and gold to the king and queen.

Visiting Today

Micklegate Bar still stands today, a square tower with its arch and turrets. Impressive even without its barbican, which was removed prior to 1816, the three-storey gatehouse sits high above the street. In medieval times the bar also had a portcullis and a double wooden gate, but these were torn down. Micklegate means 'great street' and it would have certainly lived up to its name in Richard's time.

Today the York Archaeological Trust operates the Henry VII Experience here. The museum does an excellent job of explaining the history of York under Henry VII. I was surprised by a replica of the Duke of York's head hanging on a spike in the museum. It is not for the faint of heart.

A reduced ticket for both the Richard III Experience and the Henry VII Experience is available. For more information about visiting times and ticket prices, see the website at http://richardiiiexperience.com/ or call +44 (0) 1904 615505.

Walmgate Bar

When Edward IV returned from exile in March of 1471, he was denied entry at Kingston-upon-Hull, so he made for York. As Walmgate Bar was on the principal road from Hull, he would have entered York through this gate. The tension would have been palpable as Edward, Richard and the others with them made their way through hostile territory. Three miles outside of York, the men were met by the city's recorder who told the king the city was not safe for him to enter.

Continuing onward, the group was once again met outside of Walmgate and asked to leave. Edward's troops had been left outside the walls and he only had fifteen or sixteen men with him. Using the ruse that he had only come to claim his inheritance as the Duke of York and not the crown, he asked for York's assistance.

With charm, Edward flattered the citizens, and according to the Warkworth chronicler, even cheered for Henry. The chronicler said he also wore Prince Edward's symbol of a white ostrich feather in his hat. He and his small group were finally allowed entrance into the city.

During the last siege of York in 1644, Walmgate Bar suffered damage from artillery hits. Despite repair work in the seventeenth century, the scars can still be seen today. The Gothic archway of the outer gate is the oldest part of the structure still standing. Walmgate's fourteenth-century barbican is the only one in York, and its wooden gates are from the fifteenth century. Complete with a portcullis, the gate largely appears like Richard would have remembered it, although today it is missing the moat that once passed under the barbican. The timber-framed building adjacent to the bar was not added until the sixteenth century. Above the gatehouse are two crenellated turrets, which provided an excellent view of the surrounding countryside. The gatehouse was used for a residence up until the twentieth century.

Visiting Today

There is no museum in Walmgate Bar. Still, the gate is well worth a visit because it provides a good example of medieval defences. Visitors may walk along the walls to see what the battlements were like and spend time looking for the artillery shell scars. If you are able to block out all the modern sounds, you may feel that you have slipped back in time to the day Richard and Edward stood outside the gate that day in March, knowing their future depended on gaining the citizens' trust.

Austin Friars

The Austin Friars were in York by July 1272. Originally from Tickhill, they built their new friary on the banks of the River Ouse in Lendal. Richard knew the friary well, since he lodged here several times. On one visit, the friars presented him with gifts of several gallons of wine. Richard's relationship with the friars was a positive one, and he appointed an Austin friar, William Bewick, 'surveyor of our works and buildings within our place of the friars Austin'.

Today, all that remains of the friary is a bit of limestone wall by the River Ouse and a few remnants in the Yorkshire Museum. Following the Dissolution, the prior, nine priests and four novices surrendered the friary to the king's men, and its plate was sent to the treasury of the king. The remnants of masonry from the friary are kept in a display on the lower level of the pub, Lendal Cellars.

York Guildhall

Erected in the mid-fifteenth century by the joint effort of the mayor and commonality, along with the Guild of St Christopher, the hall was used for a variety of civic purposes. Inside, ten octagonal oak pillars rested on stone bases, supporting a timbered roof decorated with both grotesques and the royal arms of Henry V. At the west end of the hall, a dais was enclosed by a wooden screen. Unfortunately, the Second World War devastated much of the original guildhall, but a new one was rebuilt keeping close to the original plan.

On 7 September 1483, Richard and Anne watched the Creed play here. Although little is known about the play itself, the Corpus Christi Guild's account rolls state that the play was for the instruction on the Christian faith and was for the glory of God. As members of the guild, Richard and Anne would have been familiar with the pageants and many of the guild's plays. However, the Creed play would have been a special treat because it was usually only performed every ten years.

Visiting Today

Today it is only possible to visit the Guildhall on special occasions. However, you can examine the outside of the structure, located behind Mansion House. It is also possible to book an event and enjoy the guildhall's atmosphere, which still retains its medieval feel. York Guildhall postcode: YO1 9QN.

Holy Trinity, Micklegate

The priory of Holy Trinity was of the Benedictine Order. It was an important establishment in York and was the starting point for the Corpus Christi pageants. Having joined the Corpus Christi guild in 1477, Richard and Anne would have been familiar with the pageantry associated with the religious festival and would have participated in the procession of the pageants of Corpus Christi performed by York's trade guilds. On the morning of the Corpus Christi festival, those who were joining in the procession met at the gates of the Priory of the Holy Trinity in Micklegate. The shrine used in the festival was housed in the priory for a time. According to Matthew Spencer in his book *Corpus Christi Pageants in England*, the shrine was gilded with six images and contained mother of pearl, silver and gilt. It also had a tablet of gold bearing the image of Our Lady in mother of pearl.

The procession began with the clergy, including the Master of the Guild, carrying the shrine. The Lord Mayor and aldermen followed, clad in their ceremonial robes, accompanied by the city officers bearing torches. Next came members of the trade associations carrying torches and banners. Along the route, houses were decorated with tapestries and flowers. Large scaffolds were placed on wheels and divided into two stages, which allowed for movement from one station to the next. At each station, one part of the play was performed. The procession would have passed through crowded streets on its way toward the minster.

Visiting Today

Unfortunately, all the monastic buildings, with the exception of the priory church, are gone. According to the church, it is the only monastic building in York to have survived as a place of worship. The church is open to visitors and is free of admission. To find out more about the church and to see a detailed virtual tour of the monastic buildings, visit the church's website at http://www. holytrinityyork.org/mpr.

Monk Bar

While Richard would have seen Monk Bar, he would not have spent time here. However, it has an association with the king that cannot be overlooked. For years it housed the informative Richard III museum, and is now home to the Richard III Experience, owned by the York Archaeological Trust.

One of York's fortified gateways, Monk Bar's top storey was added during Richard's reign, making it taller than the other gates in York. Today the bar no longer has its barbican, which was removed in the early nineteenth century.

For those unfamiliar with the York family, the Richard III Experience is informative. It offers an overview of both Richard's life and key battles in the Wars of the Roses. Visitors may buy a reduced ticket to visit both the Richard III experience and the Henry VII Experience. For more information, see the website at richardiiiexperience.com/visiting/.

York Minster

The Cathedral and Metropolitan Church of St Peter in York is the largest Gothic cathedral in England. Both a cathedral and a minster, the church's history stretches back to Roman times when the area served as a basilica, where tradition holds that Constantine was proclaimed emperor. Centuries after the Romans left, a Saxon king of Northumberland, Edwin, converted to Christianity and erected a wooden building here for his baptism. Afterwards, he ordered the building of a stone church dedicated to St Peter. Following the arrival of the Normans, a new church was built and remained until 1187 when it was destroyed by fire. The next building, built in the Gothic style, would take more than 200 years to complete.

Once he was king, Richard began plans to fund a chantry at York Minster, to be served by 100 priests who would say prayers for him and his family members. Unfortunately his early death at

Bosworth halted any further construction, and the altars that had already been built were torn down.

Following Richard's family's entrance into York after his coronation, they were escorted to the Minster, where they were met at the west door by the dean and clergy, dressed in red silken copes. Once inside the building they were sprinkled with holy water, then the Lord's Prayer was said before the services. A prayer of blessing for Richard was included in the service.

An elaborate ceremony was planned for the investiture of Edward of Middleham as Prince of Wales. More than 13,000 livery badges with Richard's device of the white boar were handed out in preparation. On 8 September 1483, the procession arrived at the Minster where the High Altar was decorated with silver and gilt figures of the twelve apostles and other relics. Richard and Anne wore their crowns, which led to rumours of a second coronation.

The Bishop of Durham performed Mass, and then the party moved to the nearby archbishop's palace, where Edward was knighted and invested as Prince of Wales by the girding on of the sword. Edward had a garland wreath placed on his head, a gold ring placed on his finger and was handed a golden staff. In addition to Edward and the Spanish ambassador, two of Richard's other family members were knighted that day – his illegitimate son, John, and his nephew, Edward. After the ceremonies, a large feast was held in the palace.

Visiting Today

From outside York Minster appears much like it did in Richard's day. The Great West Window, although not wholly original, had the same stonework. Many of the original panels in the window are also the same. As you enter the Minster through the west side, take some time to admire the Great West Doors.

As you leave the nave and move into the south transept, you are in the earliest part of the building. The entrance to the undercroft, treasury and crypt is here, but these rooms are best seen last. The tomb of Archbishop Richard Scrope is in the Lady Chapel. Scrope was executed by Henry IV, and Richard would have recognised his name. One of the fires the minster has been plagued with damaged Scrope's tomb in 1829, but it was restored in 1972.

Before making your way down the south choir aisle, take a moment to enjoy the choir screen. Many visitors spend several minutes engrossed in its rich details. The life-size statues representing kings of England would have been brightly coloured during the medieval period, and a closer examination will reveal remnants of paint in the crevices.

In the south choir aisle, look for a glass panel depicting St Cuthbert holding the head of St Oswald. Richard would have recognised the depiction, as well as the badges and shields of the nobility in the choir. In the choir clerestory are fourteenth-century windows decorated with figures of saints and kings.

The shrine of St William stood behind the high altar. After Archbishop William Fitzherbert was canonised in the early thirteenth century, his shrine became a popular pilgrimage site. Richard would have seen the shrine, but unfortunately visitors today cannot, due to its dismantling during the Dissolution. However, his story is narrated in the St William Window in the north choir aisle and fragments from the shrine are in the Yorkshire Museum.

The East Window was made in the early part of the fifteenth century and contains 117 panels which depict the days of creation and other events from both the Old and New Testaments. Both historical and mythical figures dominate the bottom row.

In the north transept is one of the more fascinating features of the church. The Five Sisters Window, which appears darker than the rest, is the oldest complete window in the building. The origin of the window's name is unknown, but one theory is that five nuns wove a tapestry for the church which was later used as a pattern for the window.

The chapter house entrance is in the eastern corner of the north transept and was in use by the thirteenth century. Richard met with city leaders in the chapter house on at least one occasion. In his day the walls would have been brightly coloured with murals, but the structure of the room is largely the same. Medieval carvings decorate the spacious room. The original ceiling panels would have easily been seen as there is no central column to block the view. Visitors today can see the panels in the undercroft display.

During the Dissolution, the chantries which dominated the Minster were demolished and many of the treasures within were seized by the Crown. The medieval character was altered with the destruction of shrines, more than fifty chantries and several altars. In the 1840 fire, many of the original medieval ceiling bosses were destroyed, but several of the key bosses were replaced with exact replicas.

Before exiting the building spend some time visiting the undercroft, crypt and treasury. Some of the minster's treasures are on display, and the exhibitions are among the best. There is still much to see once you leave the building. The Great West Door was the ceremonial entrance, so Richard would have used it upon his visits. The timber-framed building on the north-east side of the cathedral is St William's College, which was the lodging for the chantry priests in the medieval period. Today it houses York Minster's conference area. On some occasions a few of the medieval rooms are open to the public. Dean's Park lies north of the minster. The area around the minster, known as the Liberty of St Peter, would have been walled and gated during the medieval era. The Liberty functioned like its own city, complete with its own laws, and – in the event these laws were broken – its own jail. At the west end of the park is one of the surviving gates of the Liberty.

Within the gates stands the Treasurer's House, which is now open to the public through the National Trust. Further along is York Minster's Library and Archives. This building, which was the former chapel, is all that remains of the medieval archbishop's palace where Edward was invested as Prince of Wales. Richard would have been familiar with the building, since he visited on several occasions. Edward's investiture is commemorated by a plaque on the building. The only other remnant of the palace is a small bit of arcading, which may have once formed the cloister walk and is now part of the Kohima memorial.

For opening times and admission costs visit the website at https://www.yorkminster.org/visit-york-minster/opening-times-amp-admission.html/ or call +44 (0)1904 557200. York Minster postcode: YO1 7JN.

Barnard Castle, Durham

Barnard Castle sits high above the River Tees, commanding a magnificent view of the countryside, situated in a spot that was both highly defensive and strategic in its location. This area was granted to Guy de Baliol by William Rufus; however, the claim was contested by the bishops of Durham, who asserted that the land had originally belonged to them before the grant. Eventually a later earl fell into disfavour and was defeated by the king, so the area reverted to the Crown.

Guy de Baliol originally built a timber castle here, but his nephew Bernard began the stone fortifications seen today. Bernard also founded the town and gave it its first charter. His son, another Bernard, finished the work on the castle. John de Baliol's marriage to Devorguilla of Galloway brought him titles and land. John de Baliol II inherited his father's titles, and Edward I helped make him the new King of Scotland, believing he would be easy to control. This was a false assumption, because once Baliol became King of Scotland, he renounced English authority. Eventually Baliol ended up imprisoned in the Tower of London with his lands forfeited to the English king. Although the area reverted to the Crown, the Bishop of Durham saw his chance and claimed the land back for the Church. The bishopric managed to hold on to the church for a few years before the king asserted his rights and granted the land to Guy de Beauchamp, Earl of Warwick. When Richard Neville married Anne Beauchamp, the land came to him. Their daughter, Anne Neville, married Richard, then Duke of Gloucester, and the lordship passed to him.

Barnard Castle in Richard's Time

The castle originally had a large stone curtain wall surrounding the outside while the inside was divided into four wards. The town ward housed the Dovecot Tower, where the pigeons nested. The Brackenbury Tower lay to the east of the ward. North of the Dovecot Tower stood the North Gatehouse. The middle ward was separated from the town ward by a gatehouse and a drawbridge over a moat. Left of the bridge at the base of the remains of the tower are remnants of the garderobe chutes which would have emptied directly into the moat.

Most of Richard's time at the castle would have been spent in the inner ward. He would have sat at the upper end of the Great Hall in front of a heraldic tapestry, which boasted of his ties to the king. Other tapestries would have covered the wall to provide both beauty and warmth, and glazed windows would have allowed light to flood the room. Surrounded by his household, who would have been seated at tables slightly below the dais, Richard would have held lavish meals, typical of the nobility of his time.

On many occasions, Richard would have eaten in his great chamber, which abutted the upper end of the hall. An emblem of a boar is carved above the great oriel window, lending weight to the theory that Richard was the one who added the window. In his great chamber he would have taken light meals, played games and met important visitors.

Richard's private chamber was within the ashlar Round Tower, which was four storeys and 30 feet in diameter. The tower's vaulting was plain without ribs or a pillar. This chamber was easily accessible from the great chamber, and Richard would have slept here on a large bed with curtains to offer privacy. Anne's chamber is believed to have been on the second floor of the tower since this area was called a lady's chamber in the 1592 survey. Anne, too, would have had a great bed, curtained for her privacy, since some of her attendants would have also slept in the room.

The chapel and demesne land lay within the outer ward. Barnard Castle's chapel, known as St Margaret's Chapel, was described by Leland as a 'faire chapel'. Today the land is privately owned and not open to visitors. It is possible to view where the chapel once stood from the castle, but nothing substantial remains.

By the time of the 1592 survey, the castle had already fallen into a state of disrepair. This situation worsened during the ownership of the Vane family, who removed the lead from the roof, allowing the castle to fall into ruin. The artist William Bewick quoted his aunt Sarah bemoaning the castle's fate, saying, 'Oh! Misery! Can one thousand pounds worth of lead, iron, wood, and stone be more worth than a Castle which might receive a king and his whole train?'

Visiting Today
The town of Barnard Castle provides ample parking. The castle is located behind the Methodist church. For more information on opening times, visit the castle website at www.english-heritage.org.uk/daysout/properties/barnard-castle/. Before visiting the church, take some time to see stunning views of the castle from across the river. Turn left out of the castle entrance and head down the path to the river. Cross the bridge, turn right, and walk until you see a break in the trees or the river path. From this angle it is obvious that the castle was built with defence in mind. Barnard Castle postcode: DL12 8PR.

St Mary's Church, Barnard Castle, Durham

Just like he had with the church of St Mary and St Alkelda at Middleham, Richard wanted to make St Mary's church at Barnard Castle a collegiate church. In 1478, the Calendar of the Patent Rolls included a licence which granted Richard the right to found a college at Barnard Castle, consisting of a dean, twelve chaplains, ten clerks, six choristers and another clerk to celebrate divine services for his family members (including the king and his queen).

It is clear Richard intended the collegiate church at Barnard Castle to be bigger than the one he wanted to establish at Middleham. As the collegiate church was never finished, we do not know what his guidelines for it would have been, but they would have resembled the guidelines he established at Middleham, with the dean and chaplains in residence at the college. Richard's largesse for the church included raising the roof, placing windows in the clerestory, putting in the chancel arch and adding a north porch and a vestry.

Visiting Today

While the church has drastically changed from Richard's time period, there is still evidence of his importance to the town. Although much of today's church is Victorian, including the vestry, you can still see the heads carved on either side of the chancel arch. The head on the left, wearing a crown, is Edward IV, while the one on the right, with its ducal coronet, is Richard, Duke of Gloucester. The carving of Richard is quite detailed, and with binoculars it is possible to make out wavy hair and a strong chin. The north porch that Richard ordered built was where the accessible toilet entrance lies today. Before leaving the area, walk around to the back of the church where there is a carving of Richard's emblem of a boar. It is somewhat hard to see, but it is next to the window in the upper left-hand corner. St Mary's postcode: DL12 8NQ.

Nottingham Castle, Nottinghamshire

Richard III spent considerable time at Nottingham Castle, making it one of the most visited castles during his reign. From its strategic location perched high on a sandstone ridge, it towered over the surrounding countryside and commanded the crossing over the River Trent, giving him protection from a surprise uprising.

Built by William the Conqueror soon after the Norman Conquest, the castle consisted of an outer bailey, a dry moat, an inner ward and a middle bailey. Large caves were carved into the sandstone cliffs under the castle, both for storage, and if legend can be believed, secret routes in and out of the castle.

Up until Edward IV, the kings and queens who stayed at the castle lodged within the royal apartments of the inner ward in chambers over the Great Hall. By the time Edward IV took the throne, either these chambers were not large enough or were in a dilapidated state, because he began building new royal apartments within the middle ward.

Upon Richard's accession to the throne, he completed Edward's renovations. Antiquarian James Orange says that it was under Richard that the final touches 'united the splendid magnificence of a palace with the secure impregnability of a castle'. Richard built a four-storey ashlar-faced tower complete with a spiral staircase which later became known as Richard's Tower. The royal apartments, built in a crescent against the wall, were two storeys, and each storey contained large bay windows overlooking the courtyard. During the colder months, fires would have blazed in each of the apartments.

Richard and Nottingham

One of Richard's first visits to Nottingham Castle was in August of 1483 while heading to York. While here, his secretary wrote to the citizens of York advising them to have several festivals planned for Richard's visit. He also told them to hang the streets with cloths of arras and tapestry works, so that the southern lords would see city's great love for the new king. Richard, excited to get to York for his son's investiture as the Prince of Wales, stayed less than a week on this visit.

After word of Buckingham's rebellion made its way to Richard, he moved south, spending one night at Nottingham on his way. As in other castles, Nottingham had its own chapel. Perhaps Richard spent time in the room with its picture of St Katherine painted in front of the altar and the mural of her story painted above it, seeking solace from the sting of Buckingham's betrayal.

By March 1484 he was at Nottingham again. Due to Richard's affection for the castle a tradition grew that when he came to Nottingham he often retreated to a turret in the tower, giving Richard's Tower its name. Whether this tradition holds any truth, he did stay at the castle often, partly due to its central location.

Richard's pride in his son's investiture as Prince of Wales was cut short by the tragic news he received at Nottingham. As Richard and Anne listened, the messenger told them that their only child, Edward, had died at Middleham. Their response was recorded by the chronicler at Croyland, who claimed that the couple was 'almost out of their minds for a long time when faced with the sudden grief'.

Dual threats of another uprising and of an invasion by Henry Tudor forced Richard to set aside his pain at the loss of his son and focus on his country. War with Scotland was not going well, and Richard realised he needed to seek a solution that would allow him to focus his efforts on maintaining control in England. When James III sent a letter to him proposing peace, Richard wrote back offering safe conduct to the Scottish king's delegates.

As the Scottish delegation arrived at Nottingham, they crossed the bridge over the dry moat and entered through the door of the two-storey gatehouse, then passed under the raised portcullis and made their way to the Great Hall. Here Richard was sitting under his cloth of estate, surrounded by his own delegation.

A member of the Scottish delegation, Archibald Whitelaw, Archdeacon of Lothian, opened the meeting by delivering an oration in Latin. With the work of both delegations, a treaty was hammered out that included the promise of a marriage between James IV and Anne de la Pole, Richard's niece. Richard's death at Bosworth ended the marriage treaty, and James IV eventually married Margaret Tudor, the daughter of Henry VII. At the time, though, the treaty freed Richard to worry about other matters, like an invasion by Henry Tudor.

It was this threat that brought Richard back to Nottingham in June 1485. As Nottingham was a central location from which to counter any invasion attempt, Richard made it his base. To prepare, he notified his commissioners of array that they should review the soldiers and put them on alert to be ready at an hour's warning once commanded. Near the end of July, Richard received word from his spies that Henry was making preparations to embark for England. Henry soon landed in Wales and began his march towards England.

In early August 1485, Thomas Barowe, the keeper of the chancery rolls, delivered the great seal to the king at Nottingham Castle. Richard was in the oratory within the chapel, surrounded by several men, including the Earl of Lincoln. Afterwards Richard 'delivered the seal to the aforesaid Thomas Barowe to seal all manner of writs and letters patent, and appointed him keeper of the great seal'. Soon afterwards, Richard left Nottingham on his march towards Leicester, leaving his great castle of care for the final time.

Visiting Nottingham Today

Nothing substantial remains today of Richard's grand residence; the castle was ordered destroyed after the Civil War. While the gatehouse and parts of the wall are medieval, they also have been largely restored. Some fragments of the north-east tower in the middle bailey remain, but so little that there is not enough to visualise its appearance in Richard's day.

It is easy to get an idea of the scope of the castle once you enter through the gatehouse. From the bottom of the hill, look up at the inner and middle baileys. From this vantage point it becomes obvious how large the complex was. Enter the middle bailey and then walk to the centre of the grass. Here you are standing in what was the courtyard of the royal apartments completed by Richard. As you look around, try to imagine the two-storey royal apartments with their great bay windows.

The current castle, which is located in what was the inner ward, was built after Richard's time. Today it serves as both a museum and an art gallery. After spending time looking at the grounds, be sure to visit the castle museum, which contains a model of the castle in the year 1500, providing an idea of both the layout and size of the complex. The museum explores the role of Nottingham through the centuries and is well worth a visit.

It is also possible to take a tour of the caves and tunnels built into the sandstone rock. It is easy to spend a full day here if you explore everything the castle offers. One of my favourite places is the terrace, which offers exceptional views of the surrounding countryside. As the castle café is nearby, it is possible to pass a pleasant hour, nibbling on a scone and drinking a cup of piping hot tea while admiring the view.

For more information on visiting the castle, see its website at http://www.nottinghamcastle.org.uk/. If you are driving to Nottingham, take advantage of its park-and-ride scheme. For more information, visit www.nottinghamcity.gov.uk/parkandride/ or call the city council at +44 (0) 115 915 5555. High-speed trains from London St Pancras can make the journey in under two hours. For more information visit www.eastmidlandstrains.co.uk/. Postcode: NG1 6EL.

Lincoln, Lincolnshire

Given its naturally strategic location on a hill high above the surrounding countryside, Lincoln has been occupied for centuries. First the Celts, then Romans and next the Danes took advantage of the area for a settlement. After the Norman Conquest, the city was further fortified by a castle.

Located near a river, Lincoln was such an important area of trade and commerce in the medieval period that it was called one of the top three cities in England. It was in Lincoln that Empress Maud (also known by Matilda), daughter of Henry I, captured King Stephen. Other kings and queens visited – Edward I held a parliament here, and so did his son Edward II.

Richard III and Lincoln

Richard visited Lincoln in October of 1483. Making his way from Pontefract, he had stopped for a night at nearby Gainsborough Old Hall before heading to Lincoln. The visit was not destined to be a long one, because Richard had learned of Buckingham's rebellion and sent a letter to Bishop John Russell, his chancellor, requesting that his seal be sent to him at Lincoln. His frustration and sense of betrayal at Buckingham's action can be sensed through Richard's postscript to the letter, where he called Buckingham 'the most untrue creature living; whom with God's grace we shall not be long till that we will be in those parts, and subdue his malice. We assure you there was never false traitor better purveyed for, as this bearer, Gloucester, shall show you.'

From Lincoln, Richard would go on to Nottingham, and then

further south where he was able to subdue the uprising and execute Buckingham. During this stopover in Lincoln it is almost certain that Richard stayed at the Bishop's Palace. Several monarchs had lodged at the opulent ecclesiastical palace instead of the castle, and Richard probably did too.

Visiting Lincoln Today

Once you have visited the Richard III sites, I recommend you take in the other medieval sites. A visit to Lincoln is not complete without a trek down and up Steep Hill to see the buildings along the way. If you are planning on spending the night or visiting any other local attractions, the visitor centre's staff can assist you. Visitor information centre postcode: LN1 3AA.

Medieval Bishops' Palace

Today there are only ruins of the once opulent palace that was built by a succession of bishops. Bishop Hugh, who later became St Hugh, began the large hall in the complex that was later finished by Hugh of Wells. The palace was crenellated with turrets and battlements added under the eye of Bishop Henry Burghersh in the fourteenth century. At this time the garden along the south side of the building was extended.

In the fifteenth century, Bishop Alnwick embarked on a building spree. In addition to his extensive work on the cathedral, he also added several buildings to his palace, including a chapel and a square stone tower topped with a turret. The tower contained large chambers, perhaps for guests of the bishop. Richard may have stayed within one of these chambers or he may have been offered the bishop's own chamber. In the mid-nineteenth century, Edwards James Wilson wrote that a large stained-glass bay window with pictures of the kings of England and coats of arm hung above the doorway to Alnwick's tower. Richard would have seen the elaborately carved tower door while at the palace. Above the door's pointed arch was a stone carving of Bishop Alnwick's coat of arms.

Thankfully, enough surveys and early descriptions remain to tell us that the hall, 84 feet by 58 feet, was divided by eight marble columns and arches into one large centre aisle with two outlying aisles. The spacious room had large glazed windows with the lower portions closed off by shutters. A timber roof covered with lead protected the room from the elements. Here is where Richard would have conducted some of his business while in Lincoln. A fire would have roared in the middle of the room when he and his men had meals. Wine and ale would have flowed while servants bustled about bringing in each course.

Visiting Today

English Heritage oversees the ruins of the ecclesiastical palace today. Stairs to the palace are located within the cathedral close. The site offers a valuable audio tour and a guidebook. Visiting information may be found at English Heritage's website: www.englishheritage.org.uk/daysout/properties/lincoln-medieval-bishops-palace/. Postcode: LN2 1PU.

Lincoln Cathedral

Lincoln's cathedral church was started soon after the Normans arrived. The Cathedral Church of the Blessed Virgin Mary of Lincoln is a mix of several architectural styles. Built in the form of a cross, the cathedral has three towers, each one highly decorated with pillars, tracery and carvings. In the medieval era, each of the towers was topped by tall spires of timber covered with lead. The spires of the cathedral would have been seen for miles before a visitor reached Lincoln. Today's visitor can no longer see the towering spires, since one of these blew down and the others were later removed.

A large door in the centre of the immense western front is covered by an intricately decorated stone archway and is flanked on either side by four carved columns, some carved with grotesques. Above the door are carved figures of kings, which Richard would have seen painted and gilded. Each statue has its own stone canopy. The great western window sits in a place of honour above the kings. Above that is a smaller, circular window. At the building's top is a pointed arch.

On the cathedral's south side is the Galilee Porch, arcaded with slender arches. This porch was the entrance for the bishop, whose palace was to the south. As the feast of St Edward occurred during Richard's stay, he would have visited the cathedral through one of the Galilee Porch's two huge doorways, both intricately decorated with foliage.

Entering the cathedral, Richard would have seen a much different interior than we do today. Magnificently decorated chantries once graced the interior, but during the Reformation the chantries were dissolved and St Hugh's elaborate shrine was stripped of all its jewels. E. Mansel Sympson, writing in the early twentieth century, described the shrine: 'The shrine was of pure gold, and adorned no doubt with precious stones on a stone base and secured by a grille of wrought iron, the marks of which remained in the pavement till the middle of the eighteenth century.' To the right of the altar is one of the chantries that did survive the Reformation, although not completely intact – it is the chantry of Richard's great-grandmother, Katherine Swynford, who was first mistress and later wife of John of Gaunt.

It was Gaunt's legitimate son, Henry of Bolingbroke, who seized the throne from Richard II and reigned as Henry IV. In addition to his legitimate children, Gaunt, with Katherine, produced illegitimate children who had the surname Beaufort. This family, later legitimised, would become powerful in England. It was from this branch that Henry Tudor would come; his mother was Margaret Beaufort. Richard's maternal grandmother, Joan Beaufort, chose to be buried near to her mother, and her tomb of grey marble also lies here.

The cathedral's chapter house is in the shape of a decagon. Its roof is supported by a single pillar, with twenty ribs spilling out of the foliated capital at the top. Large windows with pointed arches provide the room with light. Recesses for seats where the cathedral chapter would sit surround the wall, and a visitor could spend hours examining each of the decorated grotesques. As the cathedral was never part of a monastery, this room was not used by monks for daily meetings, but by the cathedral chapter. The chapter house also played host to a parliament on at least one occasion.

Visiting Today

Before entering the minster yard through the Exchequer Gate, be sure to examine the gate itself. Several stories tall, with numerous windows, the gate includes three archways to allow pedestrian access; the centre archway is larger to permit access by horse and carriage. This gate was where tenants came to pay the church their rents, and inside the gate would have been offices for the men who kept the accounts.

In the medieval era, a large wall, embattled with turrets and with several additional gateways, would have surrounded the church. As you enter the minster yard, the west front of the cathedral stands before you. Take some time to study its intricate stonework before entering the church. In the fifteenth century, the cathedral would have dominated the skyline. If you want to see the Galilee Porch from the outside, take a walk around the cathedral's perimeter. For more information on visiting hours, see the cathedral's website at http://lincolncathedral.com/. Lincoln Cathedral postcode: LN2 1PX.

Lincoln Castle

While Richard would not have stayed at Lincoln Castle, the castle was near the cathedral and Richard would have seen it on his visit to Lincoln. Although the castle we see now was begun in Norman times, it was probably built on the site of an existing fortification. The enormous castle walls were Norman, and measured about 20 feet tall and 10 feet thick. The walls surrounded an area of about 6½ acres.

The castle was unusual in the fact it had two tall mounds, each with a tower resting on it. The keep was a typical shell keep and was constructed of wood before being rebuilt in stone. Today the keep is known as the Lucy Tower. The Norman castle consisted of the gateways, the keep, and the Observatory Tower. Most of the Observatory Tower was added in later years, although its base is Norman.

All that remains today of the once vast medieval structure are the remnants of the Lucy Tower, the Observatory Tower, the west gate and parts of the walls. The castle has marked the area where the barbican once stood with red granite, allowing visitors to have a visual representation of its size.

Visiting Today

The castle recently underwent a construction and renovation project which was completed in early 2015. The towers were restored and the wall walk was completed. A new underground vault for the Magna Carta, along with a new café and gift shop, were revealed. For more information, see its website, http://www.lincolnshire.gov. uk/visiting/historic-buildings/lincoln-castle/. Postcode: LN1 3AA.

Salisbury, Wiltshire

Before Salisbury there was Old Sarum. The first Norman cathedral in the area was established there and finished in 1092. The cathedral was eventually moved to the nearby valley, and a charter by the king established a new town there. It did not take long for the town of New Salisbury to develop into a lively centre of trade and commerce. In 1220 the new cathedral's building site was consecrated and its first stones were laid.

Salisbury also had a park. One visitor described the town in the fifteenth century:

> Close to the castle is a park, a mile wide and eight miles long. In this park is such a profusion of game as to be almost incredible. Deer exceeding several hundreds were also to be seen, also rabbits and hares without number ... Salisbury is an open town but large ... There is a very large and beautiful monastery. When one considers the elegance of the structure both within and without, it is second to none. The tower adjoins it and is built with great skill. I have nowhere seen more elegant figures.

Richard would not have had time to enjoy the park on his visit, since he had Buckingham's rebellion to put down.

Richard and Salisbury

In 1469, Richard, as Duke of Gloucester, headed a special commission of oyer and terminer in Salisbury. Henry Courtney and Thomas Hungerford had been accused of plotting with Margaret of Anjou for the death and destruction of Edward IV. The two men were found guilty and executed.

New Salisbury was one of the largest towns in England by the mid-fifteenth century. Its markets bustled with the wool trade. A prosperous place, in the autumn of 1483 it would become embroiled in the aftermath of an uprising against Richard III.

Richard had been in the north celebrating the investiture of his son Edward as Prince of Wales. While he was away, an uprising began brewing in the south. Although it would become known as Buckingham's rebellion, Henry Stafford was actually only part of the rebellion; most of the rebels were local gentry. According to the

Croyland chronicler, the gentry had become alarmed by rumours of the death of young Edward and Richard in the Tower, and had asked Henry, Earl of Richmond, to come to England to marry Edward's eldest daughter and heir.

Learning of the rebellion, Richard made his way from Lincoln towards Pontefract and then to Salisbury. The uprising in Kent had quickly been controlled by the Duke of Norfolk, and Richard began moving to deal with the Wiltshire rebels. Meanwhile Buckingham, who was not popular in Wales, was having a difficult time raising troops. Trapped by a flooded river, he slipped away from his men and tried to escape before being captured.

The cathedral's spire would have been the first thing Richard saw when he came towards the bustling town. Salisbury Cathedral had been built in the form of a cross and ran 473 feet from west to east and 229 feet from north to south. The immense structure would have been hard to miss. Built within one generation, the style kept mainly to Early English Gothic.

During the time Richard spent in Salisbury he would have visited the cathedral. In medieval times the west front was the main entrance and was one of the most elaborately decorated sections of the cathedral. Richard would have seen various layers of niches and pedestals that dominated the front with the statues and canopies covered in delicate stonework.

As they still do today, two square towers rested on either side of the front and were covered with intricate designs. After entering through one of the three decorated pointed archways, Richard would have stepped into the nave, where he would have seen the vaulted ceiling supported by solid stone pillars with slender columns of Purbeck marble. His view would have been blocked by a decorated screen, but today a visitor can see all the way down the nave and through the choir. The nave would have been adorned with intricately detailed wall paintings and a painted ceiling.

Richard probably observed Mass while in Salisbury, possibly on the day of Buckingham's execution. The peace and tranquillity of the cathedral would have offered solace to Richard, with his mind troubled by the defection of one he had trusted. He would also have visited the shrine of St Osmund in the Trinity Chapel. While not as popular as Our Lady of Walsingham or the shrine of St

Edward the Confessor, St Osmund's was also a site for pilgrimages. After Richard entered the chapel, with its slender clusters of shafts supporting delicate rib vaulting, he would have made his offering at the shrine of the saint.

Salisbury Cathedral

Today visitors do not enter the Cathedral Church of the Blessed Virgin Mary through the West Front but through the visitor's entrance located to its side. While there is no admission fee, a donation is requested. Once you are inside the nave, take a minute to absorb all its different features. Today the view to the high altar is unencumbered, giving the cathedral an open feel.

While this guide will take you through the areas with associations to Richard, take some time to explore the other areas of the cathedral. Our first stop is along the north nave aisle where an elaborate tomb rests. Richard would not have seen the tomb resting here since its occupant died several years after Bosworth. The tomb, with its effigy depicting a man with long, flowing locks of hair, his hands pressed together in prayer, holds the body of Sir John Cheyne. Cheyne had defected to Henry and fought against Richard at Bosworth. He was rumoured to have been as tall as 6 feet, 8 inches. The tomb, while slightly defaced, is still well decorated.

Make your way to the back of the cathedral to the Trinity Chapel. In the fifteenth century, St Osmund's shrine stood in the centre of the chapel. Look for the shrine tomb of St Osmund located on the floor near the centre of the room. The shrine Richard would have seen would have been a temporary one because, despite years of trying, St Osmund had only recently been canonised on 1 January 1457. St Osmund also had a head shrine, which was gilded and garnished with jewels. The mitre's point had two stones, while the mitre and base were covered with more than twenty stones.

The shrine would have been much more ostentatious when Richard visited than it is today, but its chapel is still an architectural wonder. Slender shafts of gleaming Purbeck marble gracefully support the vaulted ceiling. Although the beautiful stained glass in the lancet windows is modern, there would have been painted or stained glass here in medieval times, too.

After leaving the Trinity Chapel, move on to the chapter house.

While it is more famous for its Magna Carta exhibit, the room also contains a gorgeous medieval frieze that spans the wall. The ceiling is supported by one clustered column with ribs springing from it, and several large windows illuminate the octagonal room. Before viewing the Magna Carta, take some time to walk around the room to examine the stone frieze with its Biblical stories.

Leaving the chapter house, make your way back into the nave of the cathedral and spend time exploring the rest of the building. When you are finished, stay within the grounds of the cathedral close for a minute. This area was once entirely enclosed by embattled walls, parts of which are believed to have been built with stone quarried from the first cathedral at Old Sarum.

Salisbury Cathedral is open daily for visitors. Its website, www. salisburycathedral.org.uk/ is invaluable for information on opening times and events. Alternatively, you can call +44 (0) 1722 555120. Postcode: SP1 2EF.

King's House

From the cathedral, head straight across the cathedral green to the gateway and turn left. After a short walk, you will see King's House to your right. The house's history dates back to the thirteenth century, when it was the home of the Abbot of Sherborne. Largely renovated in the early fifteenth century, much of its main core is still visible today.

When Richard stayed here the home was still known as Sherborne House. While here, Richard received word that Buckingham's execution had been carried out in Salisbury's market square on Sunday 2 November. Now that Henry Stafford was no longer a threat, Richard continued conducting state business and making plans to deal with the other rebels.

During the seventeenth century the house was further enlarged by its owner, Sir Thomas Sadler. It was during Sadler's tenure that the home would receive the name 'King's House' because James I stayed here several times.

Visiting Today

Today the home that once received kings now houses the Salisbury Museum. Stand in the car park and face the building. After taking a moment to appreciate the fifteenth-century stonework, look to the left. This vaulted stone porch was part of the thirteenth-century home and would have been here when Richard visited. Step inside the porch and look up to see the intricate designs on the ceiling before taking time to visit the museum inside the house. The museum has several fascinating collections, including an exhibit on medieval Salisbury. There are several interesting artefacts preserved here, including a medieval rodent.

For more information on visiting the museum, see its website at www.salisburymuseum.org.uk/your-visit or call +44 (0) 1722 332151. King's House postcode: SP1 2EN.

Buckingham Marker

Leave King's House and head back towards the market. Standing in the middle of the open area, find Debenham's department store. Here on the wall of the store is a plaque commemorating Buckingham's death. Debenham's stands on the site of the former Blue Boar Inn and the Saracen's Head Inn. Buckingham's execution was carried out near here in the market square on Sunday 2 November. Although a tomb in Britford church has been attributed to him, no one knows for certain where he was buried.

An interesting story claims he was hurriedly buried nearby. In the nineteenth century, a body was supposedly uncovered during renovations at a local inn. Missing both its head and one arm, the remains were thought by some to be Buckingham. Since the skeleton was destroyed, whether it was Buckingham or not will never be known. Today, Buckingham's ghost is said to haunt the department store.

Visiting Salisbury Today

Salisbury has several associations with Richard and the Wars of the Roses. All of the sites could be visited within a half-day if rushing, but it is better to at least make a day of it. If driving in to Salisbury, take advantage of the park-and-ride scheme offered by Wiltshire Council. For more information, see www.wiltshire.gov.uk/parkingtransportandstreets/carparking/parkandride.htm. If you are inclined to drive within Salisbury, follow the signs for the city centre. Trains depart for Salisbury from London Waterloo. See www.nationalrail.co.uk/ for details.

Leicester, Leicestershire

As the final place he visited before his death at the Battle of Bosworth, Leicester has always had an association with Richard. Now that his remains have been reinterred in Leicester Cathedral, it has an even bigger tie with the king.

Leicester Castle

Richard had been to Leicester before, having stayed in the castle near the start of his reign. While here in August 1483, Richard wrote a letter to the King of France, replying to Louis XI's short letter regarding Richard's ascent to the throne. Richard's reply enquired about what protection France would offer English merchants in its country, and asked that Louis let him know by sending his reply with 'one of the grooms of my stable'. Louis did not reply, and he may never have even seen the letter since he died 30 August that year and was succeeded by his young son, Charles VIII.

By the time of Richard's visit, the castle had rested on its hill near the River Soar for hundreds of years. The first castle had been built of motte-and-bailey construction, but was rebuilt in stone by the twelfth century. The Great Hall was built soon after, and the castle served home to the earls of Lancaster and Leicester, who turned it into an opulent residence. As Richard walked through its rooms, he would have seen plastered walls which were either painted or hung with elegant tapestries.

The castle's Great Hall had been host to several parliaments, including the 'Parliament of Bats' called in 1426. Not only did Leicester accommodate parliaments, it also received other marks of royal favour. Edward IV had granted the city the right to a fair which would be held yearly for several days. This grant was witnessed by both Richard and George. In November 1484, *The Records of the Borough of Leicester* include a notation that Richard granted the city a 'certain annuity of 20 for twenty years'.

In the centuries following Richard's death, the Great Hall underwent a series of renovations. Its roof was replaced and a brick face added to the building. Despite the renovation work, it is possible to reconstruct how the Great Hall appeared by checking various accounts. Its walls were built of sandstone and the room contained large wooden columns which supported the roof and divided the nave, forming side aisles. The airy room was lighted by round-arched narrow windows. Richard would have sat on the dais at the top of the room, underneath his cloth of estate, while he and his trusted councillors discussed important matters.

The castle was in a sad state of decay by the reign of Henry VIII. It may have already been in a state of disrepair during Richard's stop in 1483, which explains the belief that he stayed at the Blue Boar Inn on his last visit. The area around the castle contained several buildings, both within and right outside the inner bailey. One of these buildings, St Mary de Castro, served as the castle's chapel. Few of the buildings which surrounded the castle survive today.

Leicester Castle and the Rebellion of 1483
Following his coronation, Richard went on progress. While Richard was watching the investiture of his young son, Edward, as Prince of Wales, men in Kent and across the south were beginning to organise to secure the release of the princes from the Tower. Richard learned of the rebellion while in Lincoln, and his letter written there grants a glimpse of his sense of betrayal by Buckingham's actions.

Buckingham had received several grants and offices from Richard, including those of the Constable of England, Chief Justice and Chamberlain in North and South Wales, and Constable and Steward of the King's Castles in Salop and Hereford. Historians still disagree as to why Buckingham, favoured like he was, chose to rebel against Richard.

The rebellion included a large number of gentry. The Croyland chronicler says that, once rumours began spreading about the deaths of Edward V and Richard, Duke of York, those involved in the uprising realised they needed a new figurehead for the rebellion and sent for Henry, Earl of Richmond. The chronicler continues by stating that it was the Duke of Buckingham who sent the message to Henry, on the advice of Bishop Morton, who was a prisoner in Brecknock Castle at the time. Perhaps it was the influence of Bishop Morton that persuaded Buckingham to turn against Richard. Whatever the reason, the Earl of Richmond was asked to come to England and marry Edward's eldest daughter, and with the princes' alleged deaths, his heir, Elizabeth.

Richard left Lincoln and began mustering troops. He stopped at Leicester Castle for a few days awaiting the men he had summoned. From Leicester, he headed towards Coventry. Fortunately for Richard, a series of events decreased the effectiveness of the rebellion. The Kentish rising occurred prematurely and the Duke of Norfolk quickly protected London. Buckingham, who was not liked in Wales, had a difficult time raising troops. Sir Humphrey Stafford blocked the exits across the upper Severn by destroying the bridges, hindering Buckingham's movements. A flood kept Buckingham trapped, leading to his capture.

Once the news of Buckingham's capture and Richard's advancing army reached the rebel leaders, many fled the country. Some of them were captured and executed, including Thomas St Leger, Richard's former brother-in-law. Buckingham was executed in Salisbury on 2 November 1483. Richard's mercy extended to a few of the leaders, who received pardons from the king.

Visiting Today

There is very little to see of the castle or its outbuildings today. Within the Castle Gardens stand the remains of the medieval castle walls. Surrounded by dense vegetation, the cleared top of the motte is now flat because it has been lowered several feet since Richard's time. Currently, the Great Hall is open for special events and private groups, but it is slated to become the De Montfort University Business School. Whether the Great Hall will be open for visitors following this is unknown. For more information, contact the Leicester Guildhall at +44 (0) 116 253 2569. Great Hall of Leicester Castle postcode: LE1 5FQ.

St Mary de Castro

A college consisting of a dean and twelve secular canons was established here in the twelfth century by Robert de Beaumont. On Whitsunday in 1426, Henry's uncle Bedford knighted him as part of the closing ceremonies of the 'Parliament of Bats'. Various accounts have the closing ceremonies happening both here and in the Great Hall, but the fact that it was a religious day supports the theory that the ceremony occurred in the chapel. After he was conferred with knighthood, the four-year-old Henry supposedly knighted the other men present, beginning with Richard, Duke of

York. Rather than the young king knighting the men, it is more likely the ceremony was performed in his name.

Richard would have visited the chapel on his visit in 1483. Church lore says his body rested here briefly after Bosworth, before being buried in Leicester. This is unlikely since Richard's body would probably have been taken immediately to the Annunciation of St Mary in the Newarke.

Visiting Today
St Mary de Castro was recently closed for safety issues but has since reopened. Check the church's website for more information on opening times at www.stmarydecastro.org.uk. The church also offers a virtual tour for the armchair traveller at http://www.stmarydecastro.org.uk/virtualtour.htm.

The Church of the Annunciation of the Blessed Virgin Mary in the Newarke
Henry, Earl of Lancaster, received a royal license to establish a hospital at Leicester in 1330, which was founded in the honour of the Annunciation of the Virgin Mary. By the middle of the fourteenth century, the hospital had become a college, with a dean, canons and vicars, and continued in its care of the poor and infirm. The college had its share of noble patrons, including John of Gaunt and William, Lord Hastings. Gaunt granted money to help with the completion of the college church and left instructions for a chantry chapel with two chaplains in his will. Hastings helped the church secure lands.

On one of his visits to Leicester, Richard would have passed by this church, which had been built in the mid-fourteenth century. It was here in August 1485, among the tombs of prominent Lancastrians, that Richard's broken body was displayed following his death at Bosworth.

Visiting Today
Following the Dissolution, the college was suppressed and fell to ruin. Today, all that is left of the college are the remains of two arches in the basement of the Hawthorn Building of the De Montfort University. These arches have recently been opened to the public for viewing. For more information, see the college website at http://www.dmu.ac.uk/about-dmu/heritage-centre/current-exhibitions.aspx.

The Turret and Magazine Gateways

The Turret Gateway separated the castle precincts from the Newarke and was built with defence in mind. When it was constructed in 1422 it was embattled, but the upper story was destroyed in the nineteenth century. The remains of the gateway can still be seen today.

Richard's body would have been brought to the church through the Magazine Gateway. The Magazine Gateway is impressive, with its height and vaulted passageways. Two arches cut through the gateway. The smaller arch allowed for pedestrian traffic, while the larger arch, with its vaulted stone ceiling, allowed carriages and horses to pass through. Richard's body, probably placed in a wagon, would have passed through here on its way to Greyfriars.

The Blue Boar Inn

Late in the day of 20 August 1485, a tired Richard made his way into Leicester. Tradition holds that on this occasion he made his way to the Blue Boar Inn. While John Ashdown-Hill makes a convincing argument that Richard never stayed in the inn, the location has been deeply engrained in the accepted tradition of Richard's story, so many people want to visit where it once stood.

Built in the fifteenth century, the Blue Boar was a large coaching inn used to wealthy travellers staying within its walls. It was demolished in 1836 to make way for other buildings. All that is left to describe the inn are engravings of the time and a written description by an architect, Mr Goddard, who examined the inn prior to its destruction.

The inn consisted of two storeys and was half timbered with oak and plaster. On the first floor there were two large windows. The second storey contained another window, which projected out, with five panels. The room was described by Goddard:

> The principal feature there was a projecting window of five lights, with moulded mullions and tracery of the fourteenth century. This window was also supported on brackets. In the interior the second storey was much like the lower one. The floor was of brick, and here was a fire-place similar to the one below, with the exception that it had three courses of brickwork between the plinth of the stone jambs and the floor, to serve as a hearth ... All

the principal beams and other parts were decorated with painted scroll-work in black, red, and yellow.

Richard would have been shown to the best room in the inn. Much of the decoration would have been the same. After awakening and breaking his fast, Richard left the inn early the next day to ride out to meet the Earl of Richmond.

Visiting Today

As the Blue Boar Inn was torn down in the early nineteenth century, nothing remains of it today. However, a Travelodge now sits on its site, so visitors who want to stay in the same location as Richard can pass a night here. The Travelodge is located on Highcross Street, which was the medieval high street. A memorial plaque is nearby.

The Bow Bridge Legends

Although it is one of the best-known sites in Leicester for its association with Richard, the Bow Bridge seen today is not the one Richard would have ridden across since the latter was demolished in the mid-nineteenth century. The bridge was rebuilt by the city of Leicester and was designed as a quasi-memorial for the king. Adorning the bridge's ironwork are emblems of the Tudor rose, the white rose of York, Richard's white boar and his motto, 'Loyaulte me Lie'.

Legend says that when Richard rode out of Leicester, his spur hit a rock on Bow Bridge. A woman in the crowd called out that where his foot had hit, there would his head hit, too. Following the Battle of Bosworth, Richard's corpse was draped across a horse, leaving his head to dangle over the side. The legend says that his head hit the exact stone, making the soothsayer's prediction come true.

Another myth regarding Richard is that after the Dissolution his body was thrown into the River Soar. When Greyfriars Priory was dissolved, a group of citizens supposedly defaced Richard's tomb, tossed his body under the Bow Bridge, and used his coffin for a water trough.

A cartographer in the early seventeenth century, John Speed, wrote that Richard's monument had been defaced during the Dissolution, that grass and weeds now covered its previous location, and that Richard's body had been put under the Bow Bridge, with his coffin being used for a water trough. Despite the fact that Speed discounted the rumours as hearsay, they were embellished by later writers.

Visiting Today
The Bow Bridge is a five-minute walk from Leicester Cathedral, near Castle Gardens. The traffic in the area is quite busy, so be careful if trying to get close to the bridge.

Leicester Cathedral, Leicester
Today, this church marks the final resting place of King Richard III. Despite the controversies surrounding his discovery and reinternment, Richard was finally laid to rest in Leicester Cathedral on 26 March 2015. His tomb has been visited by thousands of people since its reveal, allowing Ricardians and others interested in the king a place to pay their respects to this controversial ruler.

Leicester Cathedral was not a cathedral when Richard III was at Leicester. At that time it was the parish church of St Martin. Richard probably never visited the church, but he would have been familiar with its exterior, which was originally built by the Normans. Over the next few centuries the church was renovated and rebuilt. As the 220-foot spire was not added until the nineteenth century, following the addition of a new tower, Richard would never have seen it. Around the same time as the tower addition, the church was renovated and restored to its former glory. In 1927, the Diocese of Leicester was reinstated, and St Martin's was chosen to become the cathedral church.

Richard and the Cathedral
After the decision was made to rebury Richard here, the cathedral underwent a renovation process in order to prepare for his body. His tomb sits within the ambulatory between the Chapel of Christ the King and the sanctuary. The Nicholson Screen was relocated to shield the tomb from the main area of worship. His remains rest in a vault, above which sits a dark plinth inscribed with his name, dates and motto. A large block of limestone sits atop the plinth, with a cross cut into it. For information about current opening times and visits, see the cathedral's website at http://leicestercathedral.org/

visit-us. Make sure to check the website to avoid disappointment, since the cathedral is sometimes closed; available times to visit the tomb may also vary from normal cathedral opening times. At the current time, admission is free, but donations are requested. Postcode: LE1 5DE.

King Richard III Visitor Centre, Leicester

The discovery of Richard's bones led to the building of a visitor centre in Leicester dedicated to telling the story of the king. The centre stands on the site of the medieval priory of the Greyfriars, where Richard was buried. The theme of the centre is 'Dynasty, Death and Discovery'.

The ground floor of the centre contains both the 'Dynasty' and 'Death' portions of the exhibit. Audio, combined with visual images, relates the story of Richard's life, including contributions he made as well as the controversy surrounding the princes. The 'Death' part of the exhibit explains the events of Bosworth. The exhibits recounting the discovery of Richard's body, including the science behind its identification, are found on the first floor of the building. Much care has been taken to explain the science in terms the general public can easily understand.

One of the highlights of a visit to the centre is visiting the spot where Richard's body was located. Nothing remains of the priory, but by examining the area where Richard was found, we can rediscover its history.

The Greyfriars Priory, Leicester

Originally founded by Simon de Montfort II in the thirteenth century, the priory housed Franciscan monks, known as Greyfriars due to the grey habit they wore. Following Richard's death, his body was put on display at the Church of the Annunciation of the Blessed Virgin Mary in the Newarke for several days. This church held the tombs of several Lancastrians, and while Henry VII thought it a fitting place to display the body of his vanquished foe, he probably did not want to bury the former king in the building.

Vergil said Richard was brought to the Franciscans and was 'buryed ... without any pompe or solemne funerall'. Following the Dissolution, the church was sold, and throughout the next few centuries its buildings were demolished as its stone was taken to create new buildings elsewhere. Soon, nothing was left and the memory of the priory which housed the tomb of the last Plantagenet king was shrouded by time.

Visiting the King Richard III Visitor Centre Today

A visit to the centre will take the better part of two hours, and even longer if one stops to read each placard. Included in the exhibition are both a full and a partial facial reconstruction completed after the discovery of the body. Also featured is a 3D print of a replica of Richard's skeleton to illustrate his spine curvature. Another interesting exhibit includes commentary from several members of the team that located Richard's body.

The centre also has a café and a courtyard for visitors. For more information about tickets and admission, see the centre's webpage at www.kriii.com. Postcode: LE1 5DB.

Bosworth, Leicestershire

News of Henry Tudor's arrival in England had reached Richard by 11 August, and he began ordering men to meet him in Leicester. After leaving Leicester, Richard headed to intercept Tudor and his men as they made their way south on Watling Street towards London. Richard made his camp near what would become the battlefield, where he readied his troops before the battle and 'with many woords exhortyd them to the fyght to coome'.

The Croyland chronicler reports that Richard's chaplains were not ready to celebrate Mass as the day of the battle dawned. Tradition holds that Richard may have taken Mass at nearby Sutton Cheney church that morning, but there is no evidence he did so.

Henry and his men are believed to have camped near Merevale Abbey, since later in his reign Henry paid the surrounding villages for damages to their land. The next morning he made his way towards Richard's army. The two armies would meet on Fenn Lane between Stoke Golding, Shenton and Dadlington. Accounts differ as to who had the larger army, but most agree that Richard held the advantage.

As the battle continued, Richard's scouts noticed that Henry was moving away from the main army with only a small group of men. Richard advanced towards Henry, managing to kill William Brandon, Henry's standard bearer. It was then that William Stanley reached a decision, and his troops moved toward Richard, pushing him back and forcing him to fight on foot. Richard was killed and the battle soon over. While the exact location where Richard died is not known, Henry issued a proclamation which states it was at a place known by 'Sandeford'. Archaeological work in a field in the area unearthed a boar badge near to what was part of the medieval marsh. This may mean this was the location where Richard was struck down.

After Richard died, Henry made for the nearest high ground where he thanked his men. Lord Stanley took Richard's crown and placed it on Henry's head to the cries of 'God save King Henry!' from the men. Today it is believed that this occurred on Crown Hill. Henry and his men made their way to Leicester, taking Richard's body, which had been slung across a horse's back, with them.

Bosworth Battlefield Heritage Centre, Leicestershire

The location where Richard is believed to have fallen is on private land and is not accessible to visitors. However, the nearby heritage centre offers an informative account of the battle and the battle site. Bosworth Battlefield Heritage Centre was the country's first battlefield interpretation site, and it presents information in such a way that both children and adults are able to gain a clear understanding of the clash and the background of the combatants involved.

The story is told through the different viewpoints of four characters, who lead visitors through each exhibit. A large display of weaponry helps one understand the type of weapons the soldiers used in the battle. Another exhibit includes both the artefacts that have been found near the battle area and the fascinating story of how the battle site was located. Make sure to see the Bosworth Boar badge and the other finds.

After leaving the museum area, walk to the top of the hill where a memorial sundial commemorates the battle and the men who died. Three chairs at the sundial represent Richard, Henry and Stanley.

Both a two-kilometre guided battlefield walk and a longer twelve-kilometre one are available from the centre. For more information on these walks, see the centre's website. The best way to see the locations of the new battle sites is to take one of the walks. Once you have explored the area, visit nearby Sutton Cheney church. Another place to discover is St James's church at Dadlington, where many of the dead from Bosworth were buried.

For more information about the walks as well as the centre's opening times and prices, see the website at www.bosworthbattlefield.com/welcome/visit/ or call +44 (0) 1455290429. Postcode: CV13 0AD.

Part 4

Anne Neville

Anne Neville, the daughter of the Earl of Warwick, began her life within a staunchly Yorkist family. However, events would soon challenge her father's loyalty and alter Anne's future. Married to the Lancastrian heir to the throne, Anne had to adjust to both the sudden change in her family's loyalty and her new status.

Life gave her little time to become used to her change in circumstances, because within the year she would lose both her father at Barnet and new husband on the field at Tewkesbury. Her change in fortune would leave her in the custody of her brother-in-law, George, Duke of Clarence. As a Lancastrian widow in Yorkist custody, she may have envisioned a bleak future. Her fortune changed again, however, when the youngest York brother, Richard, Duke of Gloucester, offered marriage. Soon, her prospects were on the rise.

Collegiate Church of St Mary, Warwick, Warwickshire

It is thought that a Saxon place of worship may have stood here prior to the Norman building. The collegiate foundation was begun by Henry de Beaumont and was completed around 1123 by his son Roger de Newburgh, 2nd Earl of Warwick. Beaumont was the younger son of Roger de Beaumont and had been created Earl of Warwick by William II. Eventually the title of Earl of Warwick passed to the Beauchamp family, and through Anne's mother to Richard Neville.

On 11 June 1456, Anne took her first breath at Warwick Castle. The castle will be discussed in greater detail in the section on George, Duke of Clarence. Her christening took place at the Collegiate Church of St Mary in Warwick.

In preparation, her father would have gathered together the godparents, their number regulated by the church. As a girl, Anne would have been limited to one godfather and two godmothers. Godparents were carefully chosen and were expected to help guide the spiritual life of the child.

On the morning of the christening, friends, family and godparents set off from Warwick Castle in a procession to the church, where the priest waited at the door to question the godparents' knowledge of the prayers they were expected to teach Anne. Proceeding to the font, the priest put salt in Anne's mouth before anointing her with oil and immersing her in the water of the font. One of her godparents lifted her out of the water and wrapped her in her christening gown. At the altar, her godparents made a profession of faith for her. The party then left the church and hurried back to Warwick Castle where a feast was waiting.

Anne also visited the church with her family and Richard on at least one occasion. Since the family was often in Warwick, she would have been in the church on other instances as she grew older. The church had long ties with the Beauchamps, Anne's maternal family. One of the church's medieval chapels is called the Beauchamp chapel, since it was built in the mid-fifteenth century for the tomb of Richard Beauchamp.

As a collegiate church, St Mary's would have had a dean and canons, and the church complex would have been larger than it is today. According to the church, the precincts spread from the Butts to today's Old Square. At the time of Anne's christening, the hall of the vicars-choral was being built. The building stood until 1880 when it was demolished.

Following the Reformation, St Mary's was no longer collegiate and became a parish church. During the fire that swept through Warwick in 1694, much of St Mary's was destroyed and had to be rebuilt.

Visiting Today
The church has changed drastically since Anne was a young girl, yet it is still possible to catch a glimpse of it as she knew it. Today, the impressive tower with its parapet can be seen for quite a

distance. Unfortunately, it is not a tower that Anne would have known, having been constructed in the eighteenth century.

As you enter into the church through the West entrance, you pass into the eighteenth-century nave and altar. The portion of the church where Anne's christening took place fell victim to the fire, and the font in the nave is eighteenth century.

The chancel was opened to view when the medieval stone screen that once stood there was removed in the eighteenth century. The rib vaulting in the chancel overlooks the fourteenth-century tomb of Thomas Beauchamp and his wife, Katherine Mortimer. The family arms may be seen in the vaulting.

The Chapel of Our Lady, known mainly as the Beauchamp Chapel, was begun in 1442 and was still under construction at the time of Anne's christening. While not consecrated until later, this ornate chapel was finished while she was young, so she would have been familiar with the elaborate tomb of Purbeck marble for Richard Beauchamp, her maternal grandfather. The brass effigy shows him in armour with a swan next to his head, while at his feet are a griffin and a muzzled bear. The brass hearse above his head used to support a covering. Take some time to examine the weepers on the side of the tomb for familiar coats of arms.

The stained glass in the chapel is fifteenth century, but it was reassembled following the window's destruction by the Puritans. Other fifteenth-century pieces include the wall painting of the Last Judgement, which was restored in the seventeenth century. The oak stalls, with their elaborate carvings, were constructed in the mid-fifteenth century.

While not from our period, many of the other tombs in the chapel will have names familiar to those interested in British history. One of these, Robert Dudley, Earl of Leicester, was a favourite of Queen Elizabeth I.

Before leaving the church, do not forget to explore the crypt below. Of Norman origin, it has beautiful pillars and arches. According to the church, they have supported the weight of the structure for more than 850 years.

For more information on opening times, see the church's website at http://www.stmaryswarwick.org.uk/. Postcode: CV34 4RA.

The Erber, London

There are many theories as to how the fine London home of the Nevilles received its name, but Halsted believes the name was from either the French word 'auberge', for lodging house, or from 'The Harbour', from its location overlooking the Thames. The home was situated on the east of Elbow Lane, south of the Church of St Mary Bothaw, and fronted Dowgate, Carter and Bush Lanes. According to C. L. Kingsford, it was shaped as an irregular quadrilateral and was 70 yards by 50 yards.

William Latimer, whose daughter married John Neville, leased the home in the fourteenth century. It eventually passed to the Nevilles, when, in December of 1399, it was granted to Ralph, Earl of Westmorland. The Nevilles certainly made use of the lodging. Late in 1457, Henry IV, attempting to reconcile the two competing factions at court, summoned a Great Council. The Earl of Salisbury brought 500 retainers, who were said to have lodged at the Erber. By January 1458, the Duke of York was also in London at Baynard's Castle, with his retainers. Messages would have passed between the two men, and perhaps they even met at the Erber to discuss the issues plaguing them.

Anne would have been here often when she and her family were at court. According to Amy Licence in *Anne Neville: Richard III's Tragic Queen*, Anne lodged here when in London for the christening of Edward IV's daughter, Elizabeth of York.

Following the death of her father and husband, Anne was placed into the custody of her brother-in-law, George, and sister, Isabel. As George was granted the Erber, Anne spent some time here while in their custody, perhaps walking through the internal courtyard to the garden. The lady's chamber overlooked a garden, and Anne and Isabel may have spent some time together in Isabel's chamber with the fresh fragrance of flowers wafting through the room.

After Anne married Richard she probably did not visit the Erber again until he was king. However, the home was still used for state occasions. In one instance, it was used to house the ambassadors of Burgundy when Margaret, Duchess of Burgundy, visited England.

When the property came to Richard it was in need of repair, so he began renovations. Although no descriptions remain, it is possible to infer that it was an opulent home from a moniker it received, the 'King's Palace'. Unfortunately, Richard and Anne did not have the opportunity to stay here often before their deaths.

During the reign of Henry VIII, Margaret Pole, George and Isabel's daughter, was granted her family's home. In 1520, the Erber was described as having two gates, one fronting Dowgate. Hopefully Margaret had some moments of peace here before her execution during the reign of Henry VIII. Her death ended the Erber's connection with the York family.

Visiting Today

The opulent house that Anne Neville once walked through no longer exists. Today the site is under Cannon Street station. Unfortunately, while you can walk down by the station and get an idea of where the building once stood, there is really no way to 'visit' the Erber.

Anne in France

Following Warwick's flight to safety in France, he enlisted the support of the French king to persuade Margaret of Anjou to allow a marriage between his daughter, Anne, and her son, Edward. While one source says the betrothal occurred at Amboise, most sources place it at Angers and the wedding at Amboise.

Château d'Angers, Angers, France

In July 1470, the Milanese ambassador reported that the Earl of Warwick had begged forgiveness of Margaret of Anjou and had given 'homage and fealty there, swearing to be a faithful and loyal subject of the king, queen and prince as his liege lords unto death'. The site of this momentous about-face was the Château d'Angers where Anne also lodged prior to her betrothal to Prince Edward.

A fortification has stood on the site since the ninth century, but the castle was expanded in the thirteenth century. Built on a high cliff overlooking the River Maine, it had seventeen immense towers and two gatehouses. Over time, it fell into ruin and the dukes of Anjou subsequently repaired it. René, Margaret of Anjou's father, further enlarged and strengthened the fortress in the mid-fifteenth century.

Anne would have entered the building through the field gateway, or Porte des Champs. This entrance opened into the countryside and not the city, allowing the castle to remain slightly apart. She would have passed over a main bridge and then over the drawbridge, entering under the gateway with its massive double portcullis.

Anne's first glimpse of the château would be of a building much different than what is seen today. While the alternating dressed black and light stonework would have been the same, the seventeen towers were topped with coronets and were much higher. The dry moat was not as deep, and it contained René's menagerie of many exotic animals. Perhaps Anne heard the roar of a lion or an elephant trumpet when she entered the castle. The garden at the château would have been impressive, containing plants from exotic places.

While at the château, Anne would have lodged in an opulent building, since René was known for his lavish spending. Anne was not in Angers long, but she may have seen some of the artists and poets that frequented René's court. She would have walked through the Great Hall, with its large windows, painted walls and slate ceiling. The impressive spiral staircase was in a restricted area, so it is doubtful Anne would have seen its intricate carvings.

In the early fifteenth century, Louis II and his wife, Yolande of Aragon, built a remarkable chapel at the château. Anne would have attended Mass here, entering through the porch into the nave. The large Gothic windows would have flooded the room with light, allowing her to see clearly the three bays within the building. The private oratory, with its delicate tracery and sculptures, would have caught her eye. Here the dukes of Anjou could hear Mass and receive communion in private.

Anne would have been shown to her chambers in the royal lodgings. While much of the four-sided palace was destroyed throughout the years, there is still enough remaining today to demonstrate its splendour. When Anne arrived, King René's gallery was relatively new, having been completed twenty years prior. The gallery would have allowed the courtiers to have walked from their private apartments to the gardens below. Anne would have passed underneath the ceiling with its beautiful rib vaulting and out into the gardens. Wandering through the garden, with its beautiful exotic plants, Anne may have considered the twists of fate that had befallen her. At one point, her father had wanted her sister Isabel to be queen. Now his eye had fallen on her. It is impossible to know Anne's thoughts, but it is possible to walk in her footsteps through the evocative gallery.

Visiting Today

Approaching the great walls of the château, it is hard not to be impressed by its round towers projecting out of the sides of the walls. The combination of the dressed black and light stone is still striking. Visitors arriving today do not see the extent of how impressive it once was, when the towers were taller and topped with coronets. Today's moat is much deeper, and instead of containing exotic animals contains a riot of beautiful flowers.

The present entrance into the château is via a bridge over the moat and through the Porte de la Ville. Two drawbridges connected this entrance to the city in Anne's time; it also had a double portcullis, much like the Porte des Champs.

Once inside the walls, make your way to the left through the garden to the Porte des Champs. The Governor's Lodge that René built would have been here during Anne's visit, but it has been enlarged and changed over the years. Walk down through the gateway to the entrance, where you can see one of the double portcullises. This is the entrance that Anne would have come through on her way into the building.

After taking time to examine the Porte des Champs, walk towards the château. The gateway was built by René and has two turrets on either side of the arched entrance. The pepper-pot turrets resemble those that once topped the towers along the outer walls. Pass through the entranceway like Anne once did into the interior of the palace courtyard.

Walk down the stairs to the left to enter into the Apocalypse Gallery. This building was constructed in 1950 to house the remains of the fourteenth-century Apocalypse tapestry. The tapestry had been given to the cathedral by René in 1480, but it was later returned to the château after the gallery was built to protect it. In all likelihood, Anne would have seen the magnificent and intricately woven tapestry on her visit because it would have been a symbol of the Duke of Anjou's prestige. Take some time to walk through the gallery, lingering before the pieces that catch your eye. The tapestry was originally created in six sections, with each measuring approximately 77 feet long by 20 feet tall. According to the château, what remains today is approximately 338 feet long and 15 feet tall. While you are in the gallery, take some time to see the Saint-Laud chapel. While not something that Anne would have seen, the chapel was restored during the building of the gallery and still has decorative capitals and bases from the twelfth century.

After you exit the gallery area, look to your left. This was once the magnificent Great Hall. Despite being repaired and renovated throughout the centuries, little remains today. Next, walk back up the stairs and see the view of the River Maine.

The Royal Lodge, which sits across the courtyard, is not the same size it was on Anne's visit since parts have been destroyed. Try to imagine the exterior white-washed like Anne would have seen it. Its three floors included a hall and ceremonial room; the king's and queen's chambers made up the other two floors. Today, there is a short film (in French) that explains the castle's history. Multi-language placards and models depicting the castle's appearance throughout the centuries complete the exhibit.

You can then walk around to see King René's Gallery. It is easy to picture a young Anne here, walking along the gallery towards the gardens, contemplating her betrothal to her former enemy. After exploring the area, walk to the chapel where the rich, decorative entrance will take a while to examine. The niches above it once held statues. The time that the chapel was used for a prison took its toll, but the elegant simplicity of the architecture is still evident. Wander around the room, taking time to examine the duke's private oratory.

Before leaving, it is worth taking the time to walk the walls and see the view and layout of the buildings. The château also has a tea room. For more information about visiting the château, see its website at http://www.angers.monuments-nationaux.fr/ or call 33 (0)2 41 86 48 77.

Cathédrale Saint-Maurice, Angers, France

Leaving the château, walk across the Promenade du Bout-du-Monde to Rue Saint-Aignan. Several of the homes along this route would have existed when Anne made her way to the cathedral for her formal betrothal to Prince Edward. As you come to the lane and stairs leading up to the cathedral, turn right. The cathedral sits at the top of the lane, casting a striking image against a blue sky.

Officially known as the Saint-Maurice Cathedral of Angers, it was originally dedicated to the Virgin Mary but received a second dedication to St Maurice. Following a fire the cathedral was rebuilt, and the present building dates to the twelfth century. It has been renovated and restored several times throughout the years.

As Anne made her way to the cathedral she would have not have seen the twin spires, which were completed following a fire in 1533 and restored in the nineteenth century. Anne would have walked through the nave, with its Angevin Gothic vaulting, on her way to the high altar. She would not have seen the baroque altar that currently stands there. Soon, she and Edward would make their promises before the high altar, traditionally on a piece of the true cross.

If it were a sunny day, the light would have streamed in through the fifteenth-century rose windows, illuminating the room while Anne and Edward stood with their hands clasped and expressed their desire to be wed. As binding as a wedding, the ceremony sealed the pact made between Warwick and Margaret. The wedding itself would occur at Amboise.

Visiting Today

Much of the cathedral has changed following fire and renovation. The tombs of René and Louis II are still extant, but Margaret of Anjou's tomb was destroyed. Some exquisite twelfth-century stained glass remains and is worth a look. If the treasury is open, take some time to explore its riches.

For more information on visiting the cathedral, see its website at http://catholique-angers.cef.fr/Cathedrale-Saint-Maurice-Notre-Dame.

Château d'Amboise, Loire Valley, France

Settled high on a rocky promontory, Amboise was originally built for security. Claimed by Fulk of Anjou, the fortification eventually came to the lords of Amboise. In the fifteenth century, Charles VII confiscated the castle for the crown. His son, Louis XI, added to the complex, and it was here in 1470 that his son, the future Charles VIII, was born. Once king, Charles VIII made major changes to the complex, giving it an Italian flair.

Throughout the years, the château was the scene of several major events in French history. Charles VIII died here in a bizarre accident. He hit his head on a door and was dead a few hours later. During Catherine de'Medici's regency for Francois II, the Huguenots tried to take the king at the château, resulting in a bloodbath.

Eventually the château was abandoned by the royals and its fortifications destroyed; in subsequent centuries it served as a prison. Fire ravaged the structure, damaging the buildings between the chapel and the tower and these had to be demolished. More of its buildings were dismantled under the stewardship of Roger Ducos in the early nineteenth century.

Anne and Amboise

While Anne, her mother and sister were safe in Normandy, her father was busy conspiring with King Louis at Amboise. The Milanese ambassador wrote that Warwick and Clarence were well received by the French king. The men spent their day watching tournaments and discussing the marriage of Anne to Edward. Clarence and Warwick left prior to Margaret's arrival at Amboise, with Clarence going back to Isabel in Normandy and Warwick making his way to Vandoma.

After their betrothal, Anne and her fiancé, along with both their mothers, came to Amboise. Whether or not Anne was willing to marry Prince Edward or just a pawn in her father's schemes, she was now linked to a family that she had once feared. How Edward felt about marrying the daughter of his family's former enemy has not been recorded; one hopes that the two young people put aside any family differences to make the best of the situation.

During the next few months, Anne would learn more about her fiancé. Unfortunately, little is known about Prince Edward. The Milanese ambassador recorded that 'this boy, though only thirteen years of age, already talks of nothing but of cutting off heads or making war, as if he had everything in his hands or was the god of battle or the peaceful occupant of that throne'. Edward's main influence seems to have been his pragmatic, strong-willed mother rather than his pious father.

Perhaps Anne and Edward took walks in the gardens and enjoyed each other's company. Unfortunately no records exist to support whether the two young people either liked or detested each other. Given the culture of the time, both likely accepted their new status.

Anne would also have spent time with the women at Amboise. As Charlotte of Savoy had just given birth to the future heir on 30 June, Anne got to see the new baby. Entertainments would have been performed for the royal guests. The summer probably passed quickly, under the warm sun and blue skies of a French summer.

While there are still arguments as to whether or not Margaret of Anjou allowed the marriage and consummation to go ahead, it is more probable that the couple did wed, especially after Warwick landed in England. Since initial reports of Warwick's invasion were positive, there seems little reason to delay the marriage. R. A. Griffiths states that this probably occurred on 13 December. The wedding would have either taken place at the private chapel within the keep or at the Saint-Florentin church.

Soon the royal couple and their family would leave Amboise to finalise arrangements for their trip across the channel to England. A feeling of excitement would have been in the air while Prince Edward and his new wife prepared to return to what they thought would one day be their kingdom. For all of the exiles, the feeling of anticipation must have been heady. None of them could foresee the outcome of their landing.

Visiting Today

My first glimpse of Amboise was from across the river and the view was arresting. The white stone of the château glistened under a powder blue sky. Perhaps Anne felt the same sense of awe when she first saw the château that would be her temporary home.

Visitors today enter through a large ramp up into the grounds. It is hard to picture the château as Anne would have seen it because little remains of the buildings she would have known. It is possible to walk where the buildings once stood, however. Stand at the top of the ramp. The chapel of Saint-Hubert is positioned before you. Once the private chapel of the keep stood here, and it is the most likely place for the wedding of Anne and Edward. The chapel that stands today was built by Charles VIII, who was born soon before Anne's arrival at Amboise.

The royal lodgings where Anne stayed are completely gone, demolished in the seventeenth century. The lodgings were built in a triangular pattern, and Saint-Hubert was built to the outside of them. If you walk in front of the chapel, you are walking where the buildings once stood. Continue straight ahead along the walkway. The royal lodgings were here. Anne stayed in the buildings between the chapel and the remains of the twelfth-century tower. The lodgings went around to the Garçonnet tower and then to the current building. Right before the present building, they extended back out across the courtyard to join with the other side, forming a triangle.

While nothing truly remains of the Amboise Anne would have known, we can get an idea of how it would have appeared from a sixteenth-century engraving by Jacques Androuet Du Cerceau. The keep consisted of a set of buildings, many with dormer windows, situated around a triangular courtyard. The rooms were equipped with fireplaces as evidenced by the chimneys lining the roof. The towers nearby were taller than they are today and had pepper-pot tops. Inside, the walls were either plastered or covered with rich tapestries.

Even though the remaining lodging is not from our time period, it is still worth a visit. The Charles VIII wing was begun in the fifteenth century and was built adjacent to the existing keep. After exploring the royal lodging, take some time to wander the grounds. Leonardo da Vinci's grave is in the chapel of Saint-Hubert. The home where he died lies within the city and is crowded with visitors.

As with Angers, Amboise is best visited by car. For more information on visiting, see the château's website at http://www. chateau-amboise.com.

Cerne Abbey, Dorset

Tradition holds that Cerne Abbey was founded by Saint Augustine, but it is more probable that the abbey was founded in the tenth century. Another legend states that Edwold, brother of Edmund, King of the East Anglians, refused the crown after his brother's death and lived the life of a hermit near here. Following his death, Ailmer, Earl of Cornwall, translated his remains to the old church and built the monastery which was dedicated to the Blessed Virgin, St Peter and St Benedict. The Benedictine Abbey was founded in 987.

The abbey was lucky to have many royal benefactors throughout the centuries. Canute, after first plundering the monastery, became its benefactor. King John and Henry III both visited the abbey, and on Henry's visit, he granted his approval to the election of a new abbot. By the fifteenth century the monastery was a wealthy one. In 1482, Edward IV allowed it to take one third of the manor of Maiden Newton in order to sustain a chaplain, who was to pray at the altar of St John the Baptist for the good estate of the king and his wife, Elizabeth.

In 1539, the abbey was forced to surrender to Henry VIII. Through the years, the buildings fell into ruin and little is left today.

Anne and Cerne Abbey

After being battled by storms, the Lancastrian party, including Anne, was finally able to land at Weymouth, while Anne's mother landed in Portsmouth. Soon, they learned of the disastrous day at Barnet. Anne must have been devastated. To learn of her father's death after expecting to be welcomed as the wife of the heir must have been heartbreaking. Added to that was the fact that she was separated from her mother. She probably received little sympathy from Margaret who, Vergil reports, had 'swownyd for feare; she was distrawght, dismayd, and tormentyd with sorow; she lamentyd the calamyty of the time, the adversity of fortune, hir owne toyle and mysery'.

Perhaps Anne was comforted by the news her father had died bravely. Vergil credits him with invincible courage while 'manfully fyghting'. Even if she was comforted, she must have been filled with fear by the thought of her future. She was irrevocably tied to the cause of Lancaster, her father was dead, and all hope seemed lost.

The party moved to Cerne Abbey where they stayed in the abbey's guest house, built by Abbot John Vanne. Here, Margaret met with advisers to try to determine what course to take next. Should they flee back to France or continue onwards? As a fire crackled in the large fireplace, ornamented with Vanne's crest, Margaret and the Lancastrian lords began to plan for war. Edward and Anne would have been present while the plans were being made that would change their future.

Visiting Today

Although the atmosphere evokes a sense of history, little actually remains of the abbey. Part of it was incorporated into a private home, but much of it has disappeared. However, it is still possible to see the guest house where Margaret, Anne and Edward are said to have lodged. I recommend parking somewhere other than the narrow lane leading up to the buildings since it is difficult to turn around.

Enter through the fence at the right of the private home. What is left of the abbey has been restored by its owners, and an honesty box sits on the wall marked with the current tariff. Walk down the narrow lane. The Abbey Guest House is in front of you. Make your way around the front and turn right to see the ornamented oriel window. You may be able to picture a forlorn Anne looking out the window at the activity around her, thinking of her father.

While the abbot's porch was not built until after Anne's visit, it gives an idea of how opulent the abbey once was. Placards detailing the abbey's history and a conjecture of its former appearance can be found on the porch.

Head back outside the fence, then go through the archway and continue through the burial grounds out into the field. This field is where the opulent church of the abbey, decorated in the Early English style, once stood. As you walk back towards the gateway, take some time to visit the ancient St Augustine's well. According to Leland, a chapel once covered the spring, but it was destroyed following the dissolution of the abbey.

Although not York-related, the beautiful parish church is worth a visit. Built in the fourteenth century, the church still contains some medieval wall paintings. Anne may have seen the exterior of the church while visiting, but it is doubtful she ever went inside. Another must-see attraction in Cerne Abbas is the Cerne Giant. It is 180 feet tall and is the largest chalk hill figure in England. The exact age of the giant is in dispute, so it is impossible to say whether or not Anne would have seen the colossal figure while here. Cerne Abbas Postcode: DT2 7AL.

Little Malvern Priory, Worcestershire

After leaving Cerne Abbas, the Lancastrian party began to move. Turned away from Gloucester, they ended up at Tewkesbury. Some historians say that the women stayed at Gobes Hall, which is plausible. Since Tewkesbury will be discussed in the section on

Edward IV, this section focuses on Anne in the aftermath of the battle. Historians disagree about where Margaret and Anne went after the Battle of Tewkesbury. Warkworth says Margaret fled to a 'poor religious place', which some historians believe to be Little Malvern Priory.

The priory of St Giles of Little Malvern was founded in 1171 by two brothers, Jocelin and Edred. A Benedictine house, its benefactors included William de Blois and Henry III. Nestled on the side of a hill, it overlooked a wide valley. The priory fell under the supremacy of Worcester, whose prior held the right to remove monks and replace them with others. The chapter of Worcester also had to approve the prior of Little Malvern.

Anne and Margaret would most likely have lodged in the prior's lodgings. Today, this forms part of Little Malvern Court. According to *A History of the County of Worcester*, the manor had a hall on the eastern side, which adjoined the cloister's west side. The southern part of the building was four storeys and may have adjoined the cloister's southern range.

It is almost certain that Margaret and Anne would have entered the priory church to pray. While most of the church is gone, lost in the wake of the Dissolution, its nave once extended to the current site of Little Malvern Court. The tower and much of the chancel would still be recognisable to the women.

It is not known where the Yorkists took the women into custody. Sources say that Margaret was a broken woman. Little is mentioned of Anne, but undoubtedly she was also crestfallen by the turn of events. Tied to the Lancastrians by her father, she had spent the past few months expecting to be the wife of the heir to the throne. Even if she was not unhappy with the loss of her husband, she would have been frightened by her future prospects. While she and Margaret were being taken to Coventry to Edward IV, her fears may have overwhelmed her. What would her future hold?

Visiting Today
There are two locations to visit tied with Little Malvern. The first one is Little Malvern Court, which is believed to have been the location of the prior's lodging. In the care of a private family, it is open to visitors. The property has been much restored throughout the years and bears little resemblance to the lodgings that Anne would have

remembered. However, she would have seen the fourteenth-century roof of the hall which was uncovered in the 1960s. While visiting, make sure to see the gardens since remains of the priory still stand. For more information about visiting, see the home's website at http://www.littlemalverncourt.co.uk/ or phone +44 (0)1684 892 988.

The second location is the church ruins. While the nave was destroyed, the chancel and tower remain. Walk down the path towards the church. The porch you enter through was built in the 1960s and contains an interesting display of stone fragments from the priory.

Enter the chancel through the doors to your left. The arches on either side of the chancel once opened to the transepts and chapels. According to the church literature, five of the six bells were removed following the Dissolution. One fourteenth-century bell still remains, and Anne and Margaret would have heard it ringing three times a day.

One interesting feature of the church that Margaret and Anne would not have seen yet still is associated with the York family is the painted eastern window. Bishop Alcock, who had several ties with the York family, had visited the priory and found it to be in a terrible state. He initiated both physical and spiritual renovations of the house. One of his lasting contributions to the priory was the east window, which contained images of the Yorks. Although the glass was broken during either the Dissolution or the Civil War, it has been painstakingly replaced.

The window depicted Edward IV, the two young princes, Elizabeth Woodville, and Elizabeth, Cecily, Mary and Anne. Unfortunately, Edward IV and the Duke of York's images are completely gone, and Elizabeth Woodville's image is missing its head. Both Elizabeth Woodville and Elizabeth of York kneel at prayer desks beneath canopies of estate. All the women appear to be clothed in beautiful dresses. Woodville's dress is crimson, with gold trim, and her mantle is a vibrant blue. Her daughters are clad in blue dresses with crimson mantles. Although Elizabeth of York is wearing a different headdress than her sisters, the rest of their clothing is alike. Since Woodville's head is missing, it is impossible to know for certain if she was wearing a similar style; from the pattern of the missing glass, it seems she was. Edward V is also shown kneeling at a prayer desk beneath a canopy of estate. Like his sisters, he is clad in blue with a crimson mantle.

Before leaving, take a moment to look at the medieval tiles around the altar. Church literature states these were produced in the fourteenth century. Anne and Margaret would have walked on tiles much like these.

Just like with many of the locations associated with Anne, it is easiest to visit the site by car. A free car park is available across the street from the church and Little Malvern Court. The church is free to enter. Postcode: WR14 4JN.

St Martin le Grand, London

After her capture following Tewkesbury, Anne was placed in the custody of her brother-in-law, Clarence, and her sister, Isabel. Much of her time while in their custody would have been spent at Warwick Castle. While in London, the family generally lodged at Coldharbour. Warwick Castle will be covered in the section on George, Duke of Clarence, and Coldharbour in the section on Anne, Duchess of Exeter.

At some point, Richard became determined to marry Anne. How the courtship developed is a matter of speculation. That Clarence was adamantly opposed to the idea is not. While the Croyland chronicler has Clarence disguising Anne as a kitchen maid, this is unlikely. He did, however, voice his objections to the marriage. It may be that Anne did need to escape into sanctuary to wed Richard. If tradition is to be believed, she chose the church of St Martin le Grand for her sanctuary.

Two types of sanctuary privileges existed in medieval times. Temporary sanctuary allowed the individual forty days to come to terms with his accuser, acquiesce to the king's justice or leave the country. There was also a more permanent type of sanctuary, which allowed an individual to remain within the walls of the sanctuary for an unlimited amount of time. While she waited for her marriage to Richard, Anne would have stayed within the confines of St Martin le Grand.

There is dispute over what date Richard and Anne were wed. While some historians have suggested that there was no dispensation granted for the marriage, Peter D. Clarke found evidence that not only had the couple applied for a dispensation from the papal penitentiary, but that it was granted on 22 April 1472.

St Martin le Grand's History

In 1068, William the Conqueror confirmed a grant of lands made a few months before by Ingelric to the church of St Martin in London. Ingelric and his brother had built the church at their own cost. The charter also stated the church should be 'free and altogether exempt from all exaction and disturbance of Bishops, Archdeacons, Deans, or their Ministers'. As a king's free chapel, the college was immune from all but the king's authority.

In 1286, the college was granted the right to close a public road running from Foster Lane to St Nicholas Shambles. This allowed the college to be free from the inconvenience of a roadway passing through its precincts. Renovations continued throughout the years because some of the college buildings were in disrepair. In the fourteenth century, the college dean, William de Wykeham, renovated both the cloister and the church at his own expense. He also built a new chapter house, complete with a decorated stone ceiling.

Jealous over the college's exemption from its authority, the City of London began to make moves against the college's privileges. In 1402 the Commons complained that servants had been stealing their master's goods, fleeing to sanctuary at St Martin's and then living from the sale of the goods. Also, the Commons charged that murderers used the sanctuary for a hiding place, slipping away to commit more crimes.

Not content to simply complain, in the 1430s the mayor and sheriffs tried to remove a man from sanctuary. Thomas Bourchier, Dean of St Martin's, appealed to the king, who forced the man's return. Not satisfied with one attempt, they tried again in the 1440s, this time seizing more men from the sanctuary at St Martin's. According to an account by Walter Thornbury, in '1442 (Henry VI), a soldier, on his way from Newgate to the Guildhall, was dragged by five of his fellows, who rushed out of Pannier Alley, in at the west door of the sanctuary; but that same day the two sheriffs came and took out the five men from the sanctuary, and led them fettered to the Compter, and then chained by the necks to Newgate'. Infuriated, the dean once again appealed to the king and the men were returned.

In 1457, however, the council decided that the abuses of

sanctuary had gone far enough and took steps to solve the problem. They decreed that anyone claiming sanctuary had to be registered by the dean and remove their weapons. The college must keep control over well-known criminals and restore stolen goods to the owners. Other rules that appeased city officials were instituted, including that anyone in a trade had to observe the city regulations.

Throughout the years of the Wars of the Roses, St Martin le Grand housed many people. In addition to Sir William Oldhall, the Countess of Oxford came here seeking sanctuary after her husband joined Warwick to help restore Henry VI.

The privilege of sanctuary ultimately disappeared, mainly under the reign of the Tudors. The college was suppressed in 1542, and its plate and goods went to the king's coffers. Eventually the area of the sanctuary was used for the Post Office.

Visiting Today

While there is nothing remaining of the church, cloisters or chapter house of the once wealthy college, it is possible to walk the outer areas of its precincts. The best station for the walk is St Paul's. Leaving the station, head straight to St Martin le Grand. On the left side of the street would have been the precincts. Continue on across Angel Street towards the Museum of London. This area was also the site of Northumberland House.

Turn left into Postman's Park by the church. This park was once part of the precincts, and the old burial grounds of St Leonard's, Fosters Lane were incorporated into the area. One of the highlights of the park is the plaque detailing heroic acts of bravery by Londoners. Reading the plaques may bring you to tears. Postman's Park Postcode: EC1A 4AS.

Durham Cathedral, Durham

Durham Cathedral sits high above the River Wear, towering over the surrounding countryside. The cathedral's turbulent history began on the Holy Isle of Lindisfarne, when miracles were said to occur at the tomb of Cuthbert, a former bishop. He was later canonised, and his body was moved during the invasion of the Danes. After a succession of several moves, his body finally came to rest in Durham, where a Saxon church was built to house the saint's remains. When the Normans arrived, they replaced the Saxon church with one of their own and established a Benedictine Priory. The Norman foundation stone was laid in 1093. The cathedral was said to represent Noah's Ark in its proportions, and most of the church was completed by the fourteenth century.

Durham and Anne

Anne's affection for Durham was shared by her husband. The couple's generosity to religious establishments is well documented, and Durham benefited from their largesse. Richard and Anne made several pilgrimages to the shrine of St Cuthbert and were admitted into his fraternity at Durham. According to Josephine Wilkinson, this was a rare privilege meant for only those with a strong devotion to the saint.

While visiting Durham, Anne and Richard witnessed the grand procession on St Cuthbert's day. Durham historian James Raine said the clerk, with his surplice on and carrying a fine, red-painted staff, would attend the banner which 'was a yard broad and five quarters deep, and the bottom of it was indented in five parts and fringed, and made fast all about it with red silk and gold. It was also made of red velvet on both sides, sumptuously embroidered and wrought with flowers of green silk and gold.'

The couple would have made their way to the shrine. Raine's description of the shrine is a vivid one. He described it as being 37 feet long and 23 feet wide. It adjoined the choir, with the High Altar on its west and the Nine Altars to the east. The shrine itself was made of green marble, all lined and gilded with gold. The royal couple would have taken their place at one of the four areas under the shine for the pilgrims to pray.

At the west end of the shrine was a smaller altar for Mass to be said on the feast of St Cuthbert in Lent. The iron chest in which the saint's body rested had a wainscot cover which was drawn up by a strong rope on St Cuthbert's Day. The rope was attached to the north pillar and had several 'fine-sounding silver bells' fastened to it which made 'a goodly sound' when it was raised. The cover was gilded and painted with four images, including a picture of Christ sitting on a rainbow giving judgment, and a picture of Mary with Christ on her knee. Decorative carvings of dragons and beasts trimmed the top of the cover, and underneath the cover 'was all varnished and coloured with a most fine sanguine colour, that the beholders might see all the glory and ornaments thereof'. The shrine had wainscoted almeries painted and gilded with images for the relics of St Cuthbert to lie in, including all the relics that had been offered to him. When the cover was drawn up the relics were 'accounted the most sumptuous and richest jewels in all this land'.

After observing the procession and praying at the shrine, the couple would have attended the feast that the bishop and monks enjoyed on their saint's day. Since the bishop often invited visiting nobles to the feast, he would have extended the invitation to Richard and Anne.

In 1484, King Richard III presented the monks with his parliament robe of blue velvet richly fashioned with great lions of pure gold. Even with the other rich gifts royalty had given the church, his gift was specifically noted.

Both Anne and Richard had family connections to Durham, as members of the Neville family had been buried there, and Richard Neville, Earl of Salisbury, had also been a member of the fraternity of St Cuthbert.

Visiting Today

Durham Cathedral is 469 feet long, and the cathedral takes up almost the entire area in front of you on your approach. A replica of a Sanctuary Knocker hangs on the north door, a reminder of the tradition that promised sanctuary to those grabbing the knocker. Entering the nave, it is hard not to be impressed with the soaring space surrounding you. The large columns along the nave are twins, and each set is different, with every column adorned with elaborately carved detail. Taking a minute to glance around the nave, try to imagine the bright colours which would have graced the room in Richard's time.

The tomb of John, Lord Neville, can be found in the south arcade, with Ralph Neville's monument nearby. Both tombs have suffered major damage but it is possible to picture them the way they once appeared. Anne and Richard would have visited these tombs and monuments to the members of the Neville family.

The screen behind the high altar was a gift from John Neville to the cathedral. In the fifteenth century, both the screen and its more than 100 alabaster statues would have been brightly painted.

During the Reformation, these medieval statues were removed and hidden so well that they have never been found. The screen itself was divided into three parts, with the second and third parts open so that the statues could be seen from their resting place in the canopies. The Neville coat of arms was engraved above the doorways.

The Shrine of St Cuthbert appears much different now than it did in medieval times. Today a black slab marks the place where the saint's body rests, the shrine having been destroyed in the Dissolution.

The cathedral is open daily and is free to visit, although donations are suggested. As with any location, it is wise to phone or email before visiting to ensure the cathedral will be open during your visit. For more information regarding the cathedral, visit its website at www.durhamcathedral.co.uk/visit/opening-times or call +44 (0) 191 386 4266. Durham Cathedral postcode: DH1 3EH.

Part 5
Richard's Children

Edward of Middleham was Richard's only legitimate son. However, Richard acknowledged two bastards, John of Pontefract and Katherine Plantagenet, and made provisions for them during his reign. A curious legend involving a supposed third illegitimate child, Richard Plantagenet of Eastwell, sprung up many years after Richard's death at Bosworth.

Edward of Middleham

Edward's birthdate is not recorded, but fell between 1474 and 1476. He was born at Middleham, in a castle set amid the rolling Yorkshire Dales. Following his uncle's execution, Edward was granted the title Earl of Salisbury. Not much else is known of him until his father became king.

Middleham Castle, North Yorkshire

The castle where Edward drew his first breath is situated in the strikingly beautiful Yorkshire Dales. The first fortress here was built near the current location and was an eleventh-century castle of motte-and-bailey construction. It was deserted following the construction of a new stone castle nearby, which was completed with a moat and outer courtyard.

Middleham castle passed from Alan the Red to his brother before it came into the hands of the Nevilles through the marriage of Mary, daughter and heiress of Ralph FitzRanulph, to Robert de Neville. The family enlarged Middleham throughout the years, leaving an impressive fortress for the household of young Edward.

The Castle Gatehouse

Middleham's gatehouse stands three storeys high. Once complete with a portcullis, the gatehouse offered protection for those inside the castle. Its arched stone entry was not the original entrance to the castle since it was not constructed until the fifteenth century. Sculpted stone figures of armed men may once have adorned the turrets of the gatehouse like those that can still be seen on the battlements of other Neville properties. When Richard and Anne visited Edward at the castle, they would have entered through this gateway after passing through the bustling market town.

Once inside the inner courtyard, they would have walked up the massive stone staircase which led up to the keep. While a wooden staircase takes its place today, it is still possible to make out traces of the stone stairway. The huge twelfth-century keep is still the most prominent building within the complex, just like it would have been for Edward and his parents.

Perhaps Richard regaled Edward with stories of his early days at Middleham in the household of the Earl of Warwick. While here, he had formed friendships with many of the men who would eventually die fighting with him in battle. Perhaps he told Edward about these early friendships with men like Francis Lovell.

Other stories Edward may have heard regarding his family and Middleham would have included his grandfather's imprisonment of his uncle, King Edward IV. In 1469, after tensions had grown between Warwick and Edward IV, the earl took the king prisoner and held him captive at Middleham for a short time. Richard may have told his son how his uncle was able to outsmart his grandfather to gain back control of his country.

The Great Hall and Privy Chamber

When Richard came to Middleham, he would not have had much free time to spend with his son. From the Great Hall of the keep, he would have been busy administering justice for the area. His marriage to Anne Neville had helped secure the support of the people of the north, but Richard's treatment of the people would earn him their loyalty.

Richard's council would also have met in the Great Hall. Paul Murray Kendall points out in his book *The Yorkist Age* that Richard's 'council at Middleham became such an effective instrument of justice in the 1470s that after Richard became king, he created the Council of the North, which the Tudors continued'. Edward, while probably not allowed in the Great Hall during meetings, would have seen the men coming and going.

Access to both the great chamber and privy chamber would have been through the hall. Richard would have used these rooms during his tenure at the castle. Edward may have spent time with his father, playing with a whipping top in front of the chamber's fireplace.

Edward heard mass in the chapel which lies to the east wall of the keep. While there is little left of the room where the household worshipped, it is possible to make out its tracery windows. Today, a stairway leads to a platform which offers views of the site of the original motte-and-bailey castle in addition to the panoramic scene of the surrounding countryside.

The South Range

The south range of the castle was two storeys and had towers on both its south-east and south-west corners. Several rooms made up the first-floor level, and the chamber at the east end had a fireplace and large windows. Two more chambers in the west end had similar layouts. A survey in 1538 names these rooms as a lady chamber with a gallery to the presence chamber.

Edward is believed to have been born in the south-west tower. Known as the 'Prince's Tower', the 1538 survey names a room next to the tower a 'nursee'. Here, in the nursery, Edward's wet nurse, Isabel Burgh, would have taken care of Richard's heir. His governess, Anne Idley, would have been responsible for seeing to his early education.

Once Richard became king, Edward was the heir to the throne of England. Suddenly he was thrust into an important role. On 12 July 1483, York's Lord Mayor and several aldermen rode to Middleham to present a gift to the prince. Edward would have received the men and accepted the gift, presumably in the Great Hall. Soon, he would travel to York for his investiture as the Prince of Wales.

A bright future was unfolding for the young Prince of Wales, but it was not long before tragedy struck. The *Croyland Chronicle* said that Edward died after he was 'seized with an illness of but short duration'. His death in 1484 not only left both Richard and Anne heartbroken but had lasting dynastic implications because a new heir would have to be chosen.

Visiting Today

Middleham Castle is managed by English Heritage. The castle has a gift shop on site, with several interesting books and souvenirs available. Be aware that while it is possible to picnic in the grounds, the nearest toilet facility is in the town.

It is best to visit the castle by car, and parking is available on the street. The closest train station is in Leyburn, about two miles away. Bus service from Leyburn is on the Dales and District 159. Be sure to check travel information before embarking since times and lines are often subject to change.

For opening times and other visitor information, please visit the castle website at www.english-heritage.org.uk/daysout/properties/middleham-castle/ or contact the castle directly at +44 (0) 1969 62389. Middleham Castle postcode: DL8 4QG.

While in Middleham, be sure to visit the Church of St Mary and St Alkelda which is also tied to the York family. The church has several interesting displays for a lover of Yorkist history, and is just a short walk from the castle. For another site associated with Edward, you might also be interested in visiting Sheriff Hutton. For years, legend said that Edward had been buried there. While most historians do not believe this to be true, the castle ruins are striking and the church is worth a visit.

John, Richard's Illegitimate Son

We know very little about either of Richard's illegitimate children. His son, alternately called John of Gloucester or John of Pontefract, is believed to have been born in Pontefract. On 11 March 1485, Richard granted John the captaincy of Calais. (Calais will be discussed in the section on George, Duke of Clarence.)

Of John's early years, nothing is known. Following his father's death, he received a grant from the new king, 'Grant to John de Gloucester, bastard, of an annual rent of 20 l. during the king's pleasure, issuing out of the revenues of the lordship or manor of Kyngestonlacy, parcel of the duchy of Lancaster, in co. Dors.'

Kingston Lacy had been part of Edward IV's grant to Richard, so Henry VII was allowing John to claim some of his father's property. Whether John took part in a rebellion against the new king is unknown, but he is believed to have died in the Tower following the Warbeck rebellion against Henry Tudor.

Pontefract Castle, West Yorkshire

In the fifteenth century, Pontefract was a busy town crowded with people. John may have wandered through the weekly market while a young boy and visited the annual fair. Where he lived is unknown. Richard may have brought him to the castle precincts after he grew older in order to be educated. Since nobles had housed their illegitimate children before, it is within the realm of possibility that Richard did so, too. In any event, John would have seen his father at the castle on Richard's visits.

In his role of steward of the duchy of Lancaster in the north, Richard's official residence was at Pontefract Castle. While Richard would have delegated many of his duties, he would have visited to oversee works done in his name so John would have several opportunities to meet with him.

William the Conqueror granted the area where Pontefract castle stands to the de Lacy family. By 1087 the family had already constructed a motte-and-bailey castle here. Eventually, the stone castle was built on a rock high above the town.

John would have seen a castle with a main ward and two southern wards, forming a double enclosure. The wall that separated the barbicans was 5 feet thick. There were four gates that led into the castle: one on the south, one in the middle, one on the west and one on the east. A high curtain wall, nearly 21 feet thick, encircled the castle yard. At least seven towers, each of sturdy construction, stood along the castle wall.

The original keep was a round tower, 64 feet in diameter, which stood on the artificial motte. It soared high above the other towers and bore a resemblance to Clifford's Tower in York. Upon entering the structure, John would have made his way across the inner bailey, which was an irregular oval shape of more than two acres. An intimidating building, the castle was considered one of the largest and strongest in England.

Pontefract Castle's History

Pontefract had a long – and, at times, bloody – history. Several notable executions occurred here, inspiring Shakespeare to call it a prison fatal to noble peers. One of the first was Thomas of Lancaster, who was executed at Pontefract by Edward II. A legend that he was held in Swillington Tower, which used to grace the west front of the castle, is doubtful, since the tower was supposedly built after his death. It is easy to see why the legend developed, though, because it was well fortified. Richard Holmes, writing in 1878, said the tower was 46 feet square, and 10 feet, 6 inches thick.

Following the death of the Duke of Lancaster and his daughter Maud, John of Gaunt inherited the castle by right of his wife, Blanche, and enlarged it. His nephew, King Richard II, died here after Henry IV's usurpation of his throne. Whether he was murdered or died a natural death is still debated, but he probably spent his last days imprisoned in Gascoigne's Tower.

In 1460, Richard Neville, Earl of Salisbury, was brought to Pontefract following the Battle of Wakefield. On 30 December he was executed at the castle. John's grandfather and uncle, Richard, Duke of York, and Edmund, Earl of Rutland, both died at the Battle of Wakefield, along with Salisbury's son, Thomas Neville. John's grandfather and uncle would initially be buried nearby in the Priory of St John at Pontefract.

Richard III at Pontefract

John's father also made use of Pontefract as a prison. Following the death of Edward IV, Richard hurried to meet King Edward V, who was in the care of his maternal uncle, Anthony Woodville, his half-brother, Richard Grey, and his chamberlain, Thomas Vaughn. Richard arrested the men, sending Vaughn to Pontefract. The men were executed at Pontefract on 25 June 1483.

In the second year of his reign, Richard incorporated the borough and reconfirmed the ancient rights of the burgesses in Pontefract. Over the course of his short reign, he visited Pontefract several times, spending more than forty days here. Pontefract was also a base for Richard while he prepared to put down the rebellion following Buckingham's defection.

Visiting Pontefract Today

As with many sites associated with the Yorks, Pontefract is a ruin. Enough of the castle grounds remain to demonstrate its grandeur as the main residence of the lords of the Honour of Pontefract. From the top of the ruins of the keep, you can see only trefoil remains. Pontefract possibly had a quatrefoil keep with corbelled turrets since it is believed to have been built along the same plans as Clifford's Tower in York.

Making your way back down to the bailey, walk across to the area where the sandstone King's and Queen's Towers once stood. A Great Hall once stood between the towers, linking both sets of royal apartments. Little remains today, but you can walk the area where the buildings once stood.

Remains of a Saxon chapel stand within the grounds, near the gatehouse. Dedicated to St Clement, the chapel was renovated by the Normans and served as a collegiate church until the sixteenth century. Perhaps John heard Mass here, maybe even joining Richard in worship.

The castle's guidebook suggests that the gardens of the inner bailey would have been located near the retaining wall because a rare example of medieval garden seating, a stone bench, was built into the wall here.

Informative placards are placed throughout the ruins to help visitors picture the once magnificent castle. Admittance to the castle is free. For more information about opening times or special events, visit the Experience Wakefield website at www.experiencewakefield. co.uk/thedms.aspx?dms=3&feature=1&venue=2190562 or call +44 (0) 1977 723 440. Pontefract Castle Postcode: WF8 1QH.

You might also want to visit the site of the Priory of St John while in Pontefract. While it only a short walk from the castle, be aware that nothing remains of the priory where John's grandfather and uncle were first buried. To find the field, walk to Ferrybridge Road and Box Lane. An informative panel on Box Lane shows the layout of the priory. Several paths lead through the field, allowing you to get an idea of the size of the church.

Katherine Plantagenet

As with John, we know little about Katherine. We do not know if she was John's full sister, where she was born or even the name of her mother. We do know her husband's name, since Richard secured an advantageous marriage for her once he became king.

Katherine married William Herbert, the Earl of Huntingdon. The son of the powerful Earl of Pembroke, Huntingdon showed little of his father's masterful political acumen. Pembroke had been a strong supporter of Edward IV until his death following the battle at Edgcote. Huntingdon had inherited the earldom of Pembroke but was forced to exchange it for the earldom of Huntingdon. While his wife, Katherine would have spent much of her time at the family property of Raglan Castle.

Raglan Castle, Monmouthshire, Wales

The castle came into the family after Herbert's ancestor William ap Thomas married Elizabeth Berkeley. It was through Elizabeth that the family came into the property when ap Thomas purchased it from his stepson following her death.

Sir William Herbert was knighted with Richard, Duke of York, by the young king, Henry VI, in Leicester. He was appointed on 16 May 1439 to serve with York, Salisbury and others to protect the Earl of Warwick's property during his son's minority. He became a supporter of the Duke of York and received grants of land and offices from him. During his lifetime, Sir William enlarged Raglan, adding to the existing buildings and building the Great Tower, which was meant to both impress and intimidate. He is also believed to be responsible for building the South Gate, which was the main entrance to the castle until the construction of the Great Gatehouse.

Sir William's son took the name William Herbert. Born of his father's marriage to his second wife, Gwladys, he inherited Raglan following his father's death in 1445. In 1449 he married Anne, daughter of Sir Walter Devereaux. Herbert managed to safeguard his estates following Ludford Bridge, and when Edward IV came to power he helped control Wales for the young king. After securing the person of Henry Tudor, he placed him in the care of his wife Anne at Raglan. In recognition of Herbert's service, Edward IV made Raglan a lordship. Eventually, Herbert became the Earl of Pembroke. His execution following the Battle of Edgcote (also known as Edgecote Moor) was a blow to his family and to the king.

His son, also a William, married Mary, the sister of Elizabeth Woodville. With this alliance, he became brother-in-law to the king. This did not keep him from losing some of the power his father had enjoyed, however, and by the time of Edward IV's death, Mary had also died. It is not surprising that Herbert would welcome marriage to the new king's daughter.

Herbert and Katherine

At Richard's coronation, the earl bore the queen's sceptre. Following the coronation he was politically active, serving on several commissions. According to D. H. Thomas, he may have even been appointed chamberlain to Edward, Prince of Wales.

In February 1484, an indenture was made between Richard III and Huntingdon. D. H. Thomas transcribed the indenture, in which the earl 'promiseth and granteth to and with our said sovereign lord the king that, before the feast of St Michael next coming, by God's grace he shall take to wife Dame Katherine Plantagenet, daughter to our said sovereign lord'. Before the marriage, the earl would 'make or cause to be made to her behalf, a sure, sufficient, and lawfull estate of certain of his manners [*sic*], lordships, lands and tenaments in England to the yearly value of two hundred pounds'.

The king would in turn 'granteth to the said earl and to the said Dame Katherine to make or cause to be made ... a sure, sufficient, and lawfull estate of manners [*sic*], lordships, lands and tenaments in possession to the yearly value of one thousand marks ... and in the mean our said sovereign lord granteth to the said earle and Dame Katherine an annuity'. Richard also bore the cost of the marriage.

Other grants came to the couple during their marriage. Yet, when Henry Tudor came to seize the throne Herbert did not fight against him. Following the last grant to the couple, Katherine disappears from the historical record. At the coronation of Elizabeth of York, Herbert was named a widower. Katherine may have been dead by then, or, like Rosemary Horrox suggests, Herbert may have repudiated her. If so, there is no mention of her ultimate fate.

Visiting Raglan Castle

Described as 'a large and noble ruin' by R. H. Newell in 1821, Raglan Castle sits on a slight ridge. While it is possible to catch a glimpse of it from the road, nothing compares to an actual visit. The light stonework gleams on a sunny day and takes on an imposing cast when clouds roll in. One can only imagine Katherine's thoughts at her first glimpse of the masterful design of her husband's property.

The Great Gatehouse

Stand outside the entrance and look up at the gatehouse. In an article in the 22 March 1873 issue of the Antiquary, the castle is described as being 'faced with hewn freestone of a whitish-grey colour, beautifully grained, and as smooth as if it had been polished, which has so far escaped the ravages of time, that it now imparts a light and elegant appearance to the ruins'. The stonework still looks polished, and the castle, with its intricate machiolated battlements, still appears elegant. When Katherine rode up to the Gatehouse with Herbert, she would have passed by the two towers, both portcullises would have been raised and the doors flown open to welcome the castle's new mistress.

The Fountain Court

Once inside the pitched stone court, Katherine would have turned left towards the Fountain Court, which held the residential apartments. While ruined today, she would have seen a lavish chamber, likely plastered or covered with tapestries. When Sir Walter Herbert died, an inventory of his goods contained a rich tapestry with an intricate design of trees. Since much of his inventory is believed to be older and taken from Raglan, Katherine would have seen the beautiful tapestry. One of the chambers at Raglan contained a bed with rich cloth, embroidered with gold thread and silk. A fireplace would have kept her warm in the winter months, while a window seat would have allowed Katherine to watch the activity below.

Standing in the centre of the courtyard it is possible to see the ruins of the extensive accommodations that Herbert had built in the castle. The Grand Stair led to other chambers, where guests would stay while visiting. In one of the chambers, a cloth of arras telling the story of Ide would have decorated the walls; another held cloth of arras telling the Biblical story of Nebuchadnezzar. Turn around and look opposite the Grand Stair. This room was the site of the chapel. The castle's guidebook contains an image of the tile that was uncovered during work at the site. While it is hard to picture now, the chapel's floor was once covered with tiles of bright yellow and brown designs.

The chapel shared a wall with the Great Hall. On certain occasions, Herbert and Katherine would sit at the dais at the upper end of the hall where they would entertain guests or conduct business. Much of the work in the hall dates from the Tudor period, including the oriel window.

Head to the Great Tower. Built originally for defence, the tower was self-contained. By the time Katherine would have been at Raglan, it contained other residential apartments. At the top of the tower you can see a panoramic view of the rest of the property. Look down to see the moat-walk, which was built in the sixteenth century.

Before leaving the property, walk around the outside perimeter. From inside, the castle does not seem as large and imposing as it does from the outside. Raglan is under the management of Cadw and has an extensive gift shop. For more information about visiting, see the website at http://cadw.gov.wales/daysout/raglancastle/visitor-information?lang=en. Postcode: NP15 2BT.

Richard of Eastwell

While there is little evidence that Richard of Eastwell was actually a son of Richard III, this mystery is so interesting that it would be remiss not to mention it. A record was found in the Parish Register of Eastwell which stated that a Richard Plantagenet was buried 22 December 1550.

The story of this Richard was told in *Desiderata Curiosa*, and repeated in Charles Seymour's *Survey of Kent*. Much of the story is told through a transcription of a letter from Dr Thomas Brett to Dr William Warren, president of Trinity Hall in 1733. Brett learned of a family tradition while at Eastwell and recounted the story to Warren. Sir Thomas Moyle, who built Eastwell Place, saw his chief bricklayer reading a book, which he later discovered was in Latin. Upon questioning, the bricklayer recounted a curious story.

He had been boarded with a Latin schoolmaster in his youth, having no idea who his parents were. When he was a young man a man took him to a 'fine, great house' where he 'passed through several stately rooms'. He met another man at the house who was kind to him and gave him some money before sending him back to his home.

On another occasion, he was taken to Bosworth where he was conveyed to King Richard III, who embraced him and told him he was his son. The king told him that should he live through the battle he would claim him. Following the battle, the man sold anything that could connect him as a son of the king and became a bricklayer. Moyle allowed the man to live out his life in a cottage on the estate. When the bricklayer died, he was buried at the church.

The story is both interesting and romantic, and while doubtful, it is possible that Richard had another son. The story loses some credibility when one considers that, since Richard claimed both Katherine and John, why would he not claim this child?

Church of St Mary, Eastwell, Kent

Situated at the end of a dark lane, the former Church of the Blessed Mary of Eastwell lies in picturesque ruins by a lake. Vandals have defaced parts of the church, but the tomb reputed to be that of Richard Plantagenet is still there. During the eighteenth century the tomb became called Richard Plantagenet's; however, it is actually believed to be that of Sir Walter Moyle. An inscription on its side states, 'Reputed to be the tomb of Richard Plantagenet, 22 December 1550.'

You will need a car to visit the ruins. From the M20, take the A251 exit to Ashford/Faversham. Take the signposted route to Potter's Corner/Westwell on Sandyhurst Lane. Soon, there will be a sign pointing right towards Westwell. Turn right here on Linacre Street. After about one mile, there is an unmarked road that leads down to the lake.

Part 6
Edward IV and Elizabeth Woodville

Following the death of his father and Salisbury, when little hope seemed left for the Yorkist cause, Edward proved himself to be a strong commander. The battles of Mortimer's Cross and Towton helped secure his throne. His relationship with Richard seems to have been a strong one. Edward often visited his younger brothers while they were in London at Fastolf's Place, and later he awarded them land and other grants. While George initially received more grants than Richard, this was because George was older and the heir to the throne until Edward had children. While George strayed from the fold, Richard remained loyal to Edward.

Wigmore Castle, Herefordshire

Wigmore Castle came to Richard, Duke of York, as part of his Mortimer inheritance. The original castle is said to have been built by William Fitz Osbern. After his death, his son Roger de Breteuil inherited his lands in England. The lands were forfeited to the Crown when Roger entered into rebellion against the king and was imprisoned.

The king granted Wigmore, along with other lands, to Ralph de Mortimer. Most of the construction of the castle was completed in the thirteenth and fourteenth centuries. Roger Mortimer renovated and rebuilt large sections of Wigmore. Since the family was powerful and wealthy, the castle probably reflected their status. In the early fourteenth century, Mortimer hosted a large tournament here, inviting the young King Edward III and his mother, Isabella. Certainly, the castle contained lavish accommodations in which to house the royal party.

Wigmore Castle was originally of motte-and-bailey construction. The later sandstone keep was built atop the motte, and a strong curtain wall with at least four sturdy towers surrounded the entire fortress. The fortification was necessary since the castle was besieged at least once in its early history.

According to *The History of the King's Works,* there are no records of the architectural history of the castle between 1461 and 1485. The castle was in ruins by the sixteenth century, and was further dismantled during the Civil War.

Richard, Duke of York, and Wigmore

Soon after his loss of the Protectorate, York realised that he needed to leave court for a time. He first retreated to Sandal Castle, but soon decided he needed to move closer to Wales. H. T. Evans in his book *Wales and the Wars of the Roses* says Margaret of Anjou and Jasper Tudor had been busy consolidating a power base in Wales. Realising he needed to go where his support was greatest, York chose to remove himself to Wigmore sometime in October. Cecily had been at Caister Castle in Norfolk, so it is doubtful she joined him here.

Edward and Wigmore

As Wigmore was one of his father's holdings, Edward would have spent time here while a child. Perched on a ridge west of Wigmore village, the castle had three baileys. Edward and his family would have entered the castle by crossing the drawbridge to the first gatehouse, and then over another drawbridge to the inner gatehouse where the portcullis would have been raised. The keep was high on the motte, allowing for a spectacular view. While here, Edward and Edmund would have hunted in the park near the castle.

After learning of his father's death, Edward continued to raise troops among the Welsh Marches. Hearing that Jasper Tudor was heading to Hereford, Edward made his way to intercept him. Wigmore is not far from Hereford and was a logical choice to lodge Edward and his troops.

Passing by the parish church of St James, Edward and his men would have made their way up the hill to the castle where Edward lodged in the great chambers in the keep. His men would have stayed in either one of the lodging towers, in the timber-framed buildings along the curtain wall or in the Great Hall.

Knowing that his family's future rested on his shoulders, Edward possibly passed a sleepless night within the palatial rooms of Wigmore, kept warm by one of the fireplaces within the keep. Before the first rays of light flooded through the intricately cut stonework of the chamber's windows, he was organising his men to march over the frosted moors towards Tudor's troops.

Richard III and Wigmore
After Richard became king, he granted the stewardship of Wigmore to William Herbert. Herbert had married Katherine Plantagenet, who was Richard's illegitimate daughter. Wigmore was only one of the many grants that Richard gave to Herbert and to his daughter.

Visiting Today
The ruins of Wigmore Castle were described by Richard Warner in the eighteenth century:

> The noble remains of Wigmore Castle claimed our attention very early this morning. They stand to the west of the town, on a natural hill of considerable elevation, and form a very picturesque ruin ... a profuse mantle of ivy crowns its summit, which creeping also over some of the adjoining bastions, gives an air of venerable majesty to the mouldering pile.

As English Heritage has chosen to keep the site conserved as found, it appears as picturesque today as in the eighteenth century. Flowers still peep through the castle's stonework; wild flowers still carpet much of the grounds.

The best way to approach the castle is by parking at the village hall and walking up the hill. Along the route you will pass the parish church of St James. A church has stood on this spot since Celtic times, but the church in front of you was built in the eleventh century. Its tower dates from the mid-fourteenth century and stands 61 feet high. While it is doubtful that Edward visited the church, since Wigmore Abbey was nearby, he would have passed it on his visits to Wigmore.

The castle is a difficult one to visit because the walk is along steep, narrow and often muddy paths through private property. Near the top is the gatehouse. Today its large stone arch is partially filled with earth, presenting a much shorter entrance than in Edward's time. While placards are placed throughout the site, at the time of this publication the one nearest the gatehouse was overgrown by greenery. Once through the gatehouse, choose the path around to the right.

Nothing remains of the Great Hall, but a placard placed nearby shows its location. Take a moment to picture the hall like it would have been when Edward was a child. Guests would have entered through the stone archway. His parents would have sat upon the raised dais, while servants scuttled to and fro, bringing food for the guests. A large fire would have blazed in the fireplace, keeping the room at a comfortable temperature. After the picture fades, make your way towards the keep.

The keep is reached by a set of stairs. Little remains today, but a portion of the wall of the tower is still here. From an engraving of the ruins by the Buck brothers in the eighteenth century, it appears that the keep was at least three storeys high. The curtain walls would have enclosed the outside of the keep, running down to the bailey below. An extraordinary view of the surrounding countryside awaits the person who has made it to the top of the motte. Look towards the north. These plains were often swampy during the fifteenth century.

It is best to visit the castle by car, since bus service is limited. It takes about twenty minutes to walk from the village hall to the top of the keep. The site is steep at times, so it is unsuitable for those with difficulty walking. The castle is free to visit and is open during daylight hours. For more information about visiting Wigmore, see the English Heritage website at http://www.english-heritage.org.uk/visit/places/wigmore-castle/. Wigmore postcode: HR6 9UB.

Battle of Mortimer's Cross, Herefordshire

Sources disagree whether Edward was in Gloucester or Shrewsbury when news reached him of his father's death, but they do agree he learned that Jasper Tudor was coming by sea with Frenchmen, Irishmen, Welshmen and Bretons to aid the Lancastrian cause. Edward marched to Wigmore and then from there to engage the enemy at Mortimer's Cross. Edward's men included loyal Yorkists, like William Herbert of Raglan, who had a long friendship with the Duke of York, and Lord Audley.

On 2 February (some sources claim 3 February) 1461, Edward's troops advanced into formation. On the eve of the battle a strange sight appeared against the bright blue of the winter sky. The sun appeared like three suns in the east. Shakespeare immortalized the scene in *Henry VI*:

> Three glorious suns, each one a perfect sun;
> Not separated with the racking clouds,
> But sever'd in a pale clear-shining sky.
> See, see! they join, embrace, and seem to kiss,
> As if they vow'd some league inviolable:
> Now are they but one lamp, one light, one sun.

Whether Edward was quick to grasp that some might see this as a bad sign, or whether he really believed it to be a sign for his victory is unclear. Upon seeing the parhelion, he knelt down and made his prayers and thanked God. According to one chronicle, he comforted the people and told them, 'Be thee of good comfort, and dread not; this is a good sign, for these three sons betoken the Father, the Son, and the Holy Ghost, and therefore let us have a good heart and in the name of the Almighty God we go against our enemies' (Modern translation).

Little is known of the actual battle, other than that the York troops won a decisive victory. The Lancastrians may have lost nearly 3,000 men. The earls of Pembroke and Wiltshire escaped the aftermath, but Owen Tudor did not. The former husband of Queen Katherine of Valois was taken to Hereford where he was beheaded. According to *Gregory's Chronicle*, Tudor went to his death meekly after saying, 'That hede shalle ly on the stocke that was wonte to ly on Quene Kateryns lappe.' Edward had both won a decisive victory and avenged his father. After news of Warwick's defeat reached him, he headed towards London.

Visiting Today

As the precise site of the battle is not known, there is little to visit today. There are several interpretations of the battle site, but an exact location has not been determined. A stone pedestal stands at a junction of the road in Kingsland to commemorate the battle. Erected in 1799, the engraving on the stone states it was

> erected to perpetuate the memory of an obstinate, bloody, and decisive battle, fought near the spot in the civil wars between the ambitious houses of York and Lancaster on the 2 day of February 1461 between the forces of Edward Mortimer, Earl of March (Afterwards Edward the Fourth) on the side of York, and those of Henry the Sixth, on the side of Lancaster. The king's troops were commanded by Jasper, Earl of Pembroke. Edward commanded his own in person and was victorious. The slaughter was great on both sides ...

The location is worth seeing for visitors also heading to Wigmore Castle. Hopefully, like with the Battle of Bosworth, more excavation work will be done in the future to allow for a more precise battle site.

Battle of Towton, North Yorkshire

After his victory at Mortimer's Cross, Edward went to London. In St John's Fields, outside the Priory of St John, Clerkenwell, George Neville addressed a large crowd, listing the Yorkists claims and enumerating the offences of Henry VI. After listening, the crowd acclaimed Edward king; this news was brought to Edward at Baynard's Castle. Events moved quickly after that, and the next day the articles were proclaimed in London. On Tuesday 3 March a council met at Baynard's Castle and concluded that Edward should be king. On 4 March, Edward heard *Te Deum* in St Paul's before proceeding to the Palace of Westminster, where he entered the Great Hall and took his seat on the marble chair of the 'King's Bench'.

While having been declared king in London, his coronation would have to wait until he could secure his throne. Edward headed north, moving slowly to Pontefract, allowing men to join him while he went. Following a skirmish at Ferrybridge, he made

EDWARDVS. IIII.

Previous page: 1. Edward IV, first Yorkist King of England.

Left: 2. Richard III. King of England 1483–1485. Although his reign was short, Richard III remains one of the most controversial kings in history.

Below: 3. Richard III and his wife, Anne Neville. The daughter of the Earl of Warwick, Anne was first married to the Lancastrian heir, Prince Edward, before her marriage to Richard.

Right: 4. Elizabeth of York. The daughter of Edward IV and Elizabeth Woodville, Elizabeth became the wife of the first Tudor King of England, Henry VII.

Below: 5. Conisbrough Castle, South Yorkshire. This property came to the Duke of York through his father, Richard, Earl of Cambridge, who was executed for plotting against the king.

Left: 6. La Tour Jeanne d'Arc, Rouen, France. This tower is all that is left of the massive castle where Richard and Cecily lodged during their time in France. Richard, as Lieutenant Governor, and Cecily entertained Margaret of Anjou here. Joan of Arc was supposedly questioned in this tower before her execution.

Below: 7. Usk Castle, Monmouthshire, Wales. Part of the Duke of York's Mortimer inheritance, he visited the castle often enough for a rumour to arise that both Edward IV and Richard III had been born here.

Above: 8. Trim Castle, Ireland. The exterior of the castle showing the river. Boats used this river to reach the castle, which once had a harbour.

Below: 9. Trim Castle, Ireland. Pictured here are the remains of the Great Hall seen from the top of the keep. Richard and Cecily would have entertained guests in the large hall.

Above: 10. St Mary's Priory, Coventry, West Midlands. Artistic recreation of the Chapter House where William Waynflete opened the Parliament of Devils after the sack of Ludlow. The Duke of York had fled into exile and securing his attainder was a top priority of the Lancastrians. *Below:* 11. Old St Paul's Cathedral, London. A recreation of the cathedral that many of the Yorks would have visited. The Duke of York gave his oath to Henry VI here at the High Altar, and the 'loveday' between the Lancastrians and Yorkists also took place here.

Right: 12. Worcester Cathedral, Worcestershire. The nave of Worcester Cathedral looking towards the high altar where the Duke of York and the Nevilles took an oath that they were acting for the king's 'high estate'.

Below: 13. North Range of Ludlow Castle, Shropshire. A view of the North Range which held the Great Hall and the family's chamber block. The Duke of York and the Nevilles would have planned their course of action here.

Left: 14. Church of St Mary the Virgin and All Saints, Fotheringhay. The Duke of York continued construction of the college his uncle had established. The Duke of York, Edmund and Cecily are all buried within this church.

Below: 15. Raby Castle, Durham. Tradition holds that Cecily was born here at Raby Castle. The castle was one of her father's holdings in Durham, so she would have visited here often. Two of her older sisters were married in the castle's chapel, and it is possible she and Richard were also married there.

Above: 16. St Mary's Church, Staindrop, Durham. Many of Cecily's family members are buried in this church, which may also have served as the location for Cecily's christening. *Below:* 17. Neville tomb, St Mary's Church. Tomb of Ralph Neville, which was built using stone quarried from John of Gaunt's quarry in Tutbury. The effigies of his two wives, Margaret Stafford and Joan Beaufort, rest on either side of him, although Joan was buried at Lincoln Cathedral.

Above: 18. Montgomery Castle, Powys, Wales. Richard and Cecily would have spent time examining each of York's properties, and given its location, Montgomery Castle would have likely been their base in Wales.

Left: 19. Caister Castle, Norfolk. An exterior view of Caister Castle's remains. Cecily visited Fastolf's opulent castle and was so impressed she tried to convince him to let her purchase it.

Above: 20. Tonbridge Castle Gatehouse, Kent. Tonbridge Castle was part of the Duke of Buckingham's holdings in Kent, and Cecily is believed to have stayed here while in her sister's custody. In the sixteenth century, the gatehouse was described as 'a strong fortress as few be in England'.

Below: 21. Caister Castle, Norfolk. The ninety-foot tower is all that substantially remains of the castle that Cecily visited. The Great Hall would have abutted the wall to the left.

Above: 22. Berkhamsted Castle, Hertfordshire. View from the motte at Berkhamsted, which Edward IV granted to Cecily in compensation for Fotheringhay. She eventually made it her main residence, and Richard III visited her here on at least one occasion.

Below: 23. Fotheringhay Castle, Northamptonshire. Once the site of an immense fortification, all that is left of the birthplace of Richard III is a grassy mound and a bit of crumbling masonry.

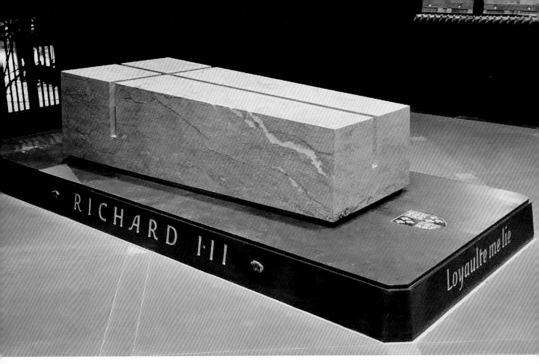

Above: 24. Tomb of Richard III, Leicester Cathedral. Richard III was reinterred in Leicester Cathedral in this tomb, which sits within the ambulatory between the Chapel of Christ the King and the sanctuary.

Below: 25. Bosworth Battlefield Heritage Centre, Leicestershire. The Heritage Centre has several educational exhibitions on the Battle of Bosworth and offers battlefield walks.

Left: 26. Cathédrale Saint-Maurice, Angers, France. Anne Neville and Prince Edward were formally betrothed in this church, which appeared much different in the medieval era.

Below: 27. Château d'Angers, Angers, France. Anne Neville lodged here prior to her marriage to Prince Edward, the Lancastrian heir. While the alternating dressed black and light stonework would have been the same, the château's seventeen towers were topped with coronets and were much higher. Pictured here is the Porte des Champs, which would have been the entrance Anne took into the château.

Above: 28. Château d'Amboise, France. Exterior shot of the château from across the river. The Earl of Warwick met with King Louis here to discuss an agreement with Margaret of Anjou.

Below: 29. Château d'Amboise, France. Sixteenth-century engraving by Jacques Androuet du Cerceau. Anne and Edward came to Amboise with their mothers after their betrothal. The apartments where Anne was lodged were constructed in a triangular shape, passing in front of the Chapel of Saint-Hubert and along the wall to the right of the current building (from this view).

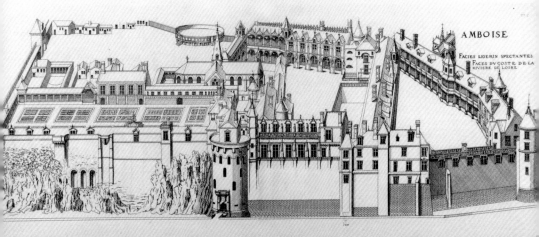

Above: 30. Little Malvern Priory, Worcestershire. All that is left of the priory are some ruins and the church. By tradition, Margaret of Anjou and Anne Neville stayed here after fleeing the Battle of Tewkesbury. *Below:* 31. Cerne Abbas, Dorset. Anne Neville, Edward and Margaret of Anjou were guests of the abbot after they arrived in England. Learning of the Lancastrian defeat at Barnet, the group made their way to the abbey and stayed in the guest house.

Above: 32. Little Malvern Priory, Worcestershire. Stained glass window in Little Malvern depicting Edward IV's family. The glass was broken during either the Dissolution or the Civil War and was painstakingly replaced. *Below:* 33. Pontefract Castle, West Yorkshire. View of the motte of Pontefract Castle across the inner bailey. The original keep would have stood atop the mound and was a round tower, 64 feet in diameter.

Left: 34. Eastwell, Kent. The reputed grave of Richard Plantagenet, who claimed to be an illegitimate son of Richard III. It is doubtful that he was, since Richard claimed his other illegitimate children.

Below: 35. Raglan Castle, Monmouthshire, Wales. Katherine, the illegitimate daughter of Richard III, married William Herbert and made Raglan Castle her home. Following her father's death, she disappeared from history.

Right: 36. Wigmore Castle, Herefordshire. Edward IV stayed at Wigmore prior to the Battle of Mortimer's Cross. Today the castle is a picturesque ruin sitting high above the town.

Below: 37. Westminster Hall, Westminster. Westminster Hall was the scene of several memorable moments in the lives of the Yorks. Here, Edward IV and Richard III were both raised to the marble seat of the King's Bench, situated on the southern side of the hall.

Above: 38. St Mary's Church, Grafton Regis, Northamptonshire. Elizabeth Woodville was born in Grafton Regis, then known as Grafton Woodville. A possible location for the wedding ceremony of Elizabeth and Edward, St Mary's Church was located close to the manor home. *Below:* 39. Tewkesbury Abbey, Tewkesbury. George, Duke of Clarence, and his wife, Isabel Neville, were both buried in the abbey. Several of the Lancastrian dead, including Prince Edward, were also buried within the church.

Above: 40. Eltham Great Hall, Kent. Exterior of the Great Hall which Edward IV had constructed at Eltham Palace. His royal apartments connected to the hall.

Below: 41. Eltham Great Hall, Kent. Interior of the Great Hall. Edward IV spent his last Christmas at Eltham, hosting a feast for 2,000 guests in his newly-finished hall.

42. Record Tower, Dublin Castle. This is the last intact tower of the large Norman castle built during the reign of King John. On 21 October 1449, Cecily gave birth to George in her chamber here at Dublin.

43. Église de Notre Dame, Calais, France. Once known as St Mary's, this church was the likely site for the marriage of George, Duke of Clarence, and Isabel Neville.

Right: 44. Tutbury Castle, Staffordshire. Margaret of Anjou was responsible for the new South Tower and may have also built the North Tower, with its spiral staircase. George, Duke of Clarence, made the castle his primary residence.

Below: 45. Warwick Castle, Warwickshire. Warwick Castle held associations for several members of the York family. George's heir, Edward, was born here.

Left: 46. Bruges Belfry, Belgium. Margaret would have seen the Belfry on her visits to Bruges. The octagonal lantern tower was not added until the late 1480s.

Below: 47. Damme, Belgium. The Stadhuis in Damme, which would have existed when Margaret of York wed Charles, Duke of Burgundy. Statues of Margaret and Charles decorate the building.

48. Church of Our Lady, Bruges. Both Margaret's stepdaughter and husband were buried in the church.

49. Cathedral Church of St Michael and St Gudula, Brussels. Margaret was present at two christenings in the church, both times standing as godmother.

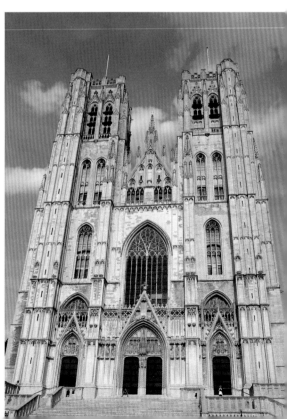

Above: 50. Margaret of York's Palace, Mechelen, Belgium. All that remains of Margaret's enormous palace is this building, which Margaret made her principal residence after Charles died. *Below:* 51. Mechelen's Grote Markt, Belgium. Margaret would have been familiar with the Grote Markt, although some of its construction has changed. St Rumbold's Cathedral can be seen soaring above the Markt, but Margaret would not have seen its tower at its current height.

52. St Rumbold's (Rombout's) Cathedral, Mechelen. Margaret would not recognise the interior of the cathedral today, but she would recognise much of its exterior.

53. Dark Gate, Ghent. All that remains of the castle of Ten Walle (later known as the Prinsenhof) is this gateway. Margaret spent much of her married life at the castle.

Left: 54. St Bavo's Cathedral, Ghent. Margaret carried the infant Charles V to his christening in this church. She would not have known the church as St Bavo's since it was originally dedicated to St John the Baptist.

Below: 55. Dartington Hall, Devon. Edward IV granted Dartington Hall to his sister Anne. It originally had belonged to her first husband, Henry Holland.

Above left: 56. Interior of the Great Hall, Dartington Hall. The Great Hall with its massive fireplace and ornate hammer-beam roof would have been extant when Anne visited, but it has been largely restored.

Above right: 57. St Andrew's Church, Wingfield. Several of Elizabeth's and John's children were likely christened here in the font donated by Michael de la Pole.

Below: 58. Wingfield Castle, Suffolk. An eighteenth-century print from a Thomas Hearne drawing of the castle. Wingfield would have been a primary residence for Elizabeth, Duchess of Suffolk, early in her marriage.

Above left: 59. Cathedral Notre Dame de Rouen, France. The church would have appeared different to Edmund's christening party. At that time, St Romain's Tower did not have its top and the Butter tower had not been added. *Above right:* 60. Priory Gate, Winchester. The fifteenth-century priory gate was extant when Elizabeth of York gave birth to her son, Arthur, in the priory. *Below:* 61. Effigies of Elizabeth and John, St Andrew's Church. Both of the alabaster effigies of Elizabeth and John were once brightly painted, and traces of paint can still be seen on John's effigy.

62. Stony Stratford, Buckinghamshire. The site of the former Rose and Crown Inn where tradition holds Edward V stayed the night before Richard took him into his care.

63. St Mary the Virgin, Ewelme. From this picture it is easy to see that the battlements at Ewelme resemble those at St Andrew's, Wingfield. John's parents largely rebuilt the church, and Alice's large tomb can still be seen inside.

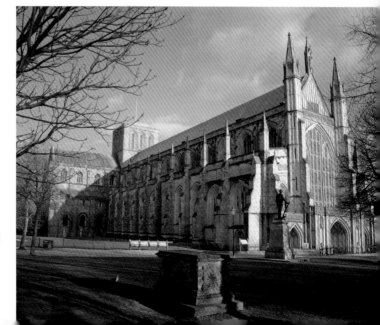

64. Winchester Cathedral, Winchester. Elizabeth's son, Arthur, was christened in the cathedral, with his grandmother, Elizabeth Woodville, standing as godmother. The church was elaborately decorated with cloths of arras for the occasion.

65. Tower of London, London. The White Tower where Edward V and Richard, Duke of York, were kept after their father's death can be seen soaring above the other buildings in the complex.

66. Windsor Castle, Berkshire. Many of the York family visited the castle, which was a favourite of Edward IV. He and several members of the York family are buried in St George's Chapel at Windsor.

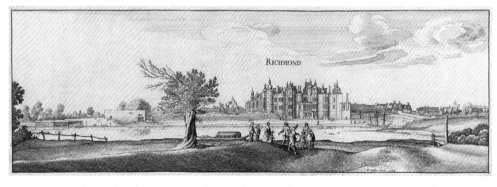

67. Richmond Palace, Surrey. Wenceslaus Hollar's image shows a view of the palace from across the Thames. Henry VII largely rebuilt the palace after it was devastated by fire.

his way toward the main body of Lancastrians who had moved near Towton.

While the armies on both sides were large, the numbers given by the chroniclers, like in most battles, were exaggerated. The Lancastrians had the advantage, in both the number of peers and the number of men. The Lancastrian forces were also fresh and ready for the battle.

As Palm Sunday dawned, the men prepared for battle in bitter conditions. When news of the Lancastrian position arrived, Edward took his place. Henry VI and Margaret of Anjou were not present, since they both had decided to stay in York.

The two groups took the field. The snow, sleet and wind were blowing directly into the Lancastrian line. The Yorkist archers released an onslaught of arrows; the Lancastrians retaliated but the wind caused most of their arrows to fall short. Edward Hall described the situation in his chronicle:

> The Lord Fauconberg, which led the forward of King Edward's battle being a man of great policy, and of much experience in martial feats, caused every archer under his standard to shoot one flight (which he caused them to provide) and made them stand still. The northern men, feeling the shoot, but by reason of the snow, not well viewing the distance between them and their enemies, like hardy men, shot their sheaf arrows as fast as they might, but all their shot was lost and their labour in vain for they came not near the southern men ... when their shot was almost spent, the Lord Fauconberg marched forward with his archers, which not one shot their whole sheaf, but also gathered the arrows of their enemies and let a great part of them fly against their own masters. (Modern translation)

The Lancastrian leaders realised that they needed to advance and, when they did, Fauconberg pulled his men out of the way and allowed the main body of the Yorks to meet them. The battle is believed to have lasted throughout the day, and the sheer number of the Lancastrians was becoming more of an advantage as the battle continued. The arrival of the Duke of Norfolk's men later in the day added fresh men to the Yorkist line at a crucial time.

Eventually the Lancastrian ranks began to break and men began to flee, the slippery sleet and snow making flight difficult. Many of the men drowned in the brook, causing Hall to state that the other men walked across on their dead bodies, and that the 'great river of Wharfe where into that brook doth run, and of all the water coming from Towton was coloured with blood'. The desperate men continued to flee and the bloody slaughter continued for miles. When the news arrived at York, King Henry, Queen Margaret and Prince Edward fled north to Scotland.

The death toll of both armies was high. The Lancastrians lost several peers, including Lord Dacre and the Earl of Northumberland. The exact number of those lost is unknown, because the chronicles all have different numbers. Executions followed before Edward moved to York. While the Lancastrian threat had only been neutralised and not extinguished, after the battle at Towton he would face no serious threat until challenged by his brother, George, and Warwick.

Visiting the Battlefield Today

Towton offers a battlefield trail to those who want to walk the route. Although we do not know for certain where the battle was fought, the trail takes you along the area where it most likely occurred. Since the walk is on privately owned land, visitors are asked to stick to the signposted path. The walk is approximately three kilometres and ends in Towton village.

Informative panels along the trail help the visitor to picture the battle scene. Be aware that the path will be extremely muddy and slippery after rain.

Palace of Westminster, London

On 26 June 1461, Edward rode triumphantly into London to await his coronation. According to Scofield, the mayor and aldermen, clad in scarlet robes, along with 400 citizens dressed in green, met Edward at Lambeth Palace and in a grand procession rode with him to the Tower of London. That evening, he created several new knights of the Bath, including his two brothers.

The next day, he rode from the Tower to the Palace at Westminster. The new knights of the Bath rode before him 'in their gowns and hoods, and tokens of white silk upon their shoulders'. He spent the night in the Palace of Westminster, preparing for his coronation at the abbey. Following the coronation, he returned to the palace to rest before a large feast was served in Westminster Hall.

A royal palace has rested here on the banks of the Thames since the reign of Edward the Confessor. Under the Normans, the palace was enlarged and the Great Hall was added. Given its close proximity to London, it was only natural for it to be a favourite among medieval rulers. The ancient palace was bounded on the north by Bridge Street, on the east by the Thames, on the west by St Margaret's church precinct and on the south by Great College Street.

Both Edward and Richard added to the palace. While king, Richard III is believed to have erected a stone gateway by the north-western end of the palace. High Tower, as it was called, sat across from the Abbey Sanctuary gate. The gatehouse was tall with spacious rooms in it. Unfortunately, it remained unfinished after Richard's death.

Queen's Chambers, Palace of Westminster

Following his coronation, Edward IV embarked on a building plan at the palace. By 1462 he had commissioned works to be done in the privy palace. Soon after he began extensive works in the garden of the Jewel Tower. After marrying Elizabeth, he began building her a new withdrawing chamber and wardrobe. Some historians believe this was due to Cecily's occupation of the current queen's chambers.

On 11 February 1466, the queen gave birth to Elizabeth of York, her first child by Edward. According to Fabyan, the child had been expected to be a boy. The physician, Dominic, had been awaiting the news in the next chamber 'that he might be the first that should bring tidings to the king of the birth of the prince'. His disappointment must have been great, when upon asking what the queen had, a lady responded, 'what so ever the queen's grace hath here within, sure it is that a fool standeth there without'.

The queen remained in her chambers until her churching. Gabriel Tetzel, who was visiting the kingdom, gave an account of the event. From him we learn that Elizabeth left her chambers in the morning and went to Westminster Abbey in a procession. Leading the procession were priests, accompanied by men singing. Behind these men were a 'great company of ladies and maidens from the country and from London'. Following the ladies were the 'trumpeters, pipers and players of stringed instruments' and 'the king's choir followed ... who sang excellently'. Twenty-four heralds and sixty nobles and knights preceded Elizabeth. She walked, under a canopy, with two dukes. Sixty ladies, including Jacquetta, followed her. After the service, she returned to the palace in the same procession. Afterwards, all who had joined the procession remained to eat. The number of guests filled four rooms.

Tetzel and his lord were shown to an alcove where they could watch the events surrounding the queen, who was seated on a golden chair in a 'costly apartment'. Tetzel reported,

> The Queen's mother and the King's sister had to stand some distance away. When the Queen spoke with her mother or the King's sister, they knelt down before her until she had drunk water. Not until the first dish was set before the Queen could the Queen's mother and the King's sister be seated. The ladies and maidens and all who served the Queen at table were all of noble birth and had to kneel so long as the Queen was eating. The meal lasted for three hours.

Following the lavish meal, the queen remained seated in her chair, while the ladies danced. The 'king's sister danced a stately dance with two dukes'. Jacquetta remained kneeling before Elizabeth, but 'at times the Queen bade her rise'. The splendour of the ceremony caused Tetzel to remark that he had never seen elsewhere the 'courtly reverence they paid to the Queen'.

While a place of comfort for Elizabeth, the palace also saw her fear. On more than one occasion, she was forced to flee into sanctuary. Her chambers at the palace would have been in a state of disarray as she gathered her children and fled to the sanctuary at Westminster.

When Elizabeth of York married Henry VII, she would have taken over the quarters formerly occupied by both her mother and her aunt at the palace. One wonders how she felt when she entered the chambers as queen. She had played many roles in this room – princess, lady-in-waiting to Queen Anne – and now she was queen.

Painted Chamber, Palace of Westminster

The Painted Chamber of the Palace of Westminster received its name from the many colourful murals painted on its wall. It was large, at

80 feet long by more than 25 feet wide, and estimated to be between 30 and 50 feet high. Seven windows originally decorated the room, but two had been closed and painted when Henry III remodelled the area. Elegant painted tracery and wainscoting graced the ceiling, while glazed tile covered the floor. According to Colvin's *History of the King's Works*, four windows in the west wall of the chamber resembled those in the Great Hall at Eltham, leaving 'no doubt that they too were among the works of the fourth Edward'.

Even the arches over the windows were covered with paintings, mostly heraldic images in deep hues of vermillion, ochre and verdigris. Paintings of the Virtues decorated the windows, while depictions of Biblical scenes filled the room. Many of these were portrayals of war. The room was warmed by a fireplace; the mantelpiece decorated with a painting of the Tree of Jesse.

The east end of the chamber once held the king's great bed, with a large painting of the coronation of Edward the Confessor hanging over it. By the time Edward IV reigned, the king had a separate, private chamber.

The Painted Chamber was often used for state business, with Parliament meeting here at times. On 29 April 1463 with 'the lord king sitting on the royal throne in the Painted Chamber within his palace of Westminster' the Bishop of Exeter announced the opening of Parliament. Several other times during Edward's reign Parliament opened in the Painted Chamber.

After the marriage of Anne Mowbray and Edward's son, Richard, a lavish feast was arranged in celebration and held in the Painted Chamber. The highly ornamented chamber would have been a suitable backdrop for the marriage feast, and it was close to the chapel where the wedding was held. Richard, Duke of Gloucester, escorted the newly married Anne Mowbray to the feast.

Visiting the Painted Chamber Today

Unfortunately a fire devastated this area of the palace and the chamber was gutted. Nothing remains on site of the elegant chamber, but fragments of the Painted Chamber were found and are on display at the British Museum. A winged seraph and a prophet had been removed from the building prior to the fire by the 'Labourer in Trust' for the palace, Adam Lee, which preserved them for future generations.

St Stephen's Chapel

Originally built by King Stephen, St Stephen's Chapel was rebuilt and refounded in a larger style by Edward I, with work continuing until the reign of Edward III. The chapel was designed like most palace chapels in the medieval period, with two storeys. The upper chapel was for the use of the royal family and the lower chapel, St Mary in the Vaults, open to the court.

According to Colvin's *The History of the King's Works*, octagonal turrets, topped with pinnacles, were constructed at all four corners of the chapel and a double porch on the west end gave access to both chapels. At 90 feet long, 30 feet wide and nearly 65 feet tall, it was a large structure. The exterior of the chapel was entirely covered with tracery. Flying buttresses supported the building, and on each side of the area above the great east window was an arcade with richly carved statues.

The chapel was connected to the Palace of Westminster with its east end close to the river. To give the king access to the chapel from his private apartments, a two-storey gallery was constructed between the south side of the chapel and the king's Painted Chamber. Most galleries resembled cloisters, with stone walls and glazed windows. Edward's gallery connected with the king's pew in the upper chapel. Above the doorway to his pew were emblazoned the arms of England and France.

While nothing remains of St Stephen's Chapel today, thanks to the works of Edward Brayley, John Britton and J. M. Hastings we know quite a bit about its interior. St Stephen's was a collegiate chapel, so stalls necessary for the dean and chapter were placed in the upper chapel.

When Edward entered the upper vestibule, he would have seen elaborate arcading. Large piers, surrounded by a cluster of columns, divided the chapel into five bays, and each wall of each bay was lavishly arcaded with columns of bright Purbeck marble, supporting ogees. The area above each arch was heavily crested, with battlements above. The mouldings in each bay were decorated with heraldic shields with grotesques in between, and the spandrels of the arches were painted with stars of gold on a blue background. Above the arcading were windows with delicate tracery filled with stained glass depicting Biblical stories of Adam and Eve, Noah, and Joseph and the Israelites, along with images of angels, knights and heraldry.

Painting, of angels and motifs of lions, fleurs-de-lis, and other gilded ornaments adorned the wall. Life-size statues stood on pedestals. Light-blue mouldings were set off by gilded bases, caps, canopies and bosses. The walls also had paintings. The Ascension of Christ and stories of other Biblical figures filled the chapel. According to Hastings, the chapel's clerestory resembled a glazed triforium.

Above the altar, at the east end of the chapel, was a painting of Edward III being presented to the court of Heaven by St George. Behind the bowing king were his kneeling sons, then his queen and daughters. The chapel's vaulted ceiling was made of wood, perhaps resembling that of Ely Cathedral's lantern tower. Large, gilded bosses ornamented the wooden ceiling.

In the lower chapel, small columns supported elaborate arches. Large bosses adorned the ceiling while ornaments of foliage, dragons and angels decorated the area. Worshippers would have entered through the chapel's arched doorways. Since the courtiers worshipped in the lower chapel, this area was just as lavish as the upper chapel.

Edward IV's youngest son, Richard, Duke of York, married the heiress, Anne Mowbray, here in 1478. The chapel was opulently decorated with tapestries and azure carpets for the ceremony. Inside the door of the chapel, the king, queen, Duke of York and other members of the royal family, standing under a canopy of cloth of gold, listened while the papal dispensation allowing the marriage was read out. Following the wedding ceremonies, the couple heard Mass at the high altar.

It is believed that the wedding ceremonies for Elizabeth of York and Henry VII also took place in the chapel of St Stephen's. Little is known about the ceremony itself, but the Archbishop of Canterbury, Thomas Bourchier, performed the wedding which united the daughter of York with Henry Tudor.

Following his death, Edward IV's body was embalmed, clothed (according to Ross) with a cap of estate on its head and red leather shoes. His body lay in state for eight days in the chapel, with both nobles and royal servants watching over it. The body was then placed on a bier, covered with cloth of gold and carried under a canopy to Westminster Abbey to be readied for the procession to St George's Chapel at Windsor.

Visiting the Chapel Today

Today, there is nothing left of the actual chapel of St Stephen's. For years it was used as a meeting place for the House of Commons and underwent much renovation. Following the fire it was rebuilt. The crypt below the chapel, St Mary Undercroft, still exists today, but is not open to the public. To see where the chapel once stood, look to St Stephen's Hall and the porch. The entrance to the hall is through the public entrance to the Houses of Parliament.

Westminster Hall

Westminster Hall would be the scene of several momentous events in the lives of many of the York family. Two of the Duke of York's sons and their consorts celebrated coronation feasts here, as did one of his granddaughters.

The Norman hall received a makeover during the fourteenth century when it became necessary to remodel it. The original Norman columns were removed and replaced by a hammer-beam roof, and its walls were heightened and refaced. The north front of the building received a new doorway with flanking towers. Statues of kings were placed in niches on the north front, while other life-sized statues stood inside the hall. All of these statues would have been colourfully painted and gilded.

It was under the immense hammer-beam roof that certain events in the lives of the Yorks would unfold. On 4 March 1461, Edward IV was raised to the marble seat of the King's Bench, which was situated on the southern side of the hall. Years later, his brother Richard would follow in his footsteps. Each of the Yorkist monarchs would leave from here for the walk to Westminster Abbey and the coronation. Following each of the coronations, a large feast would be held in the hall, with pomp and pageantry abounding. A description of how Westminster Hall was utilised prior to the coronations may be found in the section on Elizabeth of York.

Christmas of 1484

Richard III celebrated the Christmas of 1484 at the Palace of Westminster. Several celebrations were held throughout the Christmas season. Large meals, with an array of choices, were arranged, with mummers putting on plays following the feasts.

During the festivities, courtiers sang, danced and played games. Edward's daughters were present at court for the celebrations.

During the festival of Twelfth Day, Richard wore his crown at the royal banquet. Rumours began circulating that the king's niece, Elizabeth, was dressed like his queen, Anne. This led to a vicious rumour that Richard was planning to marry Elizabeth after Anne's demise. The rumours became so widely known that Richard was forced to appear before his council to denounce them. He also appeared before the leading citizens of London in the Great Hall of the hospital of the Knights of St John in Clerkenwell to deny them.

Visiting Westminster Hall Today

Most of the old Palace of Westminster was devastated by a fire. Fortunately for those interested in history, Westminster Hall survived both the conflagration and rebuilding efforts. When you enter the hall, look up at the hammer-beam roof above you. This same roof overlooked the coronation celebrations of Edward and Elizabeth, Richard and Anne, and Elizabeth of York. The statues of the kings lining the south wall also stood witness to key events in the lives of the York family.

Few other places have survived to offer the York enthusiast such a rich tapestry of history; few other places allow one to stand under the same roof where so much history has passed. The atmospheric presence of those long gone can be felt, separated from today's visitor by only the thin wall of time. You might feel hurried to move onto the next room, but find a corner and stand for a moment to experience the atmosphere. Walk around the entire room before moving on to the Houses of Parliament.

The only way to visit Westminster Hall is to visit the Houses of Parliament. At the time of writing, visitors enter into the Houses of Parliament through the hall. For information on ordering tickets for a tour, see the website at www.parliament.uk/visiting/visiting-and-tours/.

The Houses of Parliament stand directly across from Westminster Abbey. Driving in London is difficult, due to both the congestion charge and the challenge of finding parking. Fortunately, the city is easy to travel with public transportation.

The best tube stop for the Houses of Parliament is Westminster station, although Westminster is not far from any tube stop in the general vicinity. You can easily walk there from Trafalgar Square. Alternatively, you could take a boat from the Tower of London to Westminster Pier. Palace of Westminster postcode: SW1A 0AA.

Jewel Tower

One of the few remaining sections of the medieval Palace of Westminster, the Jewel Tower was built to house King Edward III's treasures. After becoming king, Edward IV began further works in the Jewel Tower garden. The tower was known as the king's privy wardrobe and was adjacent to the king's privy garden. The tower was originally surrounded by a moat on three sides and topped by battlements to protect it from thieves, since it housed the king's collection of jewels, gold, and silver. Constructed mainly with Kentish ragstone, Beer and Caen stone were used for its decorative features. Colvin describes the windows as being 'glazed ... with white glass worked with flowers and borders of the king's arms'. The tower still has its fourteenth-century vaulted ceiling embellished by decorative bosses.

Visiting Today

None of the York family would have entered the tower, but they would have seen its exterior while at Westminster. Visiting it allows one to get a sense of the medieval palace. If this tower, which was not meant to be seen often, was so richly decorated, how opulent the rest of the palace must have been. The tower is open to the public, and at the time of publication, contained an exhibit about the history of the building and a model of the medieval palace.

If you are leaving the House of Commons, cross the busy street and then turn left on Abingdon Street. The Jewel Tower is a short walk away and will be on your right. For more information about opening times and admission prices, see the Jewel Tower's website at www.english-heritage.org.uk/daysout/properties/jewel-tower/. Postcode: SW1P 3JX.

Grafton Regis, Northamptonshire

This tiny village, amid the breathtaking scenery of the hills of Northamptonshire, seems too small and peaceful to have been the scene of one of the more momentous events in the history of

England. Prior to King Henry VIII's changing its name, Grafton was known by Grafton Woodville and was home to the Woodville family. Here in Grafton manor, Edward IV's future queen was born. The eldest child of Jacquetta, Dowager Duchess of Bedford, and Richard Woodville, Elizabeth was born soon after her parents' marriage. Elizabeth first married Sir John Grey, a Lancastrian supporter. Following his death at the Second Battle of St Albans, Elizabeth tried to gain control of her jointure, but was unsuccessful. From here, the story takes on a legendary quality.

One variation of the story is that Elizabeth stood by an oak tree with her two young sons and begged Edward to help her. Hall says that Elizabeth was with her mother when Edward, out hunting, stopped by the manor. She pressed her suit to him, and he was fascinated. He thought her to be an 'excellent beautie' and neither too 'wanton nor to humble'. Impressed by her body and her 'wise and womanly demeanour', he asked her to be his mistress. Elizabeth rebuffed him, saying that if she was not good enough to be his wife, she would not be his mistress.

Mancini pushes the image further, having Edward pull a dagger, with Elizabeth coolly resisting his advances. Impressed by her character and enflamed with desire, Edward decided that she would make a fitting royal spouse.

The most accepted date for the marriage is 1 May 1464. Edward left Stony Stratford and hurried to Grafton. Here, Edward and Elizabeth were married, quietly and privately, with only the bride and groom, her mother, the priest, two gentlewomen and a young man who assisted the priest in singing. Whether this happened at the manor, the Hermitage or in the parish church is unclear, but Edward and Elizabeth did marry before she was publicly proclaimed his queen in September of that year.

Grafton Manor

The manor at Grafton officially came to the Woodville family in 1440, but it is believed they had been tenants there prior, since the family had lived in the village for years. After Earl Rivers was killed, the manor passed to his son, Anthony, who was executed after King Edward's death. His brother, Richard, inherited, and once he died, the estate came to his nephew Thomas Grey, Elizabeth's son by her first marriage. His son gave up the property to Henry VIII, who largely extended and renovated the existing manor home. The house was set on fire and ruined during the Civil War.

Visiting Today

Sadly, there is little to see of the Grafton Elizabeth would have known. The manor lands are not open to visits. It is possible to visit the parish church of St Mary, however. Some historians speculate that Elizabeth and Edward were married at the Hermitage, which was a small friary. However, the parish church was adjacent to the manor and would have offered a more private venue, especially at an early hour.

Elizabeth was almost certainly christened in the Norman font that still stands in the church today. The family was unquestionably active in church affairs, and Elizabeth's grandfather, John Woodville, built its tower. The church warden speculates that a Woodville chapel may have stood to the left of the high altar. John Woodville's alabaster altar tomb may still be seen in the church.

Grafton Regis is located just off the main Northampton road. If headed north, take the second right into the village; if headed south, take the first left. Park near the village hall and walk down the quiet country lane. After a short stroll through beautiful scenery, the church will be on the left, just past the entrance to Grafton Manor. Prior arrangements should be made by email to see the interior. The church is badly in need of funds for both maintenance and to refurbish the interior, so donations are appreciated. For more information, see the church's page on the Grafton Regis website, http://grafton-regis.co.uk/.

The village is very proud of its history and, at the time of this publication, offers several 'Walks and Talks' explaining the history of Grafton Regis. Please check the 'What's On' section of the Grafton Regis website. Grafton Regis Postcode: NN12 7SS.

Reading Abbey, Berkshire

Although she had wed Edward, Elizabeth still had to wait for a public announcement of their marriage. Some have speculated that Edward meant to put Elizabeth aside and pretend their marriage had not occurred, but there is no evidence this was the case. As aforementioned, according to Mancini, Edward 'fell in love with her beauty of person and charm of manner'.

Edward delayed publicising his marriage until September. The Earl of Warwick was promoting a marriage with France and Edward was biding his time before the announcement was made. However, in September 1464, Edward met with his council at Reading to discuss both the upcoming conference at St Omer and the condition of the currency. During the meeting Edward revealed that he had already been married for several months to Elizabeth (Woodville) Grey, the Lancastrian widow of Sir John Grey.

The announcement caused shock and consternation. A letter, written by John Wenlock, said that the king's declaration caused 'great displeasure to many great lords, and especially to the larger part of all his council'. The announcement was probably made in the Refectory at Reading, a large rectangular room with ornamental arches. The Burgundian Chronicler Jean de Waurin wrote that the men told the king that 'she was no wife for him'. The state papers of Milan also record that the marriage had upset the council:

> The greater part of the lords and the people in general seem very much dissatisfied at this, and for the sake of finding means to annul it, all the nobles are holding great consultations in the town of Reading, where the king is.

While these manuscripts were written after the fact, there seems little reason to doubt the veracity of the accounts, since they agree that the noblemen of England were upset by their king's marriage. However, the men soon realised that since the marriage had already taken place they would have to reconcile themselves to it. On Michaelmas Day, Elizabeth, escorted by both the Duke of Clarence and the Earl of Warwick, made her way into the church at Reading Abbey.

Elizabeth would have seen an immense church, built with Caen stone in cruciform shape. The nave was more than 200 feet long and 40 feet wide, while the choir was almost 100 feet long. Since the monks were of the Benedictine Order of Cluny, the church was probably highly decorated, with beautiful stained glass, elaborate wall paintings and brightly coloured paved floors. Here among the soaring columns, she was presented as Edward's queen to those assembled. A painting depicting the scene hangs today in Reading Town Hall.

At the end of the day, Elizabeth would have slept in her chamber in the abbot's lodge on a bed with silk hangings. Her room was richly decorated with tapestries depicting nature scenes hanging on the walls. Elizabeth, as queen, would have been given use of one of the residence's best chamber. The abbey was wealthy, and the abbot spent lavishly on the building, employing several servants.

Reading Abbey History

On a ridge of hill between the Kennett and Thames rivers, Henry I laid the foundation for a new monastery, dedicated to the Virgin Mary and St John the Evangelist. The abbey was surrounded on three sides by a 6-foot-thick wall covered with freestone, while a fourth side was protected by an offshoot of the Kennett. The abbey's precinct covered about 30 acres, with four gates erected to allow entrance.

The church boasted several relics, including the hand of St James, which had been given to it by Henry I. The relic may have been brought to England by Empress Matilda and enclosed in a gold case. Other reliquaries, decorated with precious jewels, would have housed the favourite relics of the monastery.

Henry I was buried in the abbey church. Most accounts say he was buried before the high altar. By the time of Richard II, his tomb was in a state of disrepair, so Richard ordered the monastery to repair both Henry's tomb and his effigy. Currently, an investigation is underway to see if the bones of Henry I can be located. Just like with Richard III, some sources claim Henry's bones were tossed into the river.

Several kings spent time at Reading and would have needed to conduct state business and hold parliaments. These meetings were usually held within the chapter house, located east of the cloisters. The room was highly ornamented and had eight rectangular columns, each decorated with a carved capital base projecting from the wall. The vaulted ceiling was about 40 feet above the tiled floor. The entrance was from the cloisters through a large door. Enormous windows on each side of the door, along with five huge windows on the opposite side, allowed light to flood the room, with its walls decorated by frescoes and intricate carvings.

Reading and Richard III

Soon after Richard's coronation, he set off on a royal progress; Reading was one of his first stops. His train included five bishops, four earls, four barons and other nobles. After arriving, he would have probably entered through the Compter Gate, which faced the great west door of the church. This gate is believed to have extended across the Forbury to St Laurence's church. Another possible entrance, if he had travelled by river, would have been the North Gate. Once inside, he would have been received by the Abbot of Reading and housed in the abbot's lodge.

While at Reading, Richard made a grant to Hasting's widow, Katheryn Neville. In his grant, he promised to be a 'good and gracious soverain lord to the said Katheryn and to hir children', granted her the marriage and wardship of Hastings' heir, including the custody of his estates during the wardship, as well as allowing her to keep other profitable wardships.

Visiting Today

Following the Dissolution, Reading Abbey was closed. Slowly the abbey buildings were dismantled for their stone and the once grand abbey fell into a state of disrepair. Visitors today are no longer able to freely walk among the ruins, as they are too dangerous for daily tours. Currently the Friends of Reading Abbey are trying to get funding to help conserve what is left of this historic building.

Occasionally, the abbey ruins are opened for abbreviated guided tours on special occasions, like Water Fest. It is worth contacting the museum to see if any tours are offered before visiting. To do so see Reading Museum's website at www.readingmuseum.org.uk/contact/.

Reading Museum, located in the town hall, is a good place to get further information on the abbey. Admission to the exhibits is free. The museum houses some recovered stonework from the abbey and features a reconstruction of how it might have appeared in medieval times. Examples of medieval tile that once covered the abbey floors are on display.

Before leaving the town hall, ask at the information desk to see the painting by Ernest Board titled *Marriage of King Edward IV and Elizabeth Woodville*. While the title is not quite accurate, given that Elizabeth was already married when she was presented at Reading, the painting is well done, with beautiful colours. For more information about visiting the museum, see its website at http://www.readingmuseum.org.uk/visiting/ or call +44(0)118 937 3400.

The abbey's inner gateway is still in existence, having been heavily restored in the nineteenth century. It is located across from Forbury Gardens, a public park erected on the site of Reading Abbey's outer court.

Driving is difficult in Reading, but the town operates a park-and-ride scheme. Alternatively, it is easy to reach Reading by public transport. For more information, see http://livingreading.co.uk/maps/getting-here-by-public-transport. Reading Museum postcode: RG1 1QH.

Tewkesbury, Gloucestershire

Following his victory at Barnet, it was not long before Edward needed to raise fresh troops and once again march to meet a Lancastrian army. Margaret of Anjou and Prince Edward had landed and were on the move, gathering men as they went.

Edward moved to meet Margaret's troops. Despite efforts by the Lancastrians to confuse him, he was eventually able to work out where they were headed and sent a messenger to Gloucester telling it to bar the gates to them. This manoeuvre forced the Lancastrians to make for the next crossing at Tewkesbury. Exhausted, they camped nearby. Edward and his army reached the area later that day and camped about three miles from the Lancastrian troops.

The next day, the king's army, separated into three divisions, marched to meet the Lancastrians. Richard held the van, Edward and George held the centre, and Hastings guarded the rear. The Lancastrians had the benefit of slightly higher ground, but Edward's troops were ready. Somerset and his Lancastrian division left its defensive ground and made its way towards Edward's army. When hand-to-hand combat broke out, it became clear that Somerset's strategy was flawed. The king's army overtook Somerset's men, who began to move back up the hill where they were attacked by other men in Edward's army. When Somerset's men broke ranks and fled, many of them were cut down.

Edward then turned on the Lancastrian centre, led by the inexperienced Prince Edward. These men began to flee while the Yorkist army surged forward, slicing them down as it advanced. Some contemporary sources say Prince Edward was slain in battle. Several of the men drowned in the river, the weight of their armour pulling them down. The Lancastrian left was the last to fall.

Many of the escaping men took refuge in Tewkesbury Abbey, claiming sanctuary, but Edward demanded they be handed over. A quick trial was held in the nearby toll house, where Richard, Duke of Gloucester, and the Duke of Norfolk served as judges. The men were found guilty and then executed. Margaret and Anne Neville were later captured, traditionally at Little Malvern. (See section on Anne Neville.) With the death of Prince Edward, the Lancastrian threat to Edward's throne was finished.

Visiting Today
The best way to explore the area around Tewkesbury is by car. The first location to visit is slightly outside of Tewkesbury in the village of Tredington.

Tredington
Tredington is located about two miles south of Tewkesbury. Tradition has it that Edward and his army stayed here on the eve of the battle at Tewkesbury. *The Historie of the Arrivall of Edward IV in England* says that Edward 'lodgyd hym selfe, and all his hooste, within three myle of them'. There is not much to substantiate the claim that Tredington was where Edward stayed, other than the village's proximity to Tewkesbury and its location on a main road. Although the manor house Edward supposedly lodged in is gone, the church nearby is still standing.

The church of St John the Baptist at Tredington has obviously been renovated throughout the years, but its layout has remained primarily the same as before the battle. The church's timber-framed tower was rebuilt in 1883. After you enter from the south porch, be sure to notice the embellishments of the stonework in the arch. The alternating zig-zag pattern of coloured stone continues on into the pillars.

The armorial bearings in the west end of the church symbolise families connected with the church, including the Neville lords of

Warwick. If Edward and his brothers observed Mass here before the Battle of Tewkesbury they would not have seen the Elizabethan pews within the nave. Take time to walk around the church looking at its decorative features before heading to Tewkesbury.

Visiting St John the Baptist Today

The church is open during daylight hours. Informative church guides are provided near the entrance and are an invaluable source of information. St John the Baptist postcode: GL20 7AB.

Tewkesbury Heritage Centre

Tewkesbury has an excellent tourist information centre, located at 100 Church Street. Be sure to pick up one of its battlefield walking tour leaflets. The centre has an informative exhibition on the battle, including a replica of the battle site. A copious amount of information about the main participants in the battle is also supplied. Since the layout of the town has not changed tremendously from medieval days, the replica allows visitors to get an idea of the scope of the battle. Because it was surrounded by water, there were no town walls, since the rivers would have offered protection. The Severn, Avon, Carron and Swilgate are all near Tewkesbury.

Tewkesbury Abbey

A monastery was built on this site in the eighth century and the site has been continuously occupied since that time. In the eleventh century an abbey was founded here by Robert Fitzhammon. Consecrated in the twelfth century, it has been the abbey church for several distinguished families. Robert, Earl of Gloucester, Henry I's natural son, held the land and helped complete the abbey. Later the lands would pass to the de Clare family and on to the Despensers. From the Beauchamps it would pass to the Earl of Warwick, and following his death at Barnet, to George, Duke of Clarence.

Hugh le Despenser renovated the church, remodelling the choir and adding pointed arches to the columns. Seven large windows, made of glass from Chartres, were also installed. At the same time, the vaulting of the apse was completed. Hugh and his wife have an intricately decorated canopied tomb in the abbey.

After the battle and executions of the Lancastrians, several of the men were buried in the church. Prince Edward was buried in the choir, with many of the lords buried in the north transept. Following his execution, George, Duke of Clarence, was also buried here, along with his wife, Isabel, behind the high altar.

After the Dissolution, the church was slated for demolition. However, the people of Tewkesbury were able to save their abbey by petitioning to use it for the parish church. Within two years they raised enough money to purchase the church from the king.

Visiting Tewkesbury Abbey Today

The outside of the church has a different appearance today than in the medieval period. The monastic buildings that abutted the south of the church are gone, exposing it to view. The cloisters of the abbey were built on the same plan like those at Gloucester, with intricate fan vaulting. The west front still has its beautiful receding arch with seven shafts, but the window that once stood within is gone, since it was replaced it in the seventeenth century.

Once inside the nave, it is impossible not to be impressed by the ceiling, with groins springing from the corbels atop each column. Imagine the church like it would have appeared in medieval days, whitewashed with colourful paintings of Biblical scenes. Much of the stained glass you see today, while beautiful, is not medieval.

The medieval stained glass is best seen from the choir. These exquisite windows are of the late Decorated style. Be sure to look up to see the soaring choir vault, which is painted and gilded. In later years, the choir was decorated with the Yorkist badge of the sun in splendour. Whether planned or not, it is ironic that the burial place of Edward, the Lancastrian heir, lies directly below the Yorkist badge. Just like with many churches, the misericords in the choir are well worth a look.

Before you leave the church, make sure to visit the north transept, since this is where many of the Lancastrian dead were buried. George and Isabel are said to be interred in a vault behind the high altar. While near the high altar, look at the Purbeck marble of the altar stone.

For more information about visiting the Church of St Mary the Virgin, see its website at http://www.tewkesburyabbey.org.uk/. Postcode: GL20 5RZ.

Obelisk

After leaving the abbey, turn right out of the abbey car park and walk across the bridge to the recreation area. At the top of the field you will see an obelisk commemorating the Battle of Tewkesbury and other important events. This is also an excellent place to take pictures of the abbey. From this vantage point, it is apparent how large the abbey once was, even with its monastic buildings gone.

Bloody Meadow

Traditionally said to be the area where many of the Lancastrians were killed while they attempted to flee, the bloody meadow is shaped in such a way that it would have been impossible for the fleeing men to escape on either side. This forced them to continue onwards, where they would have been bogged down by the soft soil. Here they were easily caught by the Yorkists and killed, causing a legend to originate that a river of Lancastrian blood flowed through the meadow. Michael Drayton's poem *The Miseries of Queen Margaret* immortalised the battle and the fleeing men:

> Never did death so terrible appear,
> Since first their arms the English learnt to wield:
> Who would see slaughter, might behold it here,
> In the true shape upon this fatal field.
> In vain was valour, and in vain was fear,
> In vain to fight, in vain it was to yield ...

The meadow is marked with a panel and is open to walkers.

Lower Lode Lane

While many of the men were killed before they made it to the river, some did make it to the ford of the river at Lower Lode Lane. Here, many of the men fleeing drowned when they attempted to escape. Author Steven Goodchild believes that Queen Margaret fled this way toward Malvern.

Lower Lode Lane is off Gloucester Road, not far from the abbey. Stay on the little lane until it ends at the river. It is hard to picture this peaceful place as the scene of gruesome death. This ford was a main crossing of the river in medieval days. Today, you can take a boat across to eat at the pub and discuss all the locations you have seen while visiting Tewkesbury.

Eltham Palace, Kent

Eltham Palace has a long and rich history. It became Crown property following the death of Antony Bek in 1311, and was a favoured residence. Edward II's and Isabella's son John was born at Eltham, which became one of the largest royal residences in the country. It frequently was under construction since each of the subsequent monarchs expanded and rebuilt to suit them.

A wall 12 feet high and 5 feet wide was built around the moat at the manor of Eltham in the fourteenth century. Large arch buttresses supported it and two towers stood in its corners on the eastern section. Originally the inner courtyard was reached by going through a gatehouse and over a drawbridge. In the fourteenth century, Richard II built a stone bridge over the moat, which Edward IV improved during his reign.

Large royal apartments were built on the western side of the complex. Built of timber, the rooms were spacious. The king's chamber and study were built over a long cloister which led to the chapel. Two fireplaces kept the kings chamber warm, while three large windows with stained glass allowed light to brighten the room. The main window's stained glass was decorated with crowns and the king's badges; in the study seven windows depicted images of saints. The ceiling of the study had carved wooden bosses depicting angels. An oratory was attached to the chapel for the king's private use.

Several royal visitors came to the palace. The Holy Roman Emperor visited the manor house, and King John II of France spent time here while a prisoner, often going on hunts and dancing and feasting with King Edward III. Parliaments were also held at Eltham on occasions.

Eltham, Edward IV and Elizabeth Woodville

Eltham was one of the royal couple's favoured residences. It was in her chambers at Eltham that Elizabeth gave birth to their daughter Bridget. In 1479, Edward spent time at Eltham avoiding the plague sweeping through London. After his treaty with France, Edward had both security and money, allowing him to embark on a period of building projects, including construction of the Great Hall at Eltham in 1475. The Croyland chronicler remarked that Edward was known for collecting valuables, like vessels and tapestries, and for building churches, palaces, castles and colleges. Eltham was no exception. In addition to the hall, Edward constructed chambers, which were so large they required eleven stone fireplaces. He spent his last Christmas here, hosting a feast for 2,000 guests in his newly finished hall.

A courtier coming to Eltham would have entered through the outer gatehouse, with its battlements, and into the outer court. The service buildings stood here, but he would have passed through the area and over the north bridge. Now in the inner court, he would turn right to the lodging set aside for the courtiers. Eltham Manor boasted several parks, so at some point during his stay he would have participated in a hunt. Eltham's gardens were also well kept, with beautiful flowers and vines. If the courtier was here during Christmas 1482, he would have celebrated the festivities inside the enormous Great Hall.

From the outside, the soft winter sun would have cast a golden glow against the buttery colours of the Kentish ragstone. Making his way inside, away from the coldness of a winter's day, he would have felt the warmth from the fire blazing in the hearth. Turning to another guest, he may have expressed amazement at the sheer size of the hall, since it was one of the largest in medieval England. Gazing up first at the enormous hammer-beam oak roof with its pendants and gilding, he turned around to see large windows placed high in the walls, with intricate tapestries hanging below.

While the feast commenced, Edward and Elizabeth would have been seated at the dais at the upper end of the hall. Light would have come through the rectangular bay windows on either side of the couple. Servants would have made their way through the screen, passing to and from the pantry and buttery. A general sense of revelry would have filled the room, none imagining that by the next Christmas this vibrant king would be dead. Elizabeth Woodville's first Christmas when queen had been at Eltham, and she may have later felt the irony that her last was, too.

Elizabeth of York and Eltham
Elizabeth visited Eltham often, because it was the residence for her younger children, including the future Henry VIII. Like most

monarchs had done before him, Henry VII refurbished the buildings and built his own set of royal apartments. Henry and Elizabeth often had their meals in the Great Hall, sitting on the dais above the courtiers. At the end of the meal, the king and queen would retire to their chambers through the doorways at the top of the hall.

Eventually, the manor house lost its status as a favourite place for monarchs, and it began to decay. During the Civil War, the manor served for a base of Parliamentary troops in Kent who ravaged the home and parks nearby. The once Great Hall became a humble barn. In the 1930s, Stephen and Virginia Cortauld took a ninety-nine-year lease on the property and built their home here. Much care was taken not to destroy the existing historic buildings.

Visiting Today

There is an overwhelming sense that so many famous figures in British history have spent time here at Eltham. From kings and queens to Froissart and Erasmus, several history makers have walked where you are walking. It is easy to see why a writer in the nineteenth century said, 'Eltham Palace was, undoubtedly, one of the most perfect specimens of a castellated mansion ever erected in this country.' After leaving the visitor centre, follow the path up towards the house. To your right is an interesting display regarding the castle's history.

When you reach the top of the path, you will see the bridge over the moat. This bridge, which is the one Edward IV improved, makes for a picturesque photo. Crossing the bridge, you will reach the turning circle and catch your first glimpse of Edward's Great Hall. Before entering, face the Great Hall and walk to the right of the turning circle. Here, you will see the ruins of the great royal chambers which once abutted the Great Hall. Today only rubble remains.

The only way to visit the Great Hall is via a ticket for the whole of Eltham Palace. The art deco palace is well worth a visit, and be forewarned, even if you believe you are not fond of the style, you will find yourself lingering in the beautifully decorated rooms. Get a map if you are only interested in seeing the areas related to the Yorks. Be sure to see the display of artefacts found at Eltham as it has several pieces from the medieval period.

Once inside the Great Hall, keep in mind that the screen at the lower end is not the original screen. Also, the doors that once led to the royal apartments now lead to the squash court. But much of the interior is similar to how it would have appeared to Edward and Elizabeth on their last Christmas together.

Eltham is easily reached by two stations – Mottingham and Eltham. It is a short walk from either station to the palace, but buses are also available. Alternatively, parking is available at the palace. A café and gift shop are on site. For more information on visiting times, see the website http://www.english-heritage.org.uk/visit/places/eltham-palace-and-gardens/.

Part 7
George, Duke of Clarence

At a young age, George had a reversal of fortunes that would have turned even an older man's head. From exile to king's heir in a short span, George's prospects changed dramatically. Immortalised by Shakespeare as 'false, fleeting, perjured Clarence', the young man was brought high by his brother only to join forces with the Earl of Warwick in an attempt to usurp Edward's throne. While his exact motives will never be known, his betrayal of Edward did not keep the king from forgiving him on more than one occasion. Finally, though, Edward had enough and George was imprisoned in the Tower of London. Although the romanticised tale of his death in a barrel of malmsey wine is thought to be fictional, he was executed on his brother's orders.

Dublin Castle, Ireland

The large Norman castle at Dublin was built during the reign of King John, who, learning that there was no place to safely keep his treasure, wrote the Justiciar of Ireland directing him to build a fortification. In his directions he told him to build a castle in a suitable spot, both for administering justice and for defending the city. He was to make it strong, with 'substantial fosses and strong walls'.

The site that Meiler FitzHenry chose was where the earlier Norman stronghold had been built, but this time building works commenced on a much grander scale. First a tower and then the curtain wall and gatehouse took shape. At Dublin, two D-shaped towers flanked an entrance that had both a drawbridge and portcullis. According to Denis McCarthy, an extensive moat encircled the castle, which had another D-shaped tower to the south and circular, projecting towers at each corner. The enclosure was about 1¼ acres.

In 1243, Henry III had a hall erected that was 120 feet long and 80 feet wide. In addition to the 30-foot circular window installed in the gable at the end of the hall, all the windows were glazed. Directly over the dais a painting of the king and queen sitting with their baronage decorated the room. Visitors would enter the room through a 'great portal'. The hall had fallen into disrepair in the early fifteenth century and was still in a state of decline by the time Richard and Cecily came to Dublin.

George and Dublin Castle

When Richard, Duke of York, came to Dublin, Cecily came with him. When she approached the town of Dublin, with its wall of more than thirty gates and towers, one wonders what she was thinking. Eventually, the couple made their way to Castle Street and entered the castle through the gate in the north wall. Once inside the quadrangular castle, Richard and Cecily would have been given the best chambers it had to offer.

Cecily went into her confinement at Dublin Castle. On 21 October 1449, ensconced in her chambers, she gave birth to George. While she had given birth to several sons, by this time only Edward and Edmund had survived. The birth of another son would have been a joyous occasion and the baby would have been christened quickly.

According to John Ashdown-Hill, the church where George was possibly christened once stood where Four Courts stands now. Following the christening, a feast was held at the castle.

George was less than a year old when the Yorks received news that troubled them. In Kent, a man named Jack Cade was fomenting a rebellion. His use of the name John Mortimer tied him to the York family, fuelling gossip that Richard was behind the rebellion. Richard wrote to Henry VI assuring him of his loyalty. Despite reassurances from the king, Richard determined to return home. In September the family, including the new addition, George, left Dublin.

Visiting Today

All that remains today of the large Norman fortress is the Record Tower. Its appearance (and name) has changed through the centuries, with the battlements being added in the nineteenth century. While there is little to see from our time period, visitors can purchase tickets to enter the undercroft, chapel royal and state apartments.

The undercroft tour allows visitors to see the tenth century Viking defence bank, the base of the Powder Tower, parts of the moat archway, flooding from the underground Poddle River and medieval town wall. The other rooms on the tour, including the chapel royal, are not part of the castle the Yorks would have known, but are quite interesting. The current Great Courtyard marks roughly the spot where the castle would have stood.

For more information about visiting Dublin Castle, see its website at http://www.dublincastle.ie/. Be aware that the castle is subject to quick closures.

Christ Church Cathedral, Dublin

While in Dublin, you might also want to visit Christ Church Cathedral, which is near the castle. With your back to the castle's entrance, turn left on Castle Street, and after a short walk the cathedral will be on your right. Although a church has stood on this spot since the early eleventh century, the present church was rebuilt by the Normans and restored in the nineteenth century.

Even though Dublin Castle had a chapel, the Yorks may have visited the cathedral. They definitely would have seen it during their time in Dublin. While we do not know where Cecily had her churching ceremony, Christ Church Cathedral is the most likely place.

Cecily would have walked to the cathedral, where she would have presented herself to the priest to give thanks to God for her delivery and to receive a blessing from the priest to assist her in raising her child in a Christian manner. According to Augustin Joseph Schulte, the ceremony would begin at the door, where Cecily would have been met by a priest. After sprinkling her with holy water, he would recite Psalms 23 and then lead her into the church, saying, 'Enter thou into the temple of God, adore the Son of the Blessed Virgin Mary who has given thee fruitfulness of offspring.' While Cecily knelt at the altar, the priest would offer a prayer. He would sprinkle her again and offer another blessing before she left the altar.

Christ Church Cathedral was also the spot where John de la Pole, Earl of Lincoln, and Gerald FitzGerald, Earl of Kildare, crowned Lambert Simnel as Edward VI. The Earl of Lincoln had been in exile at his aunt Margaret's court in Mechelen. Realising they could not secure the escape of the real Edward from the Tower, they set up an imposter in his place. This caused alarm in England as the rebels prepared to set sail.

Visiting Christ Church Cathedral Today

The church is open to visitors. For more information about opening times and admission prices, see its website at http:// christchurchcathedral.ie/visit-us/opening-hours/.

Calais, France

George's first visit to Calais came following news that his brother had defeated the Lancastrians and was now King of England. Protected by a retinue of soldiers and accompanied by courtiers from the Burgundian court, George and Richard travelled to Calais. While they slogged their way through the muddy marshland around most of the city, they would have seen the wall that surrounded Calais soaring above them. Built in the shape of a rectangle, the tall brick wall was surrounded by a deep double moat. The land they first needed to cross, to the south of the city, could be flooded by the town for added protection.

Entering through the Boulogne Gate, one of the town's four gates, they would have made their way towards the castle, whose Great Hall and chamber had recently been rebuilt. George may have noticed the rich merchants' houses, with their tile roofs, when he and Richard passed along the narrow streets and through the market squares of the city. Maybe he noticed the church of St Mary, a building which would play an important role in his future.

After they reached the north-west corner of the town, the castle's circular keep surrounded by six circular towers stood before them. The entourage crossed the bridge over the moat separating the castle from the town and went through the gatehouse. Crossing the second moat dividing the keep from the inner bailey, they entered the keep.

One other possibility for the boys' lodging within the castle walls was the stone building built in 1416 for the king. The building was large and sat against the north wall of the castle. Wherever the boys lodged, the chambers would have been fit for the brothers of the king. They would not stay here long before returning to England and their new lives.

The Duke of Clarence and Calais

Several years after his first visit to the city, the Duke of Clarence would again visit the highly fortified town. On this visit, George travelled with the Earl of Warwick. Instead of entering as the treasured brother of the king, on this visit George was embroiled in a conspiracy against his brother. Having gone against Edward's direct command, he was planning to marry Warwick's daughter, Isabel.

On 11 July 1469, Isabel and George were married by the Archbishop of York, Isabel's uncle, in a public ceremony. Since all the men wanted the wedding to be as public as possible, the most logical place for it was St Mary's church. While the castle had a chapel, it was not large enough to accommodate a crowd. Susan Rose points out in her book *Calais: An English Town in France, 1347–1558* that there was no room in the castle precincts for such a wedding. The ceremony was well attended, and, according to Scofield, five Knights of the Garter, along with several other lords and ladies, were present at the wedding which was held in open defiance of Edward's orders.

Clarence was a co-signer to the manifesto Warwick issued from Calais. Their letter stated that there were people within the country influencing the king while excluding those of his blood. To solve the problem, they planned to petition the king and requested supporters meet them in Canterbury.

The next time Clarence came to Calais, he was fleeing with his pregnant wife and his in-laws. As the tumultuous waves tossed the boat, Isabel began experiencing labour pains. Several attempts were made to convince the garrison to allow them to land, but the family was not allowed to enter the town. While plans were being made to find another place to land, Isabel gave birth, but the baby did not survive.

Calais and the Expedition Against the French

George travelled to Calais with Richard and Edward in 1475. Since England had allied with Burgundy in a planned invasion of France, five dukes (including George) and several other nobles, along with their retinues, landed in Calais. Calais was the final place of assembly, and George commanded a large group of men. The outcome of the invasion was the Treaty of Picquigny. While in Calais, the three brothers were able to see their sister Margaret once again.

Edward and Calais

Prior to George's experience in Calais, Edward had already spent time in the town. He fled here with the Nevilles after Ludford Bridge. Even though they were attainted exiles, Edward and the Nevilles were welcomed in Calais. Over the next few months, Calais served as their base of operations.

Although they were welcomed in Calais, it did not mean the men were safe here. Somerset had started towards Calais with the king's letters patent to claim the captaincy of Calais. The garrison at Calais welcomed him with gunshots, forcing him to land further down the coast. According to Scofield, he made his way to Guines Castle and won over the garrison there with promises of money. Despite Somerset's arrival, men kept joining the Yorkist earls. Soon, the Yorkists managed to make a successful raid on Sandwich, where they captured Lord Rivers, Duchess Jacquetta and Anthony Woodville and brought them back to Calais.

After several months of preparation, Somerset and his men marched towards Calais. While making their way along the Boulogne Road they were met by soldiers from Calais. In a skirmish near Newnham Bridge, the men from Calais killed several of Somerset's men and forced their retreat.

In a move that he would try again later, the Earl of Warwick, along with the other rebels, issued a manifesto claiming no harm was meant to the king. The men simply wanted to fix the problems within the country.

Elizabeth of York and Calais

Despite the fact that Elizabeth is sometimes portrayed as simply a prop for her husband's reign, she did have influence with him. She travelled with Henry to Calais for a diplomatic visit with Philip, Archduke of Austria and Duke of Burgundy. On 8 May 1500 the king and queen left England for Calais with a large retinue.

Both Henry and Elizabeth met with Philip outside Calais in St Peter's church, which had been 'richly hanged with arras' for the occasion, because Philip had refused to come within in the town itself. Henry and Elizabeth arrived with many 'lords, ladyes, knights, esquiers, gentlemen and yemen'. The church had been divided into areas for dining by hangings. Here they dined, having a 'rich banqwete'. Following the meal, the talk shifted to a more serious note, with Elizabeth playing a role in the conversation, which focused on the betrothal of Princess Mary to Philip's son, Charles. The Spanish ambassador reported,

> On Tuesday in Whitsuntide the Archduke had an interview with the King of England at Calais. They met in a church in the fields. The Queen of England also went to see the Archduke. The King and the Archduke had a very long conversation, in which the Queen afterwards joined. The interview was very solemn, and attended with great splendour. Both Princes had great honour shown them.

The queen seems to have played an active part in arranging her children's marriages, with Henry valuing her opinions.

Visiting Calais Today

The medieval section of Calais was destroyed by the widespread devastation of the Second World War; the castle known to the Yorks is gone. Most of the immense brick walls that surrounded the town are also gone, although portions were incorporated into the citadel.

The Église de Notre Dame, the probable site of George and Isabel's wedding, still stands. The church has been newly renovated and is generally open in July and August from 2 p.m. until 5 p.m. St Peter's without Calais is no longer extant. The church was torn down and the current church was built in the nineteenth century.

Getting to Calais from the UK is easy. Trains run often from London St Pancras International to Calais Frethun. Be aware that there is no cash machine at Calais Frethun, so exchange money prior to your visit. For more information on arriving by train, see www.Eurostar.com. If you prefer to travel by sea, you can catch a ferry to Calais, either as a foot passenger or with your car. Both DFDS Seaways and P&O Ferries operate a service from Dover to Calais. See their websites at www.dfdsseaways.co.uk/ and www. poferries.com/. Additionally, you could drive to Dover and travel via the Eurotunnel. For more information, see www.eurotunnel. com/uk/.

Canterbury Cathedral, Kent

For more than a millennium, people have sought God and miracles at Canterbury Cathedral. In the sixth century, St Augustine came to Canterbury on a mission to reinstate the Christian faith. In the tenth century, a Benedictine monastery was founded at Christ Church. Following a fire, the monastery was rebuilt by Lanfranc, Archbishop of Canterbury, on a grand scale.

In 1072, the office of Archbishop of Canterbury was confirmed as the chief bishop in England, making the archbishop the highest prelate in the country. While the cathedral was a place of pilgrimage to the shrines of several saints, including St Dunstan and St Anselm, it is best known for the shrine of its most famous archbishop, Thomas Becket. His violent murder in the north-west transept of the church sparked outrage. Soon, miracles were said to occur at his tomb and he became a saint not long after his death. His shrine became an important place of pilgrimage.

George and Canterbury Cathedral
After leaving England as exiles, returning as brothers to the king must have been exhilarating for George and Richard. One of their first stops on the way to London was at Canterbury Cathedral. Arriving on a Saturday during the vigil of the Holy Trinity, George and Richard were received by the prior and the monks in green copes at the doors of the church. That evening saw the boys present at vespers. The next day George and Richard were in the procession for High Mass and at second vespers.

The boys were lodged in the Archbishop's Palace. Second only in size to the Great Hall at Westminster, the archbishop's hall was often used to entertain royalty, the nobility and foreign guests.

Within the next few years, the boys may have been in the care of the Archbishop of Canterbury, Thomas Bourchier. While in his care, they would have been housed at Lambeth and not Canterbury. However, on a visit to Canterbury in August 1463, Bourchier brought Richard and George with him. On this visit both of the boys were in procession and at High Mass. George had a sword carried before him in procession to underscore his significance as the heir to the throne.

Later, in 1468, Edward, George and Richard accompanied their sister Margaret to Canterbury on her way towards Margate, where she embarked to the Low Countries to marry Charles, Duke of Burgundy. Other barons, earls, and knights escorted them, including Anthony Woodville, who would stay with Margaret until after her wedding.

While in Canterbury, the group attended the first Mass of St John and the High Mass. After Nones, they left Canterbury and headed on towards Margate. While this was a momentous occasion which furthered the family's dynastic interests, the fact that all her brother accompanied her – including the king – also underscores their close family ties.

Prior to leaving for Calais for his wedding to Isabel Neville, George spent a few days at Canterbury Cathedral in the prior's lodging. Cecily travelled to meet him at Sandwich, his departure point. On her way back to Berkhamsted, she also stayed at the prior's lodging with her small household. While at the cathedral, Cecily would have visited the shrine of St Thomas.

There were four main places within the cathedral for a pilgrim to visit, and each location had its own custodian. Meriel Connor's introduction to *John Stone's Chronicle* says that the route for pilgrims was to first visit the martyrdom next to the passage beneath the steps which rose from the nave to the monks' choir. Here, an altar dedicated to the Virgin, which was sometimes called the Altar of the Sword's Point, displayed the sword that had broken in half when it was used to brutally murder Becket during his assassination.

Cecily would then have passed the original site of the tomb on her way to the altar of the Virgin Mary in the undercroft. Here she would have donated money and prayed. Given the situation, she may have prayed for peace among her sons. She would have then made her way to the Trinity chapel to the shrine. She may have been present when the cover was raised and heard the tinkling of the silver bells adorning the canopy. Cecily would have climbed the flight of stairs to the elevated shrine on her knees, the way most pilgrims did. If she had any illness, she would have rested the diseased or injured part of her body within a recess of the shrine's stone bottom.

The shrine was embellished with gold plates, with a gold wire netting layered over it, encrusted with jewels, like sapphires, diamonds, rubies and emeralds. Polydore Vergil reported that 'on every side that the eye turns, something more beautiful than the other appears. And these beauties of nature are enhanced by human skill, for the gold is carved and engraved in beautiful designs, both large and small ... some of the cameos being of such a size, that I do not dare to mention it ... but everything is left far behind by a ruby.' This ruby was also described by the Burgundian ambassador as being half as large as an egg.

Cecily's final stop would have been the reliquary that contained the 'perforated skull of the martyr' with its forehead left bare. Kneeling in front of the reliquary, she would have been offered the skull to kiss. There were so many treasures associated with the shrine that more than twenty wagons were needed to carry them away following the Dissolution.

After his marriage to Isabel, George, accompanied by his new father-in-law, came to Canterbury to rouse support for their cause. While chance of reconciliation with Edward seemed slight, George eventually found his way back to his brother's side. Once Anne Neville married Prince Edward, the Lancastrian heir, George probably realised that he had little chance of becoming England's king.

Soon after the Lancastrians were defeated at Tewkesbury, George, Edward and Richard came to Canterbury to celebrate the feast of St Augustine the Apostle. Armed men accompanied them, because Edward was concerned about possible rebellions in the area. While in Canterbury, Edward took steps to put down an uprising. Nicholas Faunt, Canterbury's mayor, was hanged, drawn and quartered for his part in the rebellion.

Edward and Canterbury

In June 1460, Edward, Salisbury and Warwick journeyed to Canterbury after returning from exile in Calais. The earls had issued a manifesto from Calais claiming they were going to protect the country by removing the king's ministers. Archbishop Bourchier met them at Sandwich and offered them episcopal protection. A 'great company of people' had joined them by the time they reached Canterbury. Here Henry VI had sent Robert Horne, John Fogge and John Scott to confront them. After a discussion, the men reached an agreement, with Henry's men joining the Yorkist cause. After a visit to St Thomas's shrine, the men made their way to London and then to Northampton.

Edward came to Canterbury several times. In August 1461, he was received by the archbishop, prior and convent at the gate of the church; he visited again in 1462 on pilgrimage. In 1465, he was received at the gates by the archbishop, the prior and the convent, all dressed in green copes. When Elizabeth arrived, she was greeted by the archbishop, the prior and the convent, this time dressed in white copes. On this occasion, the monks greeted Elizabeth with the response of *Audi Filia*, which includes the phrase, 'the king has greatly desired your beauty'.

The next day, Edward and Elizabeth were in the procession, with the convent wearing red copes. Following vespers, the couple visited St Augustine's with the archbishop. While at Canterbury, the king and queen received the news that Henry VI had been captured. In celebration, Edward and Elizabeth heard a sermon, listened to *Te Deum* and then participated in a procession to the shrine of St Thomas.

Richard III and Canterbury
In November of 1484, Richard visited Canterbury and stayed for a little more than a week. Anne was probably with him, and they would have been lodged in the Archbishop's Palace. Her illness had not seriously weakened her by this time. From Canterbury, the couple would leave to spend their last Christmas together in Westminster.

Visiting Canterbury Today
A visitor approaching the cathedral first sees the Christ Church Gateway. This intricately embellished gate was not built until the sixteenth century, so George would never have seen it. The gateway the Yorks would have seen, though, would have been just as

beautifully carved and elaborate. After paying the admission, step into the precincts to look at the great Bell Harry Tower. This tower replaced the original Romanesque tower and was not finished until 1498.

Move on into the church. The nave seems to soar upwards, and the ceiling, supported by clusters of columns tapering into delicate rib vaulting, appears to float. Light floods the room through the stained-glass windows situated near the ceiling and through the larger windows below. While making your way through the nave, take some time to gaze upwards at the beautiful ceiling. Drawing near the choir, you will see the intricately decorated stone ceiling dividing the nave from the choir. Effigies of six kings, including Henry IV, Henry V and Henry VI, adorn the screen resting on pedestals under elaborately carved stone canopies. Statues of Christ and his apostles used to rest here, but sadly these were destroyed in the seventeenth century. Try to imagine these statues through the eyes of the York family – painted with bright colours. From a position in front of the screen, pivot left and look at the large stained-glass window which was commissioned by Edward IV and contains images of him and his family. Sadly, the Puritan Richard Culmer destroyed the images and they had to be recreated. Some early sources say the head of Edward IV was part of the original window. When Edward commissioned them, the panels were arranged differently.

Continue on down the steps near the window until you are standing in the martyrdom. When doing a pilgrimage to St Thomas's shrine, George would have approached here first. This was the area where four knights in the service of Henry I murdered Thomas Becket. The doorway to the cloisters is traditionally the doorway the men burst through in their quest to rid the king of the 'turbulent priest'. Look down at the floor to see the name Thomas cut into the stone.

Next, enter the crypt with its Romanesque features. The York family would have seen the colossal decorated columns with their carved capitals on their way to the former tomb of St Thomas. They would have also seen medieval wall paintings like the one that still exists today. Pass the Chapel of the Holy Innocents and the next large area you come to is the site where St Thomas's body was entombed from 1170 to 1220.

After visiting the former tomb, make your way back to the choir. After a fire destroyed the original building, this part of the church was rebuilt and enlarged. The vaulted stone ceiling rests on clusters of slender shafts of Purbeck marble, alternating with shafts of Caen stone. The Chair of St Augustine, which is only used as part of the triple enthronement of archbishops of Canterbury, stands at the crest of the steps leading from the altar to the Trinity Chapel and is the same chair used in the medieval era.

Exit the choir on the south aisle and work your way up to where the Trinity chapel once stood. Today a lone flickering candle marks the area where St Thomas's shrine once rested in the now demolished Trinity Chapel. Here, the Yorks would have made their offerings. The next area they would have visited was the Corona, where the cathedral believes the skull of St Thomas was kept. Head to the Chapel of the Saints and Martyrs of Our Own Time, which once was the location of the Corona.

The next area of interest is the tomb of Henry IV and his wife, Joan of Navarre, a short walk from the chapel. The tomb of the former king and queen is directly across from his chantry; steps leading to a raised platform afford a closer look at the effigies of Henry and Joan. After deposing his cousin, Richard II, Henry IV took the throne, founding the Lancastrian dynasty. After you have finished admiring the tomb, continue walking down the aisle until you see the tomb of Archbishop Bourchier. George, Edward and Richard all predeceased the archbishop and would never have seen his beautiful tomb. A loyal adherent of Edward IV, Bourchier played a vital role in securing the release of Edward's youngest son, Richard, from sanctuary. He crowned Richard III, but did not attend the coronation feasts and never disclosed how he felt about Richard's taking the throne. He also crowned Henry VII, and soon before he died, performed the wedding ceremony for Henry and Elizabeth of York.

After leaving the richly decorated tomb, head towards the cloisters. The vault tracery of the cloisters is decorated with heraldic devices and grotesques. Before moving to the chapter house, see if you can find any coats of arms you recognise. When you enter the chapter house, which is the largest in England, look up at its barrel vaulted roof before admiring the large windows. A passage from the Archbishop's Palace once connected to the Great Cloisters, so several of the Yorks probably saw the room while visiting.

Sadly, the Archbishop's Palace with its large Great Hall no longer exists. Even the ruined archway that remains is from a later time. The grand palace was located near today's Palace Street. Despite the fact that the palace is not extant, it is worth taking the time to explore the grounds of the cathedral.

While our tour only visited the spots associated with the York family, the cathedral has so much more to offer. A visit will easily take two hours. For more information about visiting the cathedral, see its website at www.canterbury-cathedral.org/visit/information/ or call +44 (0) 1227 762862. At the time of this publication, the website also offered a virtual tour at http://www.canterbury-cathedral.org/visit/tour/. Canterbury Cathedral postcode: CT1 2EH.

If you are only in Canterbury for a day and are driving, you may want to explore one of the three park-and-ride options because it is difficult to find parking in the city centre. Canterbury is easy to access with public transportation; Southeastern Railway has trains that make the journey from London in under an hour. See the webpage at www.southeasternrailway.co.uk/. High-speed trains can also be found on National Rail. For more information, see www.nationalrail.co.uk/.

Tutbury Castle, Staffordshire

Situated above the River Dove, the castle commands an excellent view of the countryside. The geography of the area makes this an obvious location for a fortress, and the region is believed to have been occupied prior to the arrival of the Normans. However, the written history of the castle begins with the Norman invasion.

The castle was first granted to Hugh d'Avranches, but was later given to the de Ferrers family, who also established the nearby Tutbury Priory. Following the rebellion of Robert de Ferrers, the castle was taken from him and given to Edmund, son of Henry III, who became the 1st Earl of Lancaster. Eventually, the title passed to John of Gaunt through his wife Blanche. Tradition holds that Gaunt rebuilt and extended the castle. Sir Oswald Mosley, writing in the early nineteenth century, romanticised Gaunt's construction efforts:

The mouldering turrets of their ancient castle arose, phoenix-like, from their ashes, with redoubled glory; the rank weeds no longer flourished within the neglected area of its walls; the breeze no longer sighed sorrowfully through the shattered casement. Crowds of attendants were now beheld bustling through the paved courts; knights and squires, in gorgeous apparel, were now seen passing and repassing from the gates on well-trained steeds, whose trampling hoofs made the massive walls resound; mirth and festivity once more resumed their sway in the baronial hall, and a state of prosperity, greater than was ever before known, now exhilarated the happy tenants of John of Gaunt.

Despite the tradition and romance of Mosley's account, Colvin states in *The History of the King's Works* that there is no record of Gaunt carrying out major building works. He attributes most of the work to the three Lancastrian kings. Margaret of Anjou was responsible for the new South Tower and may even have built the North Tower, with its spiral staircase. If so, different window patterns were used on the two ranges. The South Tower had windows with arched heads, while the North Tower windows were square.

George and Tutbury

When George reached his majority he headed to Tutbury Castle, where he established his primary residence. Even though much renovation and building had recently occurred, the Rous Roll states that he 'built much' at Tutbury. Perhaps this was to accommodate his staff, since an ordinance approved in 1468 allowed George an enormous household.

In the summer, George and Isabel's household was served breakfast at ten, with first supper being at five. In winter, breakfast was served at nine, with the first supper at four. The duke was to be 'welle and honorablye served' by the carvers, cup-bearers and other officers assigned to serve him. George required meticulous records to be kept with every bit of bread, wine, ale and messes of meat spent recorded. Meals consisted of dishes like beef, salmon, lamb, boar, veal, pork and several varieties of fish flavoured with spices like sugar, ginger, saffron and cloves. On hand was also wine, sweet wine and ale. On special occasions, meals at Tutbury would have been taken in the Great Hall, but usually the duke and duchess would have taken their meals in their chambers.

George and Isabel would have seen a triangular bailey with a stone keep resting atop the motte. Embattled walls of ashlar stone 6 feet thick surrounded the castle on three sides, while a deep moat further enclosed the structure. The castle's main entrance was on the north side, over a bridge and through the gatehouse. From his chamber in the South Tower, George could look out through the large window over the bailey while a fire burning in the huge fireplace kept the room cosy and warm.

Eventually, George lost Tutbury. According to the chronicler at Croyland, this caused a rift between the brothers. George began to withdraw from Edward's company, spending less time eating with the king. He also stopped speaking out in council meetings.

Tutbury in Later Years

During the reign of Richard III, further works were carried out at Tutbury on the domestic apartments. Tutbury also served as a prison for Mary, Queen of Scots, whose chambers were in a timber building abutting the north curtain wall. After the castle held out for the king in the Civil War, an Act of Parliament in 1647 reduced the building to ruin.

Visiting Tutbury Today

Most of the remains at Tutbury date from the fifteenth century. Parking is available on site for a charge. After parking and purchasing a ticket, make your way to the entrance. This structure is still called the John of Gaunt Gateway. Once inside the bailey make your way across to the South Range. The large red-brick building is from the seventeenth and eighteenth centuries, but remnants of the South Tower are still extant. Looking up you can see the ornamental stonework of the tower and stone tracery of the windows. You can see also stonework of the ruined North Tower. While you wander around the bailey, make sure to see the ruins of the chapel where George and Isabel would have observed Mass.

To see the view of the surrounding countryside, climb the motte which once housed an impressive cylindrical keep. On a clear day you can see the outline of the Derbyshire hills in the distance. Tutbury is an impressive ruin, and you could easily spend an hour or two wandering around the bailey.

For more information on visiting the castle, see its website at http://www.tutburycastle.com/?page_id=65/ or call +44 01283 812129. Tutbury is best reached by car. Postcode: DE13 9JF.

Warwick Castle, Warwickshire

Warwick Castle rests on a rocky cliff overlooking the River Avon. This large fortress has been the residence of several important historic figures in England's history. Edward, George, Richard and Anne all spent time inside its walls. The castle was originally built by William the Conqueror in his attempts to maintain control of the Midlands.

William built a motte-and-bailey castle near the River Avon and gave Henry de Beaumont the governance of it, creating him Earl of Warwick. The castle remained in the family, eventually passing to the Beauchamps and then to the Nevilles. Warwick Castle's entrance, as the Yorks would have known it, had a projecting barbican with a portcullis, flanked by a pair of octagonal turrets. A passage led between the barbican and the main gateway. The five-storey gatehouse was a square tower with turrets connected by arches.

George and Warwick

After the death of Warwick at Barnet, George came into possession of Warwick Castle. It is easy to imagine George and Isabel making their way across the drawbridge over the dry moat. When they entered the castle, they would have seen the machicolated Caesar's Tower connected to Guy's Tower by an embattled wall. Once inside the inner bailey, the couple would have seen the motte, where the original timber castle once stood, before making their way to each of their chambers. If welcoming guests, George and Isabel would have presided over dinner in the magnificent Great Hall.

On 25 February 1475, Isabel gave birth in her chambers at Warwick Castle. While this would have been a time of celebration for the couple, perhaps the birth also reminded them of the baby they had lost while fleeing across the sea towards Calais. This birth, however, resulted in an heir that lived and would soon join his older sister, Margaret, in the nursery.

Isabel is said to have given birth to a son, Richard, at Tewkesbury Abbey before returning to Warwick Castle, where both she and

Richard died. George had Ankarette Twynho arrested for poisoning the duchess. She was brought to Warwick, where she was tried, convicted and hanged. Her heir, Roger Twynho, later described the incident:

> The Duke, in accomplishing of his 'subtle conjected imaginations', laboured and caused her to be indicted for maliciously and damnably in tending the destruction and death of Isabel, his duchess, by falsely, traitorously, and feloniously giving unto the said Isabel a venomous drink of ale with poison to drink, of which she sickened and died. Pleading not guilty to this charge, a jury appeared, and Ankaretta was convicted.

This was one of George's last acts as he was soon arrested and placed in the Tower of London, where he was eventually executed. After this Warwick Castle came under the control of the Crown.

Edward and Warwick Castle

Edward's control of his throne was tenuous between the years 1469 to 1471. Learning of the rebellion of Robin of Redesdale, Edward slowly made his way north. Eventually understanding how many men Redesdale had managed to recruit, Edward tried to muster more men to his cause. This did not happen in time, and once news of the defeat of Pembroke and Devon reached him, all hope seemed lost. At Olney, Archbishop Neville took control of the king, and he was taken to Warwick Castle. Here, Edward found himself in the unenviable position that Henry VI had experienced as he was king in name only. While he would have had the best apartments, he was for all intents and purposes the prisoner of the Earl of Warwick. Realising that this was not the best location to secure the king, Warwick eventually moved him to Middleham.

Soon after Edward returned to England from his exile in the Low Countries, he headed south, gathering men while he went. Reaching Warwick Castle, he made it his base. Learning that his brother George was approaching, Edward, with Richard by his side, moved out to meet him. According to Polydore Vergil, Richard, taking on the role of mediator, rode out to meet George and speak with him before returning to Edward to talk with him. Vergil recounts that 'finally, not war but peace was in every man's mouth; then armour and weapon laid apart upon both sides ... and brothers gladly embraced one another'. The brothers were once again in unity, with George pardoned by Edward.

Richard III and Warwick Castle

In August 1483, Richard came to Warwick Castle. As he drew near the ancient edifice, his thoughts may have turned to his earlier times in the castle. He had visited the castle under the tutelage of the Earl of Warwick, then with Edward, and finally on visits to his brother and sister-in-law; now this grand building, which had been the birthplace of his wife, was his to command. According to Rous, while Richard was at the castle an ambassador from the Queen of Castile visited him. The queen was interested in a marriage between an Infant of Castile and Richard's heir, Edward. Unfortunately, we do not know what Richard thought about the offer.

Richard began improvements to Warwick castle, initiating construction of the Bear and Clarence towers. These two octagonal towers project outward from the wall. Although the towers are both impressive, they never reached the height that Richard intended since his death at Bosworth put an end to their construction.

Anne Neville and Warwick Castle

Anne was born at Warwick Castle on 11 June 1456. Ensconced in the nursery, she would have spent her early years under the care of a governess. While she may have gone with her family to Calais when an infant, it is equally possible she stayed in England. She was probably at Warwick when news reached the family of the disastrous rout of Ludford Bridge. Although the Nevilles spent considerable time at Warwick Castle, during her childhood she would have also visited her father's other holdings.

Visiting Warwick Castle Today

Today Warwick Castle is a major tourist attraction containing several exhibits designed for children, including one on Richard Neville. The Bear tower that Richard was responsible for building is open to the public and billed as having a bear pit.

The original motte is still evident today and offers a good view of the castle complex. One building York enthusiasts will want to see is the Great Hall. Although it has been reconstructed twice, it still stands on the same location it occupied in the fifteenth century. The rooms will not have a medieval appearance, but are still worth a visit. With the steep admission cost, you will probably want to spend at least a day at the castle, and there are plenty of activities to fill your time.

It is now possible to stay overnight on the castle grounds. For more information on visiting the castle, see its website at www. warwick-castle.com/plan/plan-a-visit.aspx. Depending on where you park, Warwick Castle has several postcodes. Stratford Road Car Park: CV34 6AH. Field Car Park: CV34 6AH. Stables Car Park: CV34 4QU.

Bowyer Tower, Tower of London

Following George's arrest he was held prisoner in the Tower of London. Most of the Tower complex will be discussed in the section on the York princes, but the Bowyer Tower is where George was imprisoned and where tradition holds he was executed.

The Bowyer Tower was built on the north side of the Tower complex. A wet moat extended around the D-shaped Bowyer tower, which sat near the Brick and Flint towers. In the nineteenth century it received a new upper floor. Today, only the ground floor is original.

George and the Tower of London

In June 1477, George was arrested and imprisoned. Initially he was housed in comfortable lodgings in the White Tower. The king brought an accusation against the duke that 'the duke be convicted of high treason and forfeit his estate as duke and all the lands he holds by the king's grant'. Edward recounted the numerous times he had pardoned and forgiven his brother, but he had reconciled himself that to pardon him again would threaten his kingdom. In early 1478, Parliament met to arraign the duke on charges of treason. On 7 February, the Duke of Buckingham was appointed to pass sentence on George. The outcome was a death sentence. The Croyland chronicler was unsure about the manner of execution, but later reports appeared saying that George had been drowned in a butt of malmsey wine. Tradition says this took place in the Bowyer Tower. Both Clarence's son and daughter were also later imprisoned in the Tower complex and subsequently executed. Henry VII executed George's son and heir Edward, while Henry VIII was responsible for the execution of his daughter Margaret.

Visiting the Bowyer Tower Today
The only way to visit this section is by purchasing a ticket to the Tower of London. To get to the Bowyer Tower from Tower Green, walk past the Waterloo Barracks and go up the stairs. The entire wall, including the Bowyer Tower, has recently been opened up to the public as part of a new display. However, the interesting exhibition does little to evoke the atmosphere George would have experienced.

The Tower of London is in the care of Historic Royal Palaces. For more information about opening times and admission costs, or to purchase tickets online, see its website www.hrp.org.uk/ TowerOfLondon/admissionsprices/toweroflondonadmission. The closest Tube stop to the Tower is Tower Hill. The Tower of London may also be reached by water. Tower of London postcode: EC3N 4AB.

Part 8
Margaret of York

The youngest surviving daughter of Richard and Cecily, Margaret was born 3 May 1446 and was closest in age to her siblings George and Richard. Her early life was overshadowed by the conflict between her father and the king, and she was still unmarried when her father died. When her brother became king, her marriage, unlike that of her sisters, was arranged as befitting an English princess. Eventually marrying the Duke of Burgundy, Margaret proved loyal to both her family and her husband's duchy. She was respected and admired, even by her stepson-in-law.

Palace of Placentia, Greenwich, Kent

Once Edward became king, Margaret stayed largely at Greenwich; she was housed there, along with Richard and George, and provided for by the king. Thomas Beaufort had been given an estate here by Henry V, but after his death it was granted to Humphrey, Duke of Gloucester, who rebuilt the home and enclosed the park. In 1433 he received a licence to crenellate the house. Humphrey built a stone and timber manor house, with a limestone tower. The palace, including the gardens, courtyards, and 200-acre park, extended from the rolling waters of the Thames to the foot of the hill, on top of which he built a stone tower. Following Humphrey's death, the home was given to Margaret of Anjou, who renamed it Placentia or Pleasaunce.

Henry and his queen each had a ward in the house. The queen's ward contained a large chamber, a parlour and a gallery, overlooking the queen's garden. Henry VI also constructed a brick wall between the home and the mighty waters of the Thames.

During the first few years of his reign, Edward IV enlarged the palace and stocked the park with deer. Margaret, George and Richard probably spent time hunting in the park. The first Christmas after becoming king, Edward celebrated at Greenwich with his younger siblings. On the anniversary of their father's death, the family may have held their father's first year's mind here in the chapel. Despite later troubles, the siblings seem to have been close. Eventually Edward granted the palace to his wife, Elizabeth.

Margaret's Visit to England and Greenwich

In 1480, Margaret returned to England as part of an embassy to her brother trying to draw Edward into an Anglo-Burgundian alliance against France. Edward Woodville, James Radcliff and other members of Edward's household were sent to Calais to escort Margaret home. Scofield says the men, wearing their jackets of 'purple and blue velvet', brought Margaret across the Channel on the *Falcon*. At Gravesend, Margaret boarded the royal barge, with the master and twenty-four bargemen decked out in their new jackets of murrey and blue, embellished with roses. The king also provided 'green velvet, garnished with aglets of silver gilt, bordered with spangles, for horse harnesses, together with crimson velvet for covering head-stalls and reins for ten hobies and palfreys' for his sister's procession.

Arriving at Greenwich, Margaret was given luxurious chambers. Intricately woven tapestries depicting the story of Paris and Helen hung within the rooms that had been fitted for her. Her feather bed had a valence of velvet. Pieces of woven wool tapestry covered the table containing the images of 'roses, sunnes and crowns'.

A large state dinner was given in honour of Margaret and her mother, Cecily. While both Edward and Richard were in attendance, along with Elizabeth, Duchess of Suffolk, one brother was conspicuously absent. Margaret seems to have favoured George, who by this time had already been executed. At one point she had even opened discussions for a marriage between George and her stepdaughter Mary. She had also interceded for him with Edward when George had sided with Warwick. Margaret was probably saddened by the loss of her brother. However, there were new nieces and nephews for Margaret to meet to ease the sadness. She stayed in England for about three months and was housed at both Greenwich and Coldharbour.

Another family event took place at the palace. When Edward's youngest son, Richard, married the heiress Anne Mowbray, a celebration occurred at Greenwich with a large tournament held in honour of the marriage of the two children.

Elizabeth of York and Greenwich

Elizabeth of York had a fondness for the Palace of Placentia that may have its roots in her early childhood, when her household was established here. From her earliest days, she could feel the fresh breeze coming off the Thames and could enjoy the palace's gardens and parks. Most of her memories of the palace would have been pleasant ones. However, one event would mar her happy childhood memories. Her sister, Mary, who was close in age to Elizabeth, died at Greenwich. We do not have a record of Elizabeth's thoughts, but since she seemed close to her other siblings throughout her life, it is probable that she also was close to Mary.

After her marriage to Henry, Elizabeth favoured Greenwich. According to Alison Weir, she stayed here when Henry went on his northern progress. She also celebrated several Christmases here. On one Christmas day at Greenwich, she and Margaret, the king's mother, ate with the ladies in the queen's chambers, while Henry dined in his chambers. On Epiphany, the king, dressed in rich clothing and crowned, led the procession to Mass, followed by the queen, also crowned. Elizabeth and Margaret, the king's mother, were both dressed in rich mantles. Following Mass, the king adjourned to the hall, where he sat on the dais under a cloth of estate, with the Archbishop of Canterbury at his right hand. Elizabeth was seated to his left, also under a cloth of estate, which hung slightly lower than Henry's. After the second course was served the crowd enjoyed the entertainment of the minstrels.

On 28 June 1491, she gave birth to her son Henry in her chamber at Greenwich. Ordinances governed how the room was to be prepared. It was richly draped in cloth of arras and the floors carpeted. One window had been ordered to be covered in such a way so that Elizabeth could have light when she wanted.

After Henry's birth, he was christened a few days later in the nearby church. The baptism ceremony was a fine one, with the church being hung with tapestries and cloth of gold. As with Arthur, Canterbury's font had been procured for the ceremony. Henry was wrapped in a crimson mantle of cloth of gold, which was trimmed in ermine. Richard Fox, the Bishop of Exeter, performed the service. Elizabeth also gave birth on 21 February 1499 to her third son, named Edmund. Between 1500 and 1501, the old palace where Elizabeth had spent so many days was demolished and a new, more palatial one begun.

It was also at Greenwich that Elizabeth and Henry received some devastating news. Their son, Arthur, had died at Ludlow Castle. News was brought to Henry first by his confessor. Then, Henry sent for Elizabeth and they mourned together, with Elizabeth comforting Henry. One account says that Elizabeth thought first of Henry and with 'full great and constant comfortable words besought his grace that he would first after God remember the weal of his own noble person, the comfort of his realm and of her'. She reminded Henry that his own mother had 'never no more children but him only and that God by his grace had ever preserved him' and that 'God had left him yet a fair prince, two fair princesses'.

Elizabeth also reminded Henry that they were young enough to have another child. She then left him and went back to her chambers before succumbing to her own grief at the loss of her eldest son. She sank into grief so deep that her ladies were worried and sent for the king. Then 'his Grace of true gentle and faithful love, in good haste came and relieved her, and showed her how wise counsel she had given him before'. These acts of affection seem to demonstrate that the couple had a loving marriage.

Visiting Today

Nothing remains today of either the Palace of Placentia from Elizabeth's youth nor the red-brick palace that she and Henry would build together. The buildings of both palaces, which housed so many of the York family, have disappeared. Following the Stuart reigns and the English Civil War, the castle fell into a serious state of disrepair, and the Royal Naval College was built on the location. Humphrey's Palace of Placentia once stood where the west wing of the Royal Naval College, currently housing the University of Greenwich, now stands. Make sure to climb the hill to the Royal

Observatory. From here the views are incredible. On a clear day, the buildings of London are visible in the distance. This was the location of Humphrey's tower, later called Greenwich Castle.

The best way to get to Greenwich is by the river. Board a boat from Westminster Pier; while you travel the Thames, try to imagine the appearance of the shore in the fifteenth century. While the river's depth has changed over the years, it still keeps to the same path that the Yorks would have travelled. If you prefer to visit from London via rail, take the Docklands Light Railway (DLR) to Cutty Sark for Maritime Greenwich. Tower Gateway is a good place to catch the DLR. Check Transport for London's site for rail updates and times. Greenwich postcode is SE10 9NN.

Sluis, the Netherlands

Accompanied by an impressive entourage, Margaret arrived in her new homeland at the port of Sluis. A bustling merchant town, Sluis was situated on the Zwin River and was a centre of trade for the area. Its growth was largely due to the silting up of the Zwin River. Successive ports had been built to assist trading when the previous port had silted up. Philip of Burgundy had reinforced Sluis with strong walls, canals and high entry gates.

According to Margaret's biographer, Christine Weightman, Margaret and her entourage landed at Sluis on 25 June. As soon as the ships of her company entered into the harbour, she was met by the Bailiff of Sluis, Simon de Lalaing. He rode out to meet her, with a great company of boats ready for her people to disembark. Margaret was also received by the Bishop of Utrecht, a man whose name was familiar, since he had helped her younger brothers when they had been in exile. Both Bishop David and the Countess of Charny were half-siblings of her future husband. They, accompanied by 'mainy lords and gentilwomen', met Margaret when she arrived. Trumpets and other instruments signalled her arrival through the Watergate, and she was presented to the town, given a gift of money and accepted as its sovereign lady. Dressed in a crimson robe trimmed with black velvet, Margaret impressed the waiting crowd.

Since it was already dark, Margaret proceeded to her lodging, with the people of the town standing in their doorways with torches to light her way. As she moved along the streets, a series of pageants were presented to welcome her. Opposite Margaret's lodging was a stage, covered with 'tappettes' and curtained. As Margaret passed by, a man drew the curtain for the last pageant. She was celebrated with pageants depicting Biblical scenes and ancient queens, such as Esther, throughout her time in Sluis.

The next morning, the Dowager Duchess of Burgundy and her granddaughter, Mary, came to greet Margaret, accompanied by several nobles, including Lord Ravenstein. Margaret met the duchess at the door, and both of them knelt to the other for a time before embracing and talking. The older duchess was impressed by Margaret and 'toke hur very moderly with grett rev'ance', leading her through the 'abundauce of the people of Englisshe and Burgoynnez' to her chamber. Here they dined with 'grett joy'. Margaret and Mary's first meeting would lead to a lasting relationship, with much affection between the two.

The Duke of Burgundy met Margaret for the first time secretly with several of the nobility from both sides present. He would visit her several times over the next few days before their formal betrothal. The museum in Sluis says this occurred in the Belfry, but Weightman places it in the house of van Baenst in the marketplace. Margaret was continuously fêted by the town during her time in Sluis. She departed from Sluis to head to Damme, where she would be officially married.

Sluis and Richard and George

Following their father's death, Richard and George had been sent to the Low Countries in exile. While they were treated courteously, they had been kept out of the way, staying with the duke's illegitimate son, David, the Bishop of Utrecht. Once Edward claimed the throne, however, things began to change. After the York victory at Towton, Richard and George began to be treated like brothers of a king. The Bishop of Elphin, Nicholas O'Flanagan, wrote to Francesco Coppino, the Bishop of Terni, about the change in the boys' treatment:

It is reported among the English lords that the Duke of Burgundy is treating the brothers of the king with respect. This pleases them wonderfully, and they believe that there will be great friendship between the duke and the English ...

O'Flanagan goes on to report that 'one of these brothers will marry the daughter of Charles'. This marriage of Mary to a York son never happened, but the duke did send for the brothers to meet in him Bruges. On their way, they stopped in Sluis. It is easy to imagine the boys being fascinated with the commotion of the cosmopolitan town.

Visiting Sluis Today

Today, Sluis is a combination of medieval and modern. A shopping area with a fine selection of restaurants is located near its medieval belfry, which has a prominent position in the heart of the town. While some of its medieval portions have been lost, Sluis has an excellent museum which preserves its history.

The home where Margaret stayed was near the town belfry. While we do not know the exact location of Richard and George's lodgings, Livia Visser-Fuchs suggests that they stayed in an inn called Teste D'Or. Unfortunately, neither Margaret nor the boys' accommodations still exist. However, it is still possible to visit both the belfry and a portion of the town walls. Visitors today cannot see the entirety of the walls because a large part was destroyed, along with the castle, in the nineteenth century. However, three of the town's gates, the Oostpoort, the Zuidpoort and the Westpoort, still exist.

The Sluis Belfry

The town's belfry was built at the end of the fourteenth century. According to the museum, the tower's four turrets were graced with the arms of Burgundy, Flanders, the duke and the town. While this is the medieval building that Margaret, Richard and George would have seen, it has been restored to its original splendour after years of war and bouts with fire. Today the belfry houses an informative museum, and a climb to its top affords beautiful views of the surrounding area. For more information on visiting the belfry, see its website at www.vvvzeeland.nl/en/vakantie/museums/23866/museum-het-belfort/west-zeeuws-vlaanderen/sluis. The easiest way to visit Sluis is by car. Parking is available near the town centre. Postcode: 4524 CD.

Damme, Belgium

Margaret journeyed from Sluis by boat to the town of Damme, where her marriage would be finalised. Damme had been a primary port for Bruges before the river silted up, and it was still a prosperous place. After arriving, the citizens of Damme received her with a procession and she was presented with a 'rich copp'. The dowager duchess awaited her there with a carriage garnished with cloth of gold pulled by several horses attired in the same cloth.

Early the next morning, between five and six, Margaret and Charles were married by the bishops of Salisbury and Tournai. The wedding was attended by the dowager duchess, the Lord Scales and several of the nobility. The couple went next to Mass at the Church of Our Lady. Afterwards, Charles left Margaret so that she could enter Bruges in full celebration. She was placed in a litter, richly decorated with cloth of gold crimson. Her mantel was of cloth of gold, and furred with ermine. She was 'rychely coroned', and, accompanied by a large group of people on horseback, left to the sounds of trumpets as she journeyed to Bruges for the next portion of her wedding celebrations.

Edward and Damme

Edward and Richard spent time in Bruges while in exile. As they prepared to go back to England to do battle with Warwick, they readied for their departure from Bruges. According to Maaike Lulofs, Edward paraded on foot from Bruges to Damme in order to please the people, before leaving for Vlissingen.

Visiting Damme Today

Today, Damme is a quiet, picturesque town, filled with cyclists enjoying a summer day. The best way to journey to Damme is by the river from Bruges. While there is not much to visit in the city related to the Yorks, it is possible to see the ruins of the church where Charles and Margaret observed Mass, and the outside of the house where the wedding occurred. The Stadhuis was also there when Margaret visited. Damme postcode: 8340.

Bruges, Belgium

The new duchess made her way towards Bruges in a splendid procession. Dressed in her rich wedding clothes and wearing a crown, Margaret rode in a carriage followed by thirteen white horses; her ladies followed in carriages.

Approaching Bruges, she passed through the Kruispoort, one of the city's magnificent gates. Here, the procession meeting her was preparing. They lined up with the clerics first and began a procession towards the ducal palace, the Prinsenhof. Everyone in the procession was elaborately dressed. Before Margaret were the trumpeters and minstrels, then a group of English archers. The duke's archers surrounded the litter to protect Margaret from the crowd, and she was followed by the knights of the Golden Fleece, splendidly attired. Also escorting the litter were the nobles from England who had accompanied her.

The streets Margaret rode through had been decorated with rich cloth of gold and silk. She passed by a series of tableaux depicting mainly Biblical representations of marriage, which had been put into place for her entry into the city. As she reached the Prinsenhof, the large, brick ducal palace in Bruges, another tableau awaited. This one was of gold and azure and full of heraldic images, including the duke's motto. Two archers painted on each side had wine flowing from their arrows into stone vats for the people to drink.

As Margaret arrived at the ducal palace, the dowager duchess came out to greet her, helping her from her litter to the sound of trumpets. According to Andrew Brown and Graeme Small, the tennis court of the enormous palace had been turned into a banqueting area, with a large wooden hall especially built for the occasion. The hall measured 40 feet long by 70 feet wide, and contained several large glass windows illuminating the scene inside. A high table, covered by 'cloth of gold of tissue' overlaid with the duke's colours of purple and black, occupied almost the entire width of the hall. Steps led up to this table, while two more tables lined the other walls. A sideboard sat in the middle of the room, almost teetering under its large collection of costly plates and jewelled cups. Intricate tapestries lined the walls, and even the roof had been covered with rich cloth of blue and white to match the candelabras.

Two immense chandeliers hung from the ceiling. Designed as large castles with mountains for their bases, the chandeliers had images of people going about their daily lives at the castle. Seven large mirrors were placed around the base of each chandelier.

On the side of the hall, seven other candelabras with four lights gleamed in the shadows, their flickering glow reflecting in the mirrors. Margaret sat at the high table, with her new stepdaughter to her left and the dowager duchess to her right. The ladies sat on one side of the room and the lords and other nobles sat on the other. This banquet was just one of several planned to welcome the town's new duchess, with each one progressively more extravagant. At one of the banquets, gilded peacocks and swans covered the table. A large tournament known as the Tournament of the Golden Tree was held in Bruges's market square in Margaret's honour, with another banquet following. The ladies arrived at the tournament in their chariots, and they watched the 'wonderful' jousts.

Years later when Mary's first child was born, Margaret had the honour of carrying the baby Philip to his christening. According to Luc Hommel, a wooden gallery had been erected across the market for the procession to walk. Torches lit the way as the large procession escorted the infant and Margaret to the Church of St Donatian. Margaret, flanked by the two godfathers, Lord Ravenstein and Pierre of St Pol, carried Philip, who was dressed in crimson cloth of gold. Rumours had flown that the baby was a girl and, following the ceremony, Margaret undressed Philip and showed him to the people to the acclamation of the crowd.

The palace would hold at least one unhappy memory for Margaret. In March 1482, her stepdaughter fell from her horse and was carried to the palace. Margaret rushed to her side, but Mary succumbed to her injuries. According to Hommel, Margaret was present for Mary's funeral at the Church of Our Lady in Bruges.

Visiting the Kruispoort Today
The ancient limestone and sandstone gate where Margaret's procession gathered for her entry into the town still stands. Rebuilt in the early fifteenth century, the large gate admitted visitors into Bruges. About a fifteen-minute walk from the Markt, the Kruispoort stands on Langestraat. To get to the gate from the Markt, head towards the Burg. From the Burg, take Hoogestraat

to Langestraat. Stay on the sidewalks until you get to the gate. Standing near it, it is easy to imagine the nervous whinnying of the horses while the people found their place in line for Margaret's procession through the gate and town.

Visiting the Markt Today

Bruges is one of the places where a tourist feels that he or she has stepped back in time. The brightly coloured guild houses, the towering belfry and the energetic crowd all give the impression that you are in medieval Bruges. The Government Palace, finished now in Gothic Revival, stands where the boats to Bruges would unload their goods. The once busy guild houses, whose members profited from the trade in Bruges, are now enticing restaurants whose meals send tantalizing aromas wafting over the square.

The Belfry

Since the thirteenth century the tower of the belfry has dominated the city's skyline. The octagonal tower was not added until after the wedding celebrations, but the building would still have been an impressive site. At the time of the tournament, the belfry was topped by a large square tower with four round turrets. Here a visitor could buy Flemish cloth in one of the market halls attached to the Belfry.

The panoramic view from the top of the belfry is worth the 366 stairs it takes to get there. The climb is broken into intervals where you will see the treasury room, which once housed the town charters, and the victory bell. If the bells chime as you climb, do not expect to hear a medieval tune, since most of the tunes are current popular songs. For information about visiting times, see https://bezoekers.brugge.be/en/belfort-belfry.

Visiting the Prinsenhof Today

Unfortunately the large complex that made up the ducal palace is gone today, but a remnant does remain, attached to a luxurious hotel known as the Hotel Dukes' Palace. Margaret would have seen the tower when her litter arrived at the complex. The hotel and site of the former palace is a short walk from the Markt. Walk along Sint-Amandsstraat until you reach Korte Zilverstraat. Here take a slight right, and then turn left onto Noordzandstraat. When you see Prinsenhof, turn right and walk up the short lane until you see the gated entrance of the hotel.

Richard and George in Bruges

Richard and George visited Duke Philip in Bruges on their way back to England. Suddenly thrust into the role of brothers to the King of England, they were now welcomed guests in Burgundy and would be received by the duke.

Unfortunately the name of the building where Richard and George lodged while in Bruges has been lost. They did not stay in the ducal palace; one source says the duke visited them at their residence. They may have lodged at the home of a rich merchant or stayed in an inn. We do know, however, that a large feast was held for the boys. Livia Visser-Fuchs's translation of the town records states that the boys were given a banquet in their honour, with the duke, the ladies of the city and the nobles present. This banquet would have occurred at the Stadhuis.

Stadhuis

The city hall in Bruges was built in 1376, making it one of the oldest in Belgium. This intricately decorated Gothic hall has served as the centre of government for the city for years. Today it contains nineteenth-century paintings in vibrant colours depicting historic moments and figures in the town's history.

For the boys' feast, a high-table would have been placed on a dais at the head of the room, with George and Richard seated beside Duke Philip as honoured guests. Entertainment would have been provided, since the duke's court was known for its sophistication and grandeur. Originally the room was divided into a vestibule and an aldermen's hall. The minstrels' balcony was above and to the left. Today the area is the demarcation line between the two rooms. The banquet would have taken place in the aldermen's hall.

In medieval times, the vaulting would have been just as richly decorated as it is now, with bright colours and vivid images covering the ceiling, and intricately woven tapestries hanging on the walls. Today the smaller hall adjoining the alderman's hall serves for a museum, where several artefacts tell the story of the region throughout several centuries.

Visiting the Stadhuis Today

The Stadhuis is open seven days a week. At the time of writing, its opening hours were from 9:30 a.m. until 5 p.m. It is always best to double check the website at https://bezoekers.brugge.be/en/stadhuis-city-hall before visiting.

Basilica of the Holy Blood

Another area of interest in the Burgh is the Basilica of the Holy Blood. The church's most revered relic was the blood of Christ. Tradition holds that Joseph of Arimathea wiped some blood from the body of Christ and kept the cloth, which was later brought back to Bruges by one of the returning Crusaders, probably Count Thierry of Alsace.

The Basilica houses two chapels. The lower Romanesque chapel is the older crypt of Saint Basil. A simple chapel, it was built in the mid-twelfth century. The Gothic chapel above was rebuilt in the fifteenth century and restored in the nineteenth century. Today, the chapel is highly decorated with a riot of colour and murals. Try to time your visit for when the vial containing the blood is taken from its golden reliquary for pilgrims and visitors to touch and pray over. On at least one occasion, Margaret and Mary took part in the magnificent procession of the Holy Blood from the Basilica through the streets. The annual procession, dating from the thirteenth century, left from the church before proceeding around the city walls. By the fifteenth century mystery plays had been added to the ceremonial procession.

Visiting the Basilica Today

The Basilica of the Holy Blood is located in the right corner of the Burg. The façade was reconstructed in the nineteenth century, so its outside appearance would have been vastly different in the medieval time. Check the website to determine when the chapel is open, and if you are interested, in times that you may touch the vial of blood. www.holyblood.com/.

St Donatian's church, which would have been one of the main buildings of the Burg, has been lost to history. It would have been an impressive church, since it was chosen for the christening of Philip.

Edward and Richard in Bruges

When Edward and Richard fled to the Low Countries as exiles, they were guests of Louis Gruuthuse, the governor of Holland and Zeeland. Much of their time was spent in his home in The Hague, but on their way to talk with Charles the Bold, they stopped in Bruges at Gruuthuse's main residence in the city. Nestled between a canal and the Church of Our Lady, Gruuthuse's home was an excellent example of Burgundian splendour. A large courtyard led to intricately decorated buildings. Louis had recently added a south wing on to his already palatial building, so the home Edward and Richard visited was quite extensive. While Edward and Richard would not have seen it, Louis may have shared his plans with them to build an oratory adjoining the Church of Our Lady.

Visiting the Gruuthuse Museum (Gruuthusemuseum) Today

Closed due to substantial renovations, the Gruuthuse museum is expected to reopen in 2017. Before its closure, the museum focused on a collection of fine lace, tapestries and other objects. Upon its reopening it is expected to focus more on the history of Bruges. Make sure to see the oratory that allowed Louis and his family to watch services in the church of Our Lady without ever leaving home. Gruuthuse was buried in the church of Our Lady, but it is not possible to visit his tomb. Be sure to visit the museum website to check for updated opening times to avoid disappointment: https://bezoekers.brugge.be/en/gruuthusemuseum

Visiting Bruges Today

Bruges celebrates its medieval heritage, and it is easy to feel the bonds of time slipping away as you wander its streets, glide along its canals and visit its museums. It would be easy to spend days in Bruges without exhausting its medieval connections. Make sure to visit several of the churches in the city, especially the church of Our Lady, where Margaret's husband and stepdaughter are buried. The church is next to the Gruuthuse museum and its spire can easily be seen from most of the surrounding area.

Traveling to Bruges is easy. Trains make the journey from Brussels several times an hour. For more information, visit www.belgianrail.be/. While you do not want to drive into the heart of the city, parking is available in large multi-storey car parks nearby. For more information, visit, www.car-parking.eu/belgium/bruges.

Brussels, Belgium

For much of Margaret's married life, she travelled from ducal residence to ducal residence across her husband's lands. During the course of her travels, she often stopped in Brussels. Today, the city is the nation's capital and home to the headquarters of the European Union. A cosmopolitan city even in Margaret's time, Brussels still hums with energy. While many of the sites she would have known are gone today, it is possible to catch a glimpse of Margaret's Brussels. The palace she once inhabited is gone, but archaeologists have uncovered its foundations. Churches she visited still exist, and a careful observer can still make out medieval buildings.

Shortly after her wedding, Margaret, accompanied by Mary, was received at the city gates on her visit to Brussels. Her entry into the city may not have been as lavish as the ones at Mons and Bruges, but the city would have greeted her with gifts and pageantry.

Coudenberg Palace, Brussels

While in Brussels, Margaret and Mary would have stayed at the ducal palace, the Coudenberg. A large complex, the palace was surrounded by an extensive park known as the Warande where Margaret and Mary could spend time hunting deer. A visitor to the castle in the early sixteenth century, Albrecht Dürer, said that behind the palace were fountains, a labyrinth and a park. The delights of the palace caused him to say, 'Anything more beautiful ... more like a paradise, I have never seen.'

From paintings of the palace, it is possible to get an idea of its appearance. A large inner courtyard was enclosed by buildings several storeys high. Many of the buildings had turrets topped with conical domes. According to Margaret's biographer, Christine Weightman, the Coudenberg was one of the few ducal palaces large enough to house both Margaret's and Charles's households at the same time. Trees had been planted within the gardens to provide delicious fruit for the ducal table.

Unfortunately, a fire destroyed the great palace in the early eighteenth century and the Place Royale was built on top of the ruins. Today a visitor can see the underground remains of the palace and the Rue Isabelle. Entrance is through the museum at Belvue-7 Place des Palais, 1000 Bruxelles. For more information about visiting the site, see the website at http://www.coudenberg. com/en/.

Cathedral Church of St Michael and St Gudula, Brussels

On two occasions Margaret stood as godmother in this church. When Mary and Maximilian had a daughter, they named her Margaret, after the dowager duchess. Weightman says that Margaret stood as godmother for this baby, who would later be known as Margaret of Austria, in this church. On another occasion she had the honour of carrying Philip and Joanna's first child, Eleanor, to her christening in November 1498. Margaret carried the baby in the procession from the palace to the Church of St Michael and St Gudula.

In 1495, Margaret was here for the proxy weddings of Margaret of Austria to Don Juan, the heir to the Spanish throne, and of Philip to Joanna of Castile. Hommel says she stood as witness to the double wedding.

As early as the ninth century people were worshipping on this spot. The church as it stands today was begun in the thirteenth century but was not completely finished until the reign of Charles V. An interesting mixture of styles, it became a cathedral in the twentieth century.

To get to the church from the Coudenburg, turn right on the Rue Royale and walk along the Parc de Bruxelles, which once formed part of the Coudenburg's Warande. After a short walk, turn left on Treurenberg. The cathedral will be in front of you.

Before entering, take some time to look at the beautiful front of the church. On a slight hill, the towers of the building are easily seen from a distance. As you enter, you will see statues of the twelve apostles adorning the columns in the nave. These baroque additions would not have been here when Margaret carried Eleanor to the font.

According to an early nineteenth-century description by John Weale, the chancel aisles had chapels, which were separated from the aisles by arches 'springing from clustered columns with crocketed capitals'. Much of what is seen within the church today dates from after Margaret's time. The beautifully carved, dark wooden pulpit dates from 1699, while the Lady Chapel was not completed until the seventeenth century. The lower part of the pulpit contains an image of Adam and Eve being expelled from the Garden of Eden, while the upper part shows Mary holding Christ and a cross and crushing the serpent below.

Visiting Today
The church is open to visitors. For more information about opening times, see its website at http://www.cathedralisbruxellensis.be/en. Be sure to walk around to the front of the church to get a close view of the statues embellishing its face.

Notre Dame de Carmes, Brussels
Another location that Margaret would have visited in Brussels is the church of the Carmelites. When the future Charles V was presented to the Order of the Golden Fleece on 21 January 1501, Margaret was selected to present the heir to his father. The knights, dressed in scarlet 'hoods and scarlet mantels that reached to the feet and were fringed with gold', proceeded to the church from the Coudenberg. Trumpeters welcomed the knights and marched with them to the church.

The church had been richly decorated with tapestries, including the famous *History of Gideon*. According to Jeffrey Chipps Smith in his work on Burgundian tapestries, the eight pieces that made up the tapestry set were together about 320 feet long and were intricately woven with gold and silver threads and silks. Precious stones were sewn into the cloth, which 'stood out and twinkled like stars'. The tapestry had also decorated the hall when Margaret and Charles had married. Prospero da Camogli described the set as 'marvelous works depicting the whole story of how the golden fleece was sent down from heaven to Gideon as a sign that he was to undertake the salvation of the people of Israel'. Following the ceremony a lavish banquet was held at the palace, resembling the banquet at Saint Omer which had consisted of fifty courses 'borne through the hall in a grand procession of trumpeters and other musicians'.

Unfortunately the Carmelite church was destroyed in the seventeenth century. Portions of it were used to build the Church

Saint-Jacques sur Coudenberg. Notre Dame de Carmes was located on the Rue de Namur, near the Place Royale.

Visiting Brussels Today

Brussels is a bustling city full of tourists and international politicians. It is easy to reach from England since Eurostar has routes straight from London. It makes a good hub for exploring the other sites in Belgium. Make sure to visit the Town Hall since the building would have existed in Margaret's time. The city has a park-and-ride scheme for drivers: http://www.car-parking.eu/belgium/brussels/pr. See the website for information and for the car parks' different postcodes.

Ghent, Belgium

Although the area had been settled from prehistoric times, a true city started to take shape at the confluence of the Rivers Scheldt and Leie under the Romans. By the twelfth century, Ghent had become an important trading centre and was one of the largest cities in Europe.

While Margaret often moved from place to place within her husband's lands, she spent much of her time in Ghent. One of the more volatile regions in her husband's duchy, the citizens of Ghent had often caused discord in Charles's domains. Prior to his marriage to Margaret, Charles had been forced to flee Ghent after an uprising by its citizens.

The city received its new duchess with a grand procession, much like the one at Brussels. Margaret stayed at the castle of Ten Walle while in Ghent, with Mary often at her side.

Ten Walle Castle, Ghent

The castle at Ten Walle was an enormous residence. Three gateways gave access to the large enclave full of chambers and courtyards. Margaret would have reached the main courtyard and palace structure by a bridge over the moat. A ducal menagerie, complete with lions, was kept within the castle gates. Margaret, Mary and Charles each had their own apartments, situated around a courtyard with a garden nearby. Since most of the Burgundian palaces had a gallery connecting the buildings, Ten Walle probably did too. Heraldic symbols decorated the structure, and intricate tapestries hung on its walls. This castle, with its opulent interior, is where Margaret spent most of her Christmases while Duchess of Burgundy.

In July 1469, Margaret received an English embassy at Ghent. She was still here when word of the rebellions in England reached her. Given her political acumen, she was probably worried for both herself and her brother. If she were not the sister of the English king, she would lose some of her political prestige. Margaret demonstrated time and time again how dedicated she was to both her family and her native country, and she probably worried about how she could help her brother.

On 31 January 1470, an embassy from England arrived, carrying a gift from Edward for Charles. The jewelled garter was a symbol of Charles's acceptance into the Order of the Garter. In a ceremony on 4 February Charles was presented the garter, along with the mantle and other symbols, when he took the oath and was received into the Order. Margaret watched as Charles accepted this symbol of brotherhood between her brother and her husband.

Margaret learned of Edward's success over the Lancastrians while at Ten Walle. It is easy to imagine her delight and relief that the main threat to her brother's throne had been eliminated. She soon welcomed another embassy from England at Ten Walle.

Weightman states that Margaret presided over the opening of the assembly of the Estates in 1476, after the defeat at Grandson, and advised them of the duke's requests for both more men and money. Another of the requests was that Mary would be able to go to her father in Burgundy. The Estates did not agree with the requests, forcing Margaret to try to persuade individuals outside the meeting.

It was at Ghent that Margaret and Mary received the devastating news that Charles was believed dead at the siege of Nancy. While they grieved, Margaret guided Mary in her next steps. Louis was an obvious threat, but the discord in Ghent was also an issue. In the period following Charles's death, two of his former advisers were executed. Eventually, even Margaret was forced to leave Ghent, leaving Mary virtually alone.

Margaret did not go quietly however. Her public proclamation that, although she was a foreigner by virtue of her birth, she was no foreigner in her heart, shows a woman with undaunted courage. She also refused to leave until she heard from Mary that she was unharmed.

Margaret's biographer, Luc Hommel, gives an account of the marriage of Mary and Maximilian. Margaret arrived back in Ghent prior to the wedding and hosted a massive celebration in Ten Walle's reception hall. As flickering candles lit the room, Margaret made sure to seat the dignitaries next to 'une jolie dame de la cour' (a pretty lady of the court). She was also present for the private wedding ceremony of Mary and Maximilian in the chapel at Ten Walle. Hommel adds details, saying that Margaret kissed them both and said, 'Here at last is the happiness you both desire.'

Visiting Ten Walle Today

The castle Ten Walle, which later became known as the Prinsenhof, no longer exists. However, it is possible to walk to where it once stood. From the Groten Markt, cross the river on Geldmunt and turn left on Burgstraat. From here you have an excellent view of the Castle of the Counts, also known as Gravensteen. Margaret would have seen this castle, with its rounded turrets, often during her time in Ghent. Turn right onto Gewad and follow it until it becomes Prinsenhof. At Prinsenhof Plein you will see the 'dark gate' of the old castle. Be sure to walk through the gate to see the unusual statue there.

St Bavo's Cathedral, Ghent

After Charles V was born, Margaret was asked to stand godmother to the young infant. The baptism of the heir was celebrated lavishly in Ghent. Red wine flowed from fountains, mystery plays were performed and mummers entertained the crowds. A gallery had been erected high above the crowd, connecting the belfry with the nearby church of St Nicholas. At night the gallery was illuminated, casting a 'brilliant glow' over the festivities. Margaret would have carried the heir from the castle to the church, where she would have taken him to the font at the church of St John, now the cathedral church of St Bavo.

Initially dedicated to St John the Baptist, the church building was replaced in the twelfth century by a Romanesque building. By the fourteenth century, a Gothic chancel had been built. In 1432, the church received one of its most enduring decorations, the *Adoration of the Mystic Lamb*. Margaret would have been familiar with the altar painting hanging in the chapel of Adam and Eve, which Albrecht Dürer said was 'very rich and grandly conceived'.

Margaret would not have seen the tower that dominates the skyline today, since work was not begun on it until 1462 and not completed until 1536. In 1540, St Bavo's abbey was abolished, and the chapter moved to St John's. Following this, the church's name changed to St Bavo's church. Margaret would not recognise the nave because it was replaced by a Gothic one in the late sixteenth century. The church also received cathedral status during the sixteenth century.

The church played host to two meetings of the Order of the Golden Fleece. The first meeting was in 1445, and the blazons of the knights can be seen in the church. More blazons from the Order's meeting in 1559 are located in the southern transept.

Margaret may have also been familiar with the crypt, which housed many of the holy relics. According to the church, Easter plays were often performed in the crypt, which also had a Holy Sepulchre Chapel. Perhaps Margaret, like her brothers, enjoyed watching religious plays.

Another painting in the crypt that Margaret may have seen is the painting of Calvary, with its two side panels depicting scenes from the life of Moses. This painting is much larger than the other Calvary painting which dates from the early seventeenth century. Before leaving the crypt, be sure to see the remains of the medieval frescoes, which date from Margaret's time. One of the paintings depicts St Margaret.

The church would hold one sad memory for Margaret. It was here that the memorial service was held for Charles. Hommel says that both Margaret and Mary attended the service, although the women were still holding out hope that Charles was still alive.

Visiting St Bavo's Cathedral Today

Visitors today will see a church much different than the one Margaret visited. The *Adoration of the Mystic Lamb* has been moved from its place in the chapel of Adam and Eve to a more secure location. It is still possible to view the exquisite painting, but be sure to check the website to see if it is open to the public on the day of your visit. Be aware that from 2013 the tower of the church is undergoing renovations that will last at least four years. For more information about visiting St Bavo's Cathedral, see http:// www.sintbaafskathedraal.be/.

Visiting Ghent Today

In addition to visiting the locations described above, you may also want to visit a few places in Ghent that do not have a deep connection with Margaret. However, these buildings all existed during her tenure in Ghent. The Gravensteen, the Belfort (Belfry), St Niklaaskerk, the Stadhuis, the Dulle Griet cannon, the guildhalls, and, if it is open, St Bavo's Abbey all help one picture the Ghent that Margaret knew. To see all that Ghent has to offer could take several days.

While it is possible to drive to Ghent, public transportation is an easy option. Trains run from Brussels several times daily. Be aware that the train station is outside of the city centre and you will need to take either a bus or a tram. You must pre-purchase tickets for the buses from a machine located outside of the terminal.

Mechelen, Belgium

Margaret spent most of her time as dowager duchess within the city of Mechelen, also known by Malines. Here she set up her principal residence, with Olivier de la Marche as master of her household. Located on the Dyle River, Mechelen was a prosperous trading town surrounded by high walls and impressive gates. Margaret's husband had made it the seat of the Grand Council, and the town had flourished under Burgundian rule, competing with Brussels for trade.

Margaret's Palace in Mechelen

Mechelen benefited from Margaret's presence there; the town contributed to the construction of her palace. Margaret and her household often participated in local events, including St Rumbold's day. When Emperor Frederick came to Mechelen in 1487, Margaret and the town ensured he enjoyed a royal welcome.

Margaret would have received most of her news from England while at Mechelen. In her palace she would have learned of

Edward's death, the disappearance of her nephews and Richard's ascension to the throne. She would also have been here when she learned of the death of her brother at Bosworth. While she may have grieved at the loss of her brothers, she had business in Mechelen that needed her attention. Although she would be a thorn in Henry's side, much of her focus was on Burgundy. This did not preclude her from hosting Perkin Warbeck and other exiled Yorkists at her court, however.

In July 1485, Philip was placed in her care in Mechelen. Margaret had spent time putting the palace in order and gathering a household for him. After Philip's father, Maximilian, was captured Margaret increased the defences in Mechelen in order to protect the young duke.

Margaret had purchased her palace from the Bishop of Cambrai. While the property was extensive, Margaret embarked on a building spree to make it even grander, building most of the palace in white stone from Brabant. She had a Great Hall erected parallel to the street, even though the complex had an existing hall standing perpendicular to the street. From an eighteenth-century engraving we can get an idea of how the palace was organised. Large gardens abutted the back of the buildings. The palace had several ranges of buildings built around courtyards. A large building towards the back of the complex was several stories with a span of gable windows. Unfortunately only a small section of the palace remains and is not open to the public.

Before Archduchess Joanna arrived, Margaret moved out of the palace and across the street to the oldest part of what would become Margaret of Austria's palace. She did not undertake extensive building works here, although a gallery was built across the street so that she could reach her private oratory in the church of St Peter and St Paul.

Visiting the Palace Today

It is possible to see the exterior of what remains of Margaret's palace. Today the building is the City Theatre, known as the Stadsschouwburg. As you walk up to the building, head to the little door in the tower where you can see the arms of Margaret and Charles the Bold. Across the street is the Palace of Margaret of Austria, which is also worth a visit.

Make your way back to the Grote Markt, where you will see the large tower of the cathedral of St Rumbold (Rombout). Margaret would not have seen the tower soar as high as it does now, since it was still under construction during her lifetime. While the interior of the church dates from the baroque, it is a beautiful church and worth a visit. After the bones of St Rumbold were dug up in the cathedral, Margaret was present at an exhibition of his relics in 1480. Following your visit to the cathedral, make your way to its west entrance.

Margaret's Burial

The church of the Franciscans once stood across the street from the cathedral. On 23 November 1503, Margaret died and was buried, according to her will, within this church in the city she had adopted as her own. While nothing remains today of her tomb, manuscripts paint a picture of its appearance. In his article in *The Ricardian*, '"Danse Macabre" Around the Tomb and Bones of Margaret of York', Paul de Win includes a translation describing the tomb. He believes that her monument was two parts, erected in an arch. On one side was Margaret kneeling with St Margaret, while on the other was her alabaster tomb, which included her crowned effigy surrounded by three friars, with an angel supporting her coat of arms.

Her monument was destroyed during the religious wars that raged in the sixteenth century, and there is still debate over where it stood. Several digs within the church produced bones, but none that could be proven to be the remains of the dowager duchess. Today the church is a cultural centre, and the only mention of Margaret is the plaque on the side of the building placed there by the Richard III Society. Perhaps one day Margaret's bones will be found and reinterred with pomp and ceremony.

Visiting Mechelen

The two locations relevant to Margaret are not all the city has to offer. Several medieval buildings remain and offer a glimpse into the Mechelen that Margaret knew and loved. I recommend Mechelen for a base from which to explore the nearby cities of Ghent and Brussels, because it is not as crowded and has a cosy atmosphere. Mechelen is easily reached by train from Brussels. If you wish to drive, the city has garages that offer 24-hour stays. For more information about travelling to the city, including opening times and accommodations, please contact the tourist information centre at http://toerisme.mechelen.be/en.

Part 9
Anne, Elizabeth and Edmund

Anne, Duchess of Exeter

Anne was the elder sister of Edward IV, George and Richard III. She was probably born at Fotheringhay in 1439. In 1446, she married Henry Holland, Duke of Exeter. The couple had one child, also named Anne. It must have been difficult for the duchess to be married to Exeter once he chose to align himself with the Lancastrians against her father and brothers.

After Exeter's attainder in 1461, Anne received grants of lands from her brother, including much of the Exeter inheritance. She also retained custody of her daughter, the heiress to the Exeter fortune. She betrothed her daughter first to George Neville, the son of John Neville, but the match was later replaced by one with the son of the queen, Thomas Grey.

Anne later divorced Exeter and married Thomas St Leger. Her first daughter, Anne, had died, and when she and St Leger had a daughter they also named her Anne. Soon after her daughter's birth, Anne died and was buried at St George's Chapel at Windsor.

Dartington Hall, Devon

Constructed on a low rise overlooking the River Dart, there has been a residence here since at least the twelfth century. The lands passed to the Crown, and Richard II granted the area to his half-brother, John de Holland, who is credited with much of the building of the immense structure. He envisioned a set of buildings laid out in a large double quadrangle. Later, the home came to

Henry Holland, and was eventually granted to Anne by Edward IV on account of 'the true and deep affection which the aforesaid Anne, our sister, has and bears towards us'.

The earliest part of the structure was the old hall, located at the north-east corner of the quadrangle, which dates from the early fourteenth century. The west side of the court contained the buildings built by Holland, including a new hall and kitchen. The hall was to lie between the two quadrangles. According to Anthony Emery, the courtyard was immense at 265 feet by 164 feet and was never spanned by any range.

Dartington Hall was described by a visitor in the nineteenth century:

> Dartington Hall is one of the most picturesque and charming seats in Devon; noble ruins, a fine old mansion, ancient outbuildings, surrounded by quaintly-terraced and beautifully-kept gardens, and lying in the midst of a richly-wooded, undulating park, almost within sound of the murmur of the rushing Dart.

Following Anne's death, the home passed through a series of hands until it came to rest with the Champernowne family. It remained with this family until the twentieth century. By the time the Elmhirst family took ownership in 1925, it had fallen into a severe state of ruin. They restored the home, including the Great Hall with its massive fireplace and ornate hammer-beam roof.

Visiting Dartington Hall Today

Not only can you visit the hall, you can also spend the night in one of its chambers. For those who want to spend a day here, the visitor centre offers a map of the grounds. The estate contains a cinema and gardens, along with a chance to visit some of the medieval sections. Once you have explored the grounds, a wide range of dining choices is available. Parking is on-site. For more information, visit the website at https://www.dartington.org/visit/. Dartington Hall postcode: TQ9 6EE.

Coldharbour, London

Coldharbour was the London home of the dukes of Exeter. It was owned and enlarged by Sir John Pulteney about 1335. During the reign of Richard II, the home came to John Holland and remained in the family; it was part of the Exeter inheritance that Edward IV later granted to Anne. When Anne came to court she would have stayed in the home, which Stow called 'a right fair and stately house'.

The home had at least forty rooms, including both a great hall and a little hall. The Great Hall fronted the water and had an entrance into the interior garden, which would have had a bench for Anne to rest. The other garden was between the river and the mansion. C. L. Kingsford believes that the mansion was quite large. He states that Coldharbour

> certainly extended from Thames Street to the river, a distance of about 300 ft. The frontage in Thames Street to the east of All Hallows Church would not have been more than about 60 ft. But ... Sir John Pulteney built the steeple of All Hallows the Less over an arched gate, and his mansion no doubt extended westwards behind the church.

Kingsford believes that the mansion extended to Wolses Gate, giving it a river frontage of about 150 feet. This was a large home, even compared to other medieval mansions. Hollar's view of the structure shows it sitting directly next to the river, but descriptions show there was a garden between it and the river. The mansion also had a watergate, but it is unclear exactly where this was positioned.

Anne probably lodged in the Great Chamber over the Great Hall, where several windows provided a view of the river. If so, she would have walked across the Great Chamber's floor with its medieval tiles to stand at the window overlooking the river. Alternatively, she may have lodged in the large chamber above the Little Hall.

The home also had its own chapel, which had several windows. The walls would have been lined with tapestries or brightly coloured paintings. Statues of the Virgin Mary and of other saints would have adorned the interior.

Other Yorks and Coldharbour

Margaret of York stayed at the riverside mansion on her state visit to England in 1480. For this occasion, two curtains of green sarsenet were procured for the chapel, and sheets, fustians and a tapestry with the story of Paris and Helen were issued to decorate the home. Red worsted, green sarsenet with a green silk ribbon and sheets of Holland cloth were also provided for her stay.

After taking the throne, Richard III granted the home to the College of Heralds. It was only in the heralds' hands a short time, since Henry VII soon gave it to his mother, Margaret Beaufort. By this time, the home was again in need of repair. New chimneys were added, along with new lattice and glass for the windows. The walls had to be 'recoloured with red Motty, Cole, and Oker'. The lady's chamber windows were re-glazed with 28 feet of Normandy glass, and the Great Chamber received 8 feet of 'florysche' glass, probably stained or otherwise ornamented.

After Bosworth, Henry had Elizabeth and her mother installed in his mother's mansion so he could meet with Elizabeth privately. For a short time, Henry stayed nearby at Baynard's Castle. Alison Weir believes that Elizabeth's sisters also joined her at Coldharbour, along with the Earl of Warwick. Chambers were set aside for Elizabeth's use and one of the rooms in the mansion became known as Lady Elizabeth's Chamber. According to Kingsford, 'for the Lady Elizabeth's Chamber there were provided a table and two trestles ... and four boards which cost 8*d.*, and six sawdelet bars were fitted to the west window'.

Apparently this time together allowed affection to flourish between the couple. In the *Calendar of Papal Registers Relating to Great Britain and Ireland*, Stanley's testimony states that he heard Henry and Elizabeth

> often and at divers times treating and communing of and about a marriage to be contracted between them ... And further he says that the same king is moved and led thus to contract marriage with the said lady for the sake of the peace and tranquillity of his realm ... And further he says that the aforesaid lady has not been captured nor compelled, but of great and intimate love and cordial affection desires to contract marriage with the said king ...

The Earl of Nottingham agreed, adding that Henry wanted to marry Elizabeth 'both on account of the singular love which he bears to her, and also on account of the special prayers and entreaties of the lords and nobles, both spiritual and temporal, and of the whole commonalty of his said realm of England'. Elizabeth would stay at the mansion for several weeks awaiting her marriage to Henry. George's son, Edward, would only spend a short time within the mansion's walls before he was moved to the Tower of London.

This would not be Elizabeth's only visit to the mansion. According to Weir, when news of rebels reached Sheen, Henry sent Elizabeth with an escort to retrieve her young children at Eltham and return to London. Once she was in London, she first stayed at Margaret's home before removing to the Tower for safety.

Visiting Coldharbour Today

Sadly, as with other London mansions, including the Erber, there is nothing left of this once palatial residence on the banks of the Thames. It is possible, however, to visit the general location of the former home. The nearest tube stop is Cannon Street station. Turn left on Cannon Street and then left again on Dowgate Hill. Turn left on to Upper Thames Street and then right on to Angel Lane. At the bottom of the hill, turn right on to Hanseatic Walk. This area is the general spot where the home would have been located. While in the area, you might also want to visit the location of the Erber and Baynard's Castle.

St George's Chapel, Windsor

St George's Chapel is one of only three Chapels Royal and has played a significant role in the spiritual life of those worshipping here. A church has stood here since the reign of Henry III, who established a church dedicated to Edward the Confessor in the Lower Ward. Very little is left of Henry III's church, which stood on the site of what is now the Albert Memorial Chapel.

Anne, Duchess of Exeter and St George's Chapel

After her death (prior to 1476), Anne, Duchess of Exeter, was buried in St George's Chapel. She and her second husband, Thomas St Leger, were interred in the Rutland chantry, in the north nave aisle. While chantry priests were arranged to pray for Anne, the magnificent tomb in the chantry is that of her daughter and her daughter's husband, George Manners. Anne was already dead by the time Thomas took part in Buckingham's rebellion and was executed by her brother, Richard. When mt-DNA testing was completed on the bones found in Leicester, the DNA used for comparison came from Anne's descendants.

Edward IV and St George's Chapel

When Edward III established the Order of the Garter, he founded the College of St George and made the chapel the spiritual home of the Order. The chapel eventually fell into decay, and Edward IV decided to renovate it. His program involved extensive works, as he almost rebuilt the entire chapel, although it would not be completed until the sixteenth century. By the time of his death, the choir and aisles had been completed, with carvings of the canopies and stall already underway. He doubled the size of the college and number of priests and choristers serving the chapel and spent lavish amounts on the rich vestments and wall hangings, as well as statues and carvings.

Edward IV left detailed instructions for the design of his chantry in his will. He wanted to be buried beneath a stone which was 'wrought with the figure of death with scutcheons of our arms and writings convenient about the bordure of the same remembering the day and year of our decease, and that in the same place or near to it an altar be made'. Above the 'figure of death', he wanted a vault to be placed and on his tomb an image for 'our figure, which figure we will be of silver and gilt or at the least copper and gilt'. Unfortunately, Edward's untimely death occurred before his tomb was finished, and neither his figure of death nor his effigy were ever completed. In the eighteenth century, his burial was marked with the current stone. Richard III had Henry VI's body brought from Chertsey Abbey and had it reinterred in St George's Chapel, directly across from Edward's tomb.

The Order of the Garter and St George's Chapel

The Order of the Garter is the oldest chivalric order in England and consists of the sovereign and twenty-five knights. There is some confusion surrounding the dating of the order, but most historians agree that it was established by 1348. Tradition holds that it was founded after a lady dropped her garter, which Edward III picked up to give back to her. Seeing the stares of those around him, he said, 'Evil unto him who thinks evil of it.' This gave him the idea to form an order using a garter as its emblem and to make St George its patron saint. Another theory is that the order came out of war with the French.

While Edward IV was king, a celebration was held each year for the Order which included the installation of new knights and a service in St George's Chapel. Several Knights of the Order were installed in Edward's time, including his brothers George and Richard, as well as Anthony Woodville and Charles, Duke of Burgundy. During Richard's reign, the new Knights of the Order included Thomas Stanley, Thomas Howard, Edward Brampton and Francis Lovell. Lovell and Howard were both later degraded (stripped of their honour), although Howard was ultimately reinstated.

Visiting the Chapel Today

There are several memorials and tombs related to the Wars of the Roses in the chapel today. Entrance to the chapel is through the south door. Walk through the south nave aisle and make your way to the centre of the nave. Even though construction of the nave started during Richard's lifetime, he would never see the stone vaulting spanning it since the nave was not completed until the sixteenth century.

The Rutland Chantry where Richard's sister Anne was buried is located in the north choir aisle, and so is the Hastings Chantry. William, Lord Hastings, had been an ardent supporter and friend of Edward IV. After Edward's death, Hastings supported Richard as protector, and for a time the two men were united in a common goal. However, on 13 June 1483, Hastings was executed at the Tower on Richard's orders. The charge was conspiracy, and whether or not such a conspiracy existed has been hotly debated by historians throughout the centuries. The chantry is constructed in exquisite detail, with four scenes from the life and death of St Stephen decorating it.

After leaving the chantry, make your way up the north choir aisle until you reach the tomb of Edward IV. Edward and Elizabeth's grave is marked with a stone slab placed there in the eighteenth century. The elaborately decorated chantry chapel is only a portion of what Edward had envisioned, but it is still beautiful.

Make your way back down the aisle to the choir. Above the stalls in the choir hang the banners of the Knights of the Garter. Below each banner is a crest on top of a helm. Unlike the banners and other regalia, the stall plates on the back of each seat are not removed upon the death of the knight and many of the plates from the earliest Knights of the Garter still remain. The Sovereign's stall is the largest and contains a misericord which commemorates the Treaty of Picquigny; you can see a replica of the misericord in the south choir aisle. The oriel window overlooking the choir was constructed in the Edward IV chantry on the orders of Henry VIII, who built it so Katherihe of Aragon could view the services.

The tomb of Henry VI is located in the south choir aisle. A large marble slab marks the location of the king's grave. Soon after his reinterment, miracles began to occur at his tomb, so an alms box was placed there to collect money from the pilgrims. On your way out of the chapel, pause to see the Albert Memorial Chapel and the fragment of a medieval wall painting nearby.

Windsor Castle will be discussed in the section on the nieces and nephews of Richard, but it and St George's Chapel are popular tourist spots and become crowded in the summer months. At certain times, St George's Chapel is closed. It is best to check out the website before visiting. For more information on admission, see www.royalcollection.org.uk/visit/windsorcastle. Postcode: SL4 1NJ.

Elizabeth, Duchess of Suffolk

Elizabeth was the fifth child and second daughter born to Cecily and Richard. She was born during their tenure in Rouen on 22 April 1444 and was christened in Rouen Cathedral (see section on Rouen Cathedral), with Jacquetta, Duchess of Bedford, standing as her godmother. In 1458, Elizabeth married John de la Pole, Duke of Suffolk. At the time of their marriage, John was still in his minority. Elizabeth had not yet achieved the status of sister to the king, but she was daughter of a duke and married as such.

Her husband John was the son of William de la Pole and Alice Chaucer. Their marriage may have been a way to try to reconcile the York and Lancastrian parties. Richard had been one of the voices calling for the attainder of John's father, William, but by 1458, his daughter was marrying William's son. If it were an attempt to bring the Yorks into the Lancastrian fold, it failed miserably since it brought the young duke to the Yorkist side instead. John fought on the side of the Yorks both at St Albans and at Towton.

John did not come into his lands right away, and despite his ties to the York family failed to receive the many grants of lands and offices he may have expected as both the king's supporter and brother-in-law. He and Elizabeth had several children, and it seems unusual that John did not push for more lands. Elizabeth stayed in contact with her family and was present at great state events like funerals and weddings. It is unclear how much time Elizabeth and John spent at court, but it appears they spent much of their time on their lands.

Wingfield, Suffolk

The young couple spent most of their early married life at their manor at Wingfield since Alice Chaucer still retained rights to Ewelme Manor and spent much of her time there. The first lord of Wingfield was Robert de Wingfield. The land passed to the de la Pole's through the marriage of the Wingfield heiress to Michael de la Pole.

Wingfield Castle

Elizabeth and John would have spent much of their time at Wingfield Castle. In this moated manor house a few miles from Eye, the couple would begin their marriage. Elizabeth would have crossed the drawbridge over the moat before entering through the gateway. The portcullis would have been drawn up for her entry into the home. On each side of the gateway were the arms of her new family – the De la Poles and the Wingfields. After passing through the gatehouse with its turreted towers flanking each side, she would have entered into the courtyard.

Michael de la Pole had been given a licence to crenellate the home in April 1385 'with stone and lime or paling of timber, and also enclose all their woods, lands, meadows and pastures'. He converted the existing home into a sizable residence and enclosed his lands. Unfortunately, he did not have long to enjoy his new lands before he was accused of treason. He escaped to Paris where he died in 1389. His son, another Michael, inherited. By the time the home came to Elizabeth and John, the de la Poles were firmly established in the region.

The castle was set up in a quadrangle plan, with the Great Hall along the west side of the building. Elizabeth's chambers would have been nearby. Here she would have given birth to several of her seven sons and four daughters.

Her husband seems to have taken to heart the advice his father had written to him prior to the elder William's death. He had written,

> Thirdly, in the same wise, I charge you, my dear son, alway as ye be bounden by the commandment of God to do, to love, to worship, your lady and mother; and also that ye obey always her commandments, and to believe her counsels and advices in all your works, the which dread not but shall be best and truest to you. And if any other body would steer you to the contrary, to flee the counsel in any wist', for ye shall find it naught and evil ...

John was apparently willing to do his mother's bidding, because when Alice wanted to choose a sheriff, she sent her son and new daughter-in-law to plead the case with the Duke of York. Alice and John had several land disputes with the Paston family. According to Helen Castor in her work on the family, the Pastons thought they might have better luck petitioning Elizabeth than the duke.

While she seemed content to stay on her husband's lands, Elizabeth did go to court on family occasions. In one instance, there seems to have been no place available for her to stay. She wrote to John Paston, asking him 'to lend your lodging for three or four days until I may be purveyed of another and I shall do as much to your pleasure. For God's sake, say me not nay' (modern translation).

Following the death of the last de la Pole son, the manor was granted to Charles Brandon, Duke of Suffolk, who exchanged it for other lands. The home passed through a series of hands, undergoing renovations throughout subsequent centuries.

The castle is in private hands today and is not open to visitors. Most of the castle that Elizabeth and John would have known has been restored and renovated, and a portion of the wall and the gatehouse are the only extensive remains. The castle entrance is a short walk away from the church, but little can be seen from the road.

St Andrew's Church, Wingfield

Construction on the present church was begun in the mid-fourteenth century on the site of an earlier church. Built of a mixture of flint and stone and topped with red-bricked battlements, it was a collegiate church founded by Sir John de Wingfield and his wife. According to the church, William de la Pole erected arches, lengthened the chancel and inserted a large East Window into the building. Portions of the medieval glass still remain in the upper tracery. Much of his construction was done with Lincolnshire stone.

Entrance to the church was through the South Porch, built by Michael de la Pole. The niche over the outer doorway would have contained a statue, probably of its namesake, St Andrew. According to the church, the Chapel of the Holy Trinity, which now serves as the vestry, was once the Wingfield Chantry Chapel. When Elizabeth entered the church, she would have seen the nave with its brightly painted panelled ceiling. The timbers in the ceiling today are fairly modern, since they are part of the reconstruction work on the church done in the nineteenth century. She would not have seen the pews since these were added later.

The font was brought to the church by Michael de la Pole and sits in the west end of the Nave. It is tempting to imagine the infant de la Pole children being christened here. The family would have observed Mass here, as well. Several of the family members are buried in the church, including Michael de la Pole, 2nd Earl of Suffolk, and his wife, Katherine. Both John and Elizabeth are also buried here.

Their effigies are located in the north side of the church. Carved out of alabaster, the figures of both Elizabeth and John were once brightly painted, and traces of paint can still be seen on John's effigy. A drawing from C. A. Stothard shows the details of the rich colouring. John's effigy is that of a knight wearing his ducal coronet, his head resting on a Saracen's head. At his feet is a lion and by his side is his dagger. Elizabeth is wearing a gown with bright hues of crimson and blue. On her head is her coronet. The canopy above them is decorated with the *rose-en-soleil*. Other heraldic devices once decorated the front of the tomb.

Visiting Today

Wingfield's church has an ancient air, as if history has surrounded the church in a cloak protecting it from outside encroachment.

Once inside, even with the modern improvements, the church still exudes history. It is open during daylight hours, but as always it is best to check ahead to avoid disappointment. Wingfield church is proud of its historic ties to the Wingfields, the de la Poles and to Charles Brandon and Mary Tudor. Several informative panels are located throughout the building. Be prepared to spend quite a bit of time perusing this church as it is full of history. For more information, see its website at http://www.wingfield-suffolk.org.uk. Parking is available, and at the time of this publication, a pub sat near the church. Postcode: IP21 5RB.

Ewelme, Oxfordshire

Ewelme came to the de la Poles through the marriage of Alice Chaucer and William de la Pole. Alice's father, Thomas, son of Geoffrey Chaucer, married Maud Burghersh (also known as Matilda). Maud's father, Sir John Burghersh, held Ewelme, and after his death, Ewelme ultimately passed to Chaucer. Alice was born at the manor, as was her son, John. She and William are responsible for building the almshouse and school, as well as rebuilding the church.

While Alice was alive, John and Elizabeth would have visited her at the manor in Ewelme. An inventory from 1466 shows how opulent the manor was. One of the bits of furnishings that had been moved to Ewelme from Wingfield was an iron chair of estate, with a canopy of purple satin and leather. Another chair of estate, this time of wood, with its canopy of blue cloth of gold and four 'pomells of coper and gilt', was also moved. Several cushions stuffed with feathers and covered with leather were brought, too. Following Alice's death, the couple would have continued to visit their holdings in Oxfordshire.

Ewelme Manor

After their marriage, William and Alice enlarged and renovated the manor house at Ewelme. The home was built of brick and timber and was surrounded by a moat. A letter from Charles Rudge, whose grandfather purchased the property from the Crown, says that the home had embattled cornices running around its roof, perhaps like that of the church. A large park encircled the property. Leland described the home:

The inner part of the house is sette with in a fair mote, and is buildid richely of brike and stone. The haul of it is fair and hath great barres of iren overthuart it instede of crosse beames. The parler by is exceeding fair and lighstum: and so be al the lodginges there.

An engraving by Buck in the eighteenth century shows the accommodation block of the handsome home, with chimneys topping the roof. As lovely as it appears even in a ruinous state, it must have been a beautiful home when John and Elizabeth stayed there. The accommodation block was large, consisting of ten rooms with five on each floor. The large hall was to the right of the chamber block.

The manor had a chapel, and John Goodall says that William and Alice had received a papal dispensation to have a font within the home. He suggests that the delivery of a valence and cushions for the font may suggest that at least one of Elizabeth's children was christened in the manor's chapel. A portion of the inventory at Ewelme appears in an appendix to the *Eighth Report of the Royal Commission on Historical Monuments*, and from it we are able to get an idea of how the chapel looked at the time. The front of the altar would have been draped with red cloth of gold of damask, with a front covering of red 'cloth of baudekyn' embroidered with swans. The walls were hung with arras cloth, one featuring a depiction of St Anna.

The walls would have been covered with plaster and a roaring fire would have kept the cold of an Oxfordshire winter at bay. Large windows flooded each room with light. Despite the misfortune that would ultimately destroy the family, it is easy to imagine them happy here.

Henry VII and Elizabeth of York also visited Ewelme on occasion. David Starkey believes that it is possible Henry VIII was conceived at Ewelme Manor during a visit by the royal couple.

Following the death of Edmund de la Pole in 1513, the manor was seized by the king. A record for payment to repair Ewelme, along with other manors, was recorded in February 1518. As with most of the de la Pole holdings, Henry VIII granted Ewelme to Charles Brandon. Eventually the king took the property back. By the early seventeenth century, the manor had already fallen into ruins. Most of it was destroyed, but a small portion of the hall and chambers was converted into a Georgian home.

Today, only that small portion of the home remains and it is in private hands. It is possible to see the gate into the home, but the house and lands are not open to visitors. The nearby church, however, is open.

Ewelme St Mary the Virgin and Almshouse

Alice and William largely rebuilt the church at Ewelme shortly after their marriage. Its appearance resembles the church at Wingfield, with its flint and stone building topped with red-bricked battlements. The church was dedicated to St Mary the Virgin.

After Alice's death, her son and daughter-in-law had an elaborate tomb placed in the church between the nave and the chapel of St John the Baptist. Made of alabaster, the intricately detailed tomb contains an effigy of Alice wearing a ducal coronet with the Order of the Garter on her arm. Her head rests on a pillow supported by angels. Under the tomb is her enclosed cadaver effigy; if you lie on the floor you can see the paintings above it. Alternatively, you can see a copy of the paintings displayed on the Chaucer tomb, depicting the Annunciation, St John the Baptist and St Mary Magdalene.

Carved angels surround the tomb, standing on pedestals and bearing shields with arms of the families associated with Alice. The shields were restored in the early nineteenth century. The tomb would have been brightly painted, and some traces of crimson and blue paint still remain today.

Tradition holds that Queen Victoria made a trip to see Alice de la Pole's effigy in order to find out the correct way for a female to wear the garter. Whether this legend is true or not, it demonstrates that this effigy is special.

The enormous font cover was given to the church by John de la Pole in memory of his mother, and the carving on the font was restored in the nineteenth century. The head on the arch above the font is supposedly Edward III. Portions of the tile in the sanctuary are medieval, and the window in the chantry chapel contains remnants of medieval stained glass. The West Tower remains from the earlier building, but its upper sections were rebuilt in the eighteenth century.

Alice and William were also given licence to establish an almshouse at Ewelme and the foundation was completed in the 1440s. Two priests and thirteen almsmen made up the residents of the house. One of the priests was to teach the boys in the region, and the thirteen almsmen of the house were to be chosen largely from the men of the surrounding area. William, as lord of the manor, was to make a visitation each year. Once William died, this obligation fell to John.

A covered walkway from the church leads down to the almshouse, also known as God's House at Ewelme. The thirteen men of the almshouse were required to attend Mass and Evensong daily so access to the church was necessary.

The almshouse was constructed of red brick containing a herring-bone pattern and was built in a quadrangle. A gallery surrounds the courtyard where today plants and residents soak up the sunlight.

Visiting Ewelme Today

A door along the west side of the church provides access to the stairway leading down to the almshouse. After pushing the door open, it is tempting to picture the men, wearing their cloak with its red cross on the breast, passing by you as they make their way to the chantry chapel to pray for the souls of William and Alice. After walking through the inner courtyard, take the corridor to your right to exit into the lush formal garden. A short walk will lead you to the school, which Alice and William were also responsible for starting. The original aim of the school was to educate local boys. The master was to be from the University of Oxford and was to be chosen by the lord of the manor. Today the building houses a primary school. For more information about visiting, see the church's website at http://www.achurchnearyou. com/ewelme-st-mary-the-virgin/.

It is easiest to park outside the gates of the church since this provides access to the rest of the village. After spending time meandering through the church, walk through the almshouse and past the school. Continue walking down the High Street. After you pass Parson's Lane, you will see a red-brick wall that marks the boundary of today's current manor house. Unfortunately, the manor is closed to the public. As you make your way back towards the village, you will see a pond known as King's Pool. Two legends surround the name of the pool. One states that Henry VIII used to bathe in the pool; the other says that Catherine Howard once pushed the king into the pool. I prefer the latter, more popular, tradition. If you are hungry or thirsty from your walk, a shop located in the former Wesleyan chapel offers refreshments. Ewelme postcode: OX10 6HS.

Edmund, Earl of Rutland

Born 17 May 1443 while the couple was in Rouen, Edmund was the second surviving son of Cecily and Richard, Duke of York. He was christened in an elaborate ceremony in Rouen Cathedral, giving fodder for later rumours that his brother Edward was illegitimate. Most of his early years were spent with Edward at Ludlow Castle. When his father fled from England, Edmund accompanied him to Ireland, while Edward and the Nevilles fled to Calais. Following the rout at Ludford and his subsequent flight, Edmund was named in the bill of attainder issued from Coventry.

In early December 1460, the young earl left London with his father and Salisbury and headed north, arriving at Sandal Castle on 21 December. A few days later, on 30 December, he and his father perished in the Battle of Wakefield. Salisbury was captured and executed soon afterwards. Edmund was buried in the priory of St John at Pontefract. In July 1476, his body, along with that of his father, was removed from the priory and transported to Fotheringhay for reburial. For more information about Rouen, Ludlow and Sandal, see those sections.

The Cathedral Notre Dame de Rouen, France

People have worshipped on this spot for more than a thousand years. Construction of a new cathedral on the site of the earlier church was begun around the turn of the first millennium and finished in 1063, with William the Conqueror present at its dedication. This church did not stand long, and it was rebuilt in the mid-twelfth century. Throughout the next few centuries, renovations and embellishments continued, only stopping during the English occupation.

When baby Edmund was carried to his christening, the upper part of the twelfth-century St Romain's tower was unfinished and the Butter tower had not yet been started. Entering the cathedral, the members of the party would have seen a soaring nave with large columns surrounded by clusters of pillars, supporting large arches. Near the ceiling, windows flood the area with light, showcasing the graceful arches springing from the columns.

The priest met the party at the door, so all the members would have seen the graceful, richly ornamented West Front of the cathedral before they entered. The height of St Romain's tower would have been lower, because the upper storey was not added until the late fifteenth century. The front would also have looked much different without the Butter tower.

For Edmund's christening in the north transept, the ornate relics of the cathedral were displayed on the high altar and the tombs were uncovered. The choir was hung with splendid tapestries, which was usually only done during Christmas and Easter.

Visiting the Cathedral Today

A visit to Rouen's cathedral could take half a day, so budget your time accordingly. Several figures whose names will be familiar to those interested in medieval history have tombs or memorials here, including Henry the Younger, Richard the Lionheart and William Longsword. As you make your way around the cathedral, be sure to see the medieval stained glass located in the north aisle (the best view is from the south aisle). The windows in the choir date from the mid-fifteenth century, and the ambulatory also has a fine selection of medieval glass. Today, the font for christenings stands within St Romain's tower, but this is not the font in which Edmund or Elizabeth would have been christened. For more information about visiting the cathedral, see its website at http://www.cathedrale-rouen.net/accueil.php/ or call +33 2 35 71 71 60.

Wakefield Bridge, West Yorkshire

The Lancastrians attacked the Yorkists at Sandal Castle on 30 December. While it is impossible to know exactly what occurred, one theory proposes that the duke's men were out foraging for food when the Lancastrians appeared. Hearing the cries of their fellow soldiers, the men joined the fray instead of staying within the safety of the castle. The Lancastrians waited until the Yorkists were on level ground before attacking with their full force. Richard, Edmund's father, was slain during the battle.

Edmund apparently tried to escape, but was struck down on nearby Wakefield Bridge. Lord Clifford, who later earned the nickname 'The Butcher' for his actions, killed Edmund, perhaps while he tried to reach sanctuary in the chapel on the bridge. Edmund was seventeen, and not a young child as portrayed by both Hall and Shakespeare.

Hall's Chronicle says that Edmund pled silently with Clifford for his life. Clifford's response was cold: 'By God's blood, thy father slew mine, and so will I do thee and all thy kin.' He then drove his dagger into Edmund's heart. Afterwards, he turned to the priest nearby and coldly told him to take word to Edmund's mother and brother.

Shakespeare further immortalised the scene in his play *Henry VI*. Edmund's tutor begs Clifford for the young earl's life. Clifford has the priest removed by soldiers before turning to Edmund. A young Edmund repeatedly begs not to die, and Clifford says, 'The sight of any of the house of York is as a fury to torment my soul; And till I root out their accursed line and leave not one alive, I live in hell,' before stabbing Edmund with his dagger.

St Mary's Chapel on Wakefield Bridge

A touching legend appeared over the centuries that the chantry chapel on Wakefield Bridge had been built by Edward IV in remembrance of his father, brother and the others who died at Wakefield. However, the chapel on the bridge was already in existence in the fourteenth century. A record in the patent rolls, 13 May 1356, grants a licence for two chaplains to celebrate 'divine service daily in the chapel newly built on Wakefield Bridge'.

On 30 May 1397, the king issued a licence allowing for two chaplains 'celebrating divine service daily in the new chapel of St. Mary upon Wakefeld Bridge, and in consideration of that fine and for 5 marks paid in the hanaper by the king's uncle Edmund, duke of York'. Edmund soon signed a foundation deed in which the chaplains were to pray for him. Following his death, his lands passed down to Richard, Duke of York.

After the Dissolution the chantry chapel served as a warehouse. It was rebuilt in the mid-nineteenth century, although traces of the old stonework may be seen at the base. The bridge itself is still beautiful, with its delicate arches, and the chapel was actually built in to the bridge, with part of its foundation on an island. A new front had to be erected in the early 1930s due to decay. Restoration work was also done in the 1990s, and an interesting feature of the chapel today is that the carved heads on its south wall represent people from the late twentieth century, including the vicar and patrons.

Visiting St Mary's Chapel on Wakefield Bridge

Today the chapel is only open on certain days. It is best to check the website at http://www.chantrychapelwakefield.org/open-days.html. Unfortunately, the crypt is all that remains of the original chapel. For armchair travellers, the friends of the chantry have put together an informative video which currently may be viewed at http://www.chantrychapelwakefield.org/.

Part 10
Edward V; Richard, Duke of York; Elizabeth of York

Richard had several nieces and nephews, many of whom played a role in the history of England. For the purposes of this book, however, we will focus on the two sons and eldest daughter of Edward IV and Elizabeth of York.

The Princes in the Tower

Edward V was born 2 November 1470 in the sanctuary at Westminster. He was made the Duke of Cornwall, Earl of Chester and Flint, and Prince of Wales. His household was soon moved to Ludlow and it was here where he learned of his father's death.

Richard, Duke of York, was born 17 August 1473. In 1478, he married Anne Mowbray, heiress to the Mowbray estates, in a ceremony in St Stephen's Chapel in Westminster. The young couple had not been married long when his bride died at Greenwich in 1481. Richard was with his mother when he learned of his father's death; he fled with her to sanctuary.

These two sons of Edward IV are commonly known as the Princes in the Tower due to the mystery and controversy surrounding their imprisonment and death. While many people believe that Richard III had them murdered, the lack of incontrovertible evidence allows for the existence of other plausible scenarios. The controversy surrounding the death of the two boys is beyond the scope of this book and will only be discussed within the context of the place where the young princes were imprisoned.

Sanctuary, Westminster Abbey

Edward V and the First Flight to Sanctuary

The privilege of sanctuary had existed for centuries in England. Throughout these years, the abbots of Westminster had challenged any violation of its sanctuary. Elizabeth Woodville would make use of its rights of sanctuary on two occasions. The first occasion would see the birth of her eldest son, while the second would mark the release of her second son into his uncle's custody.

A royal birth was a time of anticipation – for both the royal couple and the country alike. Certainly, though, no one could have anticipated the conditions of the birth for Edward V at the start of Elizabeth's pregnancy. When news reached Elizabeth that rebels were nearing the city, she left the Tower of London and fled into sanctuary. She then sent word to the mayor and aldermen that the rebels were planning to enter the city and take the Tower of London. She had delivered the Tower into the hands of the city so that the rebels would not 'invade the said sanctuary of Westminster to despoil and kill the said Queen'.

Elizabeth, along with her daughters and mother, stayed in sanctuary. Elizabeth was in her eighth month of pregnancy. Where exactly the party stayed while in sanctuary is unknown, but the most plausible scenario is they stayed within one of the untenanted houses in the sanctuary. It is possible, as some sources suggest, that the group stayed in the Abbot's house like they did the second time Elizabeth felt forced to flee. At first the queen must have been frantic, worried that Warwick would violate sanctuary. According to Cora Scofield, Warwick had decided to keep Henry's restoration as peaceful as possible; upon his arrival he issued a decree that

> no man, of what degree or condition so ever he be, presume attempt or be so hardy to defoul or distrouble the churches or holy places of seintwaries of Westminster and Saint Martin's within the city of London or elsewhere ... upon pain of death.

The decree may have lessened Elizabeth's fears, but she still had no idea when, or even if, her husband would return. The birth of his heir on the feast of All Saints, or shortly thereafter, would have been a bittersweet event. The young prince's birth offered 'some consolation and hope' to Yorkists, but 'King Henry's supporters, much the more numerous at this state, thought the birth of the child to be of little importance'. His christening would have occurred at Westminster Abbey.

Although Elizabeth and her family were in sanctuary, it does not necessarily mean they were in a cramped, gloomy place. In his thesis, *The Westminster Contradiction: Sanctuary Privileges During the Ricardian Usurpation,* Jeff Wheeler states that William Stukeley drew and incorrectly identified the fourteenth-century belfry as the sanctuary. Wheeler contends that 'the sanctuary of Westminster was not limited to the walls of the abbey, nor was it a special shrine within its gardens'.

While the family was not treated like royalty by Henry VI, he did allow for 'half a beef and two muttons a week' to be sent to the household. He was also paying Lady Scrope to attend Elizabeth. Records of the Exchequer include his desire that 'vnto oure right trusty and welbeloued Elizabeth ladie Scrope for hir attendance by oure commaundement by thauis of oure Counsail aboute Elizabeth late calling hir Quiene ye doo paie of oure Tresore the somme of x li'.

Under what exact conditions that Elizabeth gave birth is unknown. Her mother and Lady Scrope were with her, and other women, including a midwife, were probably brought in to assist her.

Luckily, Edward and his family would not have long to wait before being rescued from the sanctuary. News would have reached Elizabeth that her husband had made it to his brother-in-law's court, and that he was making plans to retake his throne. By March Edward IV was in England and he soon marched on London. The city admitted him on 11 April and the chronicler of the *Arrivall* says that after making prayers at the abbey, the king went to Elizabeth

and comforted her that had a long time abided and sojourned at Westminster, assuring her person ... in right great trouble, sorrow, and heaviness, which she sustained with all manner patience that belonged to any creature, and as constantly as hath been seen at any time any of so high estate to endure; in which season nonetheless she had brought into this world, to the king's greatest joy, a fair son, a prince, wherewith she presented him at his coming, to his hearts singular comfort and gladness, and to all them that him truly loved and would serve. From then, that night, the king returned to London, and the Queen with him ... (Modern translation)

The young prince had been presented to his father, and then the family moved to Baynard's Castle. Edward V's entry into the world may not have been marked by a triumphant celebration, but his birth certainly pleased his father.

Richard, the Young Duke of York, and the Second Flight to Sanctuary
Following Edward IV's death, Elizabeth once again fled into sanctuary. This time, her youngest son, Richard, was part of the group seeking the protection of the Church. Mancini records that 'the queen and marquess withdrew to the place of refuge at Westminster Abbey standing close to the royal palace, and called by the English a sanctuary. They had with them the Duke of York, a boy of eight years, and the queen's already grown-up daughters'.

More says that this time Elizabeth and her children lodged in the residence of Abbot John Esteney. According to the Croyland chronicler, Richard kept close watch around the precincts, and Mancini reported that Richard surrounded the sanctuary with troops by the consent of the council. With the coronation date for Edward set, Richard insisted that the Duke of York come out of sanctuary to be with his brother. Archbishop Bourchier was sent to discuss the matter with Elizabeth.

After Bourchier had spoken to Elizabeth, personally guaranteeing that her youngest son would be safe with Edward V in the custody of their uncle, she agreed to relinquish him. More paints a romantic scene where Elizabeth begs the men to consider the trust that Edward IV had in them, before she turns to her young son and says, 'Farewel, my own swete sonne, God send you good keping, let me kis you ones yet ere you goe, for God knoweth when we shal kis togither agayne. And therewith she kissed him, and blessed him, turned her back and wept and went her way, leauing the childe weping as fast.' A less tender account is given by Simon Stallworthe, who said that the Duke of York was delivered to 'my lord Cardinal, my lord Chancellor ... and with him met my lord of Buckingham in the middle of the hall of Westminster', before

Richard greeted him at the Star Chamber door with 'many loving words'.

In 1486, Elizabeth would lease Cheyneygates from the abbot. It is puzzling why she would pick the place where she had once been forced to flee for her residence. She would not stay there long; she soon retired to Bermondsey Abbey.

Visiting Sanctuary Today

While the medieval version of sanctuary at Westminster Abbey no longer exists, remnants of it remain in the names of the streets Broad Sanctuary and Little Sanctuary. The present Deanery was built on the site of the Abbot's house, also called Cheyneygates, and some of its stone was incorporated into the building. A few of the medieval rooms remain, including the Jerusalem Chamber, which was added by Abbot Litlyngton. Unfortunately the rooms are not open to the public.

Westminster Abbey, London

Since his family was in sanctuary, Edward V was christened at Westminster Abbey in a quiet ceremony. There were other chapels in the sanctuary, but since he was the son of a king, it is most likely the family had him christened in the abbey church.

Little remains to remind a visitor that the area where the large church rests was once called Thorney Island. A marshy area covered by thorns, an ancient manuscript deemed it 'in loco terribili'. Legend has it that the king of the East Saxons, Sebert, erected an early church here in the seventh century in honour of St Peter. Certainly by the tenth century, a group of Benedictine monks had been established here by St Dunstan.

King Edward the Confessor took a great interest in the church and built a larger church here. After his death in 1066, Edward was buried before the high altar of the church and miracles were soon being attributed to him. The church as we see it today was built largely under the direction of Henry III. The eastern tower was taken down, rebuilt and then connected to the western part of the church. Henry's new church was different than the one today in that its interior was full of bright colours. According to Christopher Wilson, 'larger areas were fully polychromed ... the arch and rib mouldings projecting parts were gilt and hollows were red, blue or green ... the main arcades had alternate lengths of dark and light colouring spotted like marbles'. This plethora of colours would have been normal to a medieval visitor.

Henry III is also responsible for building a shrine for the body of Edward the Confessor behind the high altar, to which he carried the chest containing the bones of the former king. The new shrine was elaborate, decorated with gold and precious jewels. The shrine was not the only gift Henry III gave to the abbey. He also presented the church with the standard of a dragon of red and gold, with large sapphire eyes and a tongue that appeared to be continuously moving.

As you visit the abbey, keep in mind that coronations, including those of Edward, Richard, Anne, Elizabeth Woodville and her daughter were held here. Standing in the middle of the crowded abbey church, try to picture the parade of kings and queens throughout the centuries entering here for their coronation rites.

Another location of particular interest for those interested in the York family is the chapel of Henry VII. This large chapel sits on the site of the thirteenth century Lady Chapel. After entering, look up to see the magnificent vaulting; one can certainly understand why Leland called it a 'wonder of the world'. Here you may visit the tomb of Elizabeth of York and Henry VII, as well as see the tomb of Anne Mowbray, the wife of the young Richard, Duke of York. The remains thought to be those of the two princes rest within a marble urn in the chapel.

While you are in Westminster Abbey, be sure to look for the tombs of Sir Thomas Vaughan, Sir Humphrey Stanley and Sir Humphrey Bourchier. Vaughan's canopied tomb is located in the chapel of St John the Baptist, while Bourchier's tomb rests in St Edmund's Chapel. Stanley's brass can be found on the floor of the chapel of St Nicholas.

Also take time to visit the museum, where the heads of the wooden effigies carried at Elizabeth and Henry's funerals may be seen. There is so much to see within the abbey and its surrounding buildings that a visit can take several hours.

Visiting Westminster Abbey Today
As the abbey is one of the busiest tourist attractions in London,

it takes careful planning to be able to see what you want without being crowded by other tourists. When I have visited, I have found that either arriving prior to opening to be first in line or later in the day works best. The abbey offers an informative audio tour. Entrance to the church is through the Great North Door, located near St Margaret's church. For more information about visiting hours and costs, see www.westminster-abbey.org/visit-us.

Stony Stratford, Buckinghamshire

Stony Stratford still retains a medieval feel. Located near the River Ouse, Stony Stratford was a market town along a main coaching road. On the night of 29 April 1483, the young King Edward V lodged here with his half-brother, Richard Grey. The next morning, Edward and his entourage prepared to leave in search of larger accommodations in order to house all the men in both his party and his uncle Richard's.

His uncle Woodville had spent the night before in Northampton with Richard and Buckingham. While some chroniclers say the meeting was prearranged, Croyland says that Woodville was sent there by the king to greet the dukes. The men had enjoyed a meal and conversation, but the next morning Woodville was unexpectedly arrested before he could make his way back to Stony Stratford. After arresting him, Richard, accompanied by Buckingham, journeyed to the inn where Edward was staying and also arrested Richard Grey and Thomas Vaughan.

Richard and Buckingham then made their way to Edward, who had watched his paternal uncle arrest his half-brother. While Richard and Buckingham treated him with courtesy, he was helpless when the two dukes sent the rest of his men away. Explaining that Woodville, Vaughan and Grey had conspired against him, Richard told the king he had arrested the men for protection. According to Mancini, Richard and Buckingham approached Edward with 'a mournful countenance' and expressed 'profound grief at the death of the king's father', yet blaming his ministers

> as being such that they had but little regard for his honour, since they were accounted the companions and servants of his vices, and had ruined his health ... the dukes said that these ministers

should be removed from the king's side ... besides Gloucester ... accused them of conspiring his death and of preparing ambushes ...

Despite Edward's protestations that the men were good and honourable, they were sent north. As Edward watched his uncle and half-brother led away, it is impossible to know what he was thinking. This would be his last glimpse of these two members of his family, since they would soon be executed. With all of his men gone, the young king was left with little choice but to submit to his uncle's authority.

For centuries, people have debated about the events at Stony Stratford. What was in Richard's mind when he made such a move? Richard's supporters say that the Woodville faction had left him little choice. He would have been shut out of the government and may have even been in danger. Others say that Richard made up his mind to be king the moment he learned of his brother's death. One thing is clear – Stony Stratford was the site of a crucial event in the nation's history.

Visiting Stony Stratford Today

Stony Stratford is proud of its ties to historic events and makes it easy for visitors to locate items of significance through its informative website. The website includes information about where to park and printable booklets detailing various walks through town. As Stony Stratford also played host to Edward IV when he was courting Elizabeth Woodville, it is an important place for someone interested in the York family. Before your visit, be sure to check the website at www.stonystratford.gov.uk/Visit_The_Area/Visitor_essentials/ to get valuable information.

Once in Stony Stratford, make your way to the Market Square. From here turn left in front of the library and then right on Church Street. A short walk will lead you to the high street where you will turn right again. After passing New Street on your left and The George on your right, you will see a red building on the left. This is the former Rose and Crown Inn, where it is believed Edward V was lodged while in Stony Stratford. A small plaque on the building recounts the story.

While the town does not have many specific locations to visit associated with the York family, it is still worth a visit. It was the site of a moment of chaos and confusion in young Edward V's life. Its location near to both Northampton and Grafton Regis is an added benefit. There are river walks, as well as several shops and restaurants in the area. Stony Stratford postcode: MK11 1AH.

Tower of London, London

Anyone who has visited London in the last 900 years would at least partially recognise this bastion of the city. Work on the immense structure commenced during the reign of William the Conqueror and was finished by 1100. The White Tower was built to dominate the land surrounding it, and at 90 feet tall, dwarfed the other structures near it. Over the next few centuries, succeeding monarchs would add to the Tower. Henry III had two new waterfront towers built to serve as luxurious lodgings for the royal family. He also built a curtain wall and reinforced it with nine towers and a moat. Edward I filled in the existing moat and added another curtain wall and a moat.

The young princes would have seen a group of buildings whose general layout is much the same as today. Unfortunately, several of the medieval buildings have been lost to time, including buildings the boys would have known.

Edward V was moved here soon after his arrival in London. This was not unusual, since kings often stayed at the Tower prior to their coronation. The fact that his mother was in sanctuary at Westminster may have also played a role in the decision.

After Richard, Duke of York left sanctuary, he joined his older brother here at the tower. At some point between then and Richard's coronation, the boys were moved from the king's lodgings to the White Tower. Tradition says that the boys were kept in the Garden Tower, which later became known as the Bloody Tower, but more likely they would have been held in the White Tower. If the boys were murdered, this would also have occurred in the White Tower. At the time of this publication, there was an interesting exhibit in the Bloody Tower regarding the princes.

Once you are inside the White Tower, enjoy the exhibitions on the ground floor before heading up to the first floor where the Chapel of St John the Evangelist is located. The room looks different than it would have appeared to Edward V and Richard. Imagine it whitewashed, with brightly coloured paintings marking its walls; picture light streaming through the exquisite medieval stained glass installed by Henry III. Take a minute to examine the columns to see the carvings along their bases. Once Edward V and his brother were placed in the White Tower, he began coming to confession daily. It is a poignant picture to imagine the two young boys praying in this chapel, their heads bent low, almost touching.

The large room adjacent to the chapel were the king's lodgings before the newer buildings replaced it. This larger room may have then been used for public meetings, while the smaller room was a private chamber. Perhaps the boys were lodged in this area.

It was in the White Tower that the bones of two boys were discovered in 1674. Near the former entrance to the White Tower, about halfway up the staircase is a break in the wall. Under the remnants of the staircase was where the two bodies were found. These bones were ultimately placed in Westminster Abbey because they were thought to be those of Edward and Richard.

As modern forensic science was not available at the time, it has been hotly debated whether these bones are actually those of the princes. At this time, however, the bones are not available for further testing, so this will remain one of the many mysteries surrounding the tragic story of the two boys. *Were the boys killed? If so, who did it? Are the bones those of the young princes?* These questions may never be answered.

Elizabeth of York

In January 1503 everything seemed well with the queen. Although she was pregnant, she kept a busy itinerary, travelling often. She spent Christmas at Richmond and then travelled to the Tower to celebrate Candlemas with King Henry. She was received here and made her way to her chambers.

The queen's chambers that Elizabeth would have used have disappeared. In order to get an idea of what they may have looked like, visit St Thomas's Tower, which was built by Edward I to provide royal accommodations and to create another watergate. Eventually, this entrance, now known as Traitor's Gate, became the main entrance for prisoners accused of treason. The first room in the tower is the King's Great Chamber. This room is unrestored, and it is harder to picture in its original state. Entering the next room you will see what once served as the king's private hall. Today it is decorated like a bedchamber. While this tower was no longer the royal apartments in Elizabeth's time, this room allows you to imagine how bright and colourful her chambers would have appeared.

On Elizabeth's last visit to the Tower things seemed to be progressing fine. She and Henry celebrated Candlemas and later that night she 'travailed of child suddenly and was delivered of a daughter', named Katherine. Following the birth, Elizabeth, 'upon the 11th day of the said month being Saturday in the morning, died the most gracious and virtuous princess the Queen'. The baby died several days later on 18 February.

By all accounts, Henry was devastated at the loss of his queen. He ordered her body wrapped in Holland linen. Her lead coffin was enclosed in a wooden chest covered with white and black velvet and a cross of white damask. Her body was then conveyed to the chapel of St Peter ad Vincula, which had been hung with black mourning cloths 'furnish'd with scochins of her Armes'. Here, surrounded by burning tapers, the queen's body lay in state for several days.

Richard III and the Tower

Leaving St Thomas's Tower, make your way to the Wakefield Tower. Once inside, look for the painted timber screen. Behind the screen is a tiny chapel with a beautiful stained glass window. Look down at the tiled floor where a memorial stone states 'by tradition Henry VI died here'. Although this is a possibility, by the time of Henry's death, the Wakefield Tower had not been used for royal lodgings for many years, making it more probable that he would have been kept in either the Lanthorn Tower or St Thomas's Tower instead. Exit the Wakefield Tower via the spiral staircase and make your way along the south wall walk. Stop here for a moment to look out over the grassy area towards the south-west corner of the White Tower. From here you will see the remaining foundations of the gatehouse known as Coldharbour Gate, which was the entrance to the innermost ward of the castle. The area below you was where the Great Hall stood.

Constructed during the reign of Henry III, the Tower's Great Hall has completely disappeared. While we do not definitively know what it looked like, it is reasonable to assume it resembled others of that date. Windows, with glazed frames, were placed under arches set on slender columns. The large room would have been whitewashed, with tapestries adorning its walls under a wooden, high-beamed roof.

Before the coronations of Richard and Anne, a large dinner was served here in the Great Hall. It would have been a time of great feasting and joy for the couple, as they sat on the dais above the crowd. The next day, Richard, sitting under the cloth of estate in the hall, created several Knights of the Bath before adjourning to his chambers to prepare for his procession to Westminster.

Jolt yourself back to the present and walk inside Lanthorn Tower. The present building was reconstructed on the same location after a fire destroyed the original. This tower was a possible lodging place for Henry VI and may have been the scene of his death. After the defeat of the Lancastrians at Tewkesbury and the death of Henry's heir, Edward, the only remaining threat to Edward's throne was Henry VI.

The Croyland chronicler does not name the murderer, only saying, 'May God have mercy upon and give time for repentance to him, whoever it might be, who dared to lay sacrilegious hands on the Lord's Annointed!' Other chroniclers are not so kind. Philip de Comines says that Richard 'slew this poor King Henry with his own hand, or caused him to be carried into some private place and stood by himself while he was killed'. Fabyan and the *Great Chronicle of London* also lay the deed at Richard's feet, with Fabyan stating that 'the most common fame went that he was stabbed with a dagger by the hands of the Duke of Gloucester'. This 'common fame' does not agree with evidence from an exhumation of Henry's grave in 1911 which showed a fractured skull to be the cause of death. Certainly, he did not die of 'melancholy' like the chronicler of the *Arrivall* claims.

When Richard and Anne came to the Tower on 4 July, prior to their coronations, Richard would have lodged in the Lanthorn Tower since Edward V had by this time been moved to the White Tower. After exiting the Lanthorn Tower, make your way towards the Bowyer Tower. Here is the traditional site of the execution of George, Duke of Clarence. More details can be found in the section on George.

Richard and the Execution of Hastings

On Friday 13 June, two council meetings were called. One occurred at Westminster, while the other was held in the Tower. According to Paul Murray Kendall, the council chamber was in an upper room of the White Tower. At the meeting in the Tower were Hastings, Morton, Stanley and others. At some point in the meeting, Hastings was accused of treason, dragged out to the green beside St Peter ad Vincula, shriven, and then beheaded on a squared piece of timber without a trial. The other men accused were not beheaded and eventually released. The motive behind the execution of Hastings is still a matter of contention today.

From the White Tower, head to Tower Green where a sculpture of a glass pillow was erected on the scaffold's site to commemorate the people beheaded here. Another name on the list of people executed here is Margaret Pole, Countess of Salisbury. Margaret was the daughter of George, Duke of Clarence, and was executed here during the reign of Henry VIII in 1541. The details of her execution are particularly bloody. The inexperienced executioner's first blow hit her shoulders and it took several blows to remove her head. Stories later circulated that the elderly woman ran around the block shrieking while she tried to escape the blows.

Visiting the Tower Today

A visit to the Tower can take an entire day. The best time to come to the Tower is as soon as it opens. Pre-purchase your ticket so that you can enter quickly. At the time of this publication, you can buy a fast-track ticket from a tour bus operator (even if you do not have a tour bus ticket). If you plan to see the Crown Jewels, do that first. Then either take a Yeoman Warder tour or see the York-related sites on your own. Taking a Yeoman Warder tour is the only way to gain entrance to the chapel of St Peter ad Vincula unless you visit late in the afternoon.

You might also want to obtain tickets to the 700-year-old Ceremony of the Keys. Entering the Tower after dark, you will see the locking of the Tower gates. To get tickets, you must write ahead. For more information, visit the website at www.hrp.org.uk/TowerOfLondon/WhatsOn/theceremonyofthekeys.

For more information about opening times and admission costs, or to purchase tickets online, visit the website at www.hrp.org.uk/

TowerOfLondon/admissionsprices/toweroflondonadmission.   The closest tube stop to the Tower is Tower Hill. Tower of London postcode: EC3N 4AB.

Elizabeth of York

The eldest child of Edward IV, Elizabeth was born 11 February 1466 at the Palace of Westminster. Unmarried when her father died, she went with her mother into sanctuary for the second time. Eventually, after her uncle Richard took the throne, she left sanctuary and soon was back at court. A rumour that Richard planned to marry her swirled through court, and he felt forced to make a public announcement to discredit it.

Henry VII had made a public vow to marry Elizabeth, and tradition holds that Richard had her secreted away to Sheriff Hutton when news arrived of Tudor's intent to enter England. After Richard's death, Elizabeth was brought to London where she lodged at Coldharbour, then in the hands of Margaret Beaufort. Henry and Elizabeth were married in 1486, making Elizabeth of York the first Tudor queen consort.

Windsor Castle, Berkshire

All the children of Edward IV would have been familiar with Windsor Castle, with its gleaming stone walls. The first building on this spot was a wooden structure built on the order of William the Conqueror as one of the fortifications surrounding London. It quickly became a royal favourite. In the twelfth century, the castle was rebuilt in stone. Subsequent monarchs enlarged and renovated it.

Throughout the centuries the castle has served both as a fortress and a birthplace of royalty. The Lancastrian king Henry VI was born at Windsor. Kings of both France and Scotland have been imprisoned here. Edward IV spent a great deal of time at the castle, perhaps because of its close proximity to London and spacious hunting grounds.

When Louis Gruuthuse, who had lodged Edward IV and Richard when they were in exile, came to visit, Elizabeth was present at the festivities, getting to meet the man who had sheltered her father. Bluemantle Pursuivant states that:

The King had him to the Queen's chamber, where she sat playing with her ladies ... which sight was full pleasant to them. Also the King danced with my lady Elizabeth, his eldest daughter. [The next night] the queen did order a great banquet in her own chamber. At the which banquet were the king, the queen, my lady Elizabeth the king's eldest daughter, the duchess of Exeter, my lady Rivers, and the lord Gruuthuse, sitting at one mess; and at the same table sat the duke of Buckingham, my lady his wife ... and when they had supped, my lady Elizabeth the king's eldest daughter, danced with the duke of Buckingham, and divers other ladies also. (Modern translation)

Following the dancing, the king and queen, along with her ladies, brought the Lord Gruuthuse to his chambers, which had been carpeted and decorated with wall hangings of white silk and linen cloth. A large bed had been made for him, of the finest down that could be procured. His sheets were of 'Reynes, also fine fustians, the counterpoint cloth of gold, furred with ermine. The tester and the canopy were also shining cloth of gold'. His chamber was elaborate, with his sheets and pillows of the queen's ordinance.

The next morning, Edward observed Mass in his chapel and afterwards presented Gruuthuse with a jewel-encrusted cup of gold. They then went hunting in the little park, where the king further gifted Gruuthuse with a crossbow with strings of silk. Given her age, Elizabeth would not have been present at the hunt.

Elizabeth was also not present years later when the body of her mother arrived by boat at Windsor, because she was nearing her confinement. Her mother was laid to rest in St George's Chapel at Windsor with a small funeral. Woodville's biographer David Baldwin suggests that she may have requested the small burial because she was aware that the deceased's estate was to bear the expense and she did not have funds for an elaborate funeral. While Elizabeth of York was not able to attend the funeral, she did name her next child Elizabeth.

Elizabeth would recognise many of the buildings in the castle today. There are some changes she would not have known, however. The Round Tower was shorter in her time. Her son, Henry VIII, would add the range that contains the Royal Library and the entrance gateway to the Lower Ward. The houses on the south side of today's Lower Ward were not added until the reign of Mary I. In Elizabeth's time, the entrance on the south side was reached via a bridge over the ditch and through a gateway. However, many of the buildings she knew are still extant.

Edward IV and Windsor

As part of his refurbishment of his castles near London, Edward IV made extensive improvements to Windsor Castle. He visited Windsor often, preferring to be there for St George's Day whenever circumstances would allow.

Following the Battle of Barnet, Edward rode into London and quickly learned that Margaret of Anjou had landed and was drawing a large number of men to her cause. Dispatching runners to several counties, Edward moved to Windsor where he and Richard celebrated St George's Day before heading off to thwart Margaret's army. Later, Richard III would set off from Windsor on his first royal progress.

Visiting Windsor Castle Today

Windsor Castle is a prime tourist spot and is incredibly busy. It is best to visit early in the morning or later in the day. The castle is still one of the residences of the monarch and at certain times it or some of its rooms may be closed. It is always best to check the website at https://www.royalcollection.org.uk/visit/windsorcastle/ before visiting for planned closures.

It is easy to reach the castle from London by train. From London Paddington or Waterloo, take the train to Windsor and Eton Riverside or Windsor and Eton Central. For more information, see the National Rail website at www.nationalrail.co.uk. A coach service to Windsor leaves from London Victoria.

If you plan to visit Windsor by car, you will want to park in one of the car parks in the town centre since the castle has no public parking. A list of public car parks may be found at www.windsor. gov.uk/visitor-info/parking. If you do not feel comfortable driving in a crowded city centre teeming with tourists, you may want to use the park-and-ride scheme. More information may be found at www3.rbwm.gov.uk/info/200359/park_and_ride/245/park_and_ride. Windsor Castle postcode: SL4 1NJ.

Winchester, Hampshire

As Elizabeth neared the time for the birth of her first child, she moved to Winchester where a round table fabled to be King Arthur's hung in Winchester Castle. Henry presumably wanted his heir to be born here surrounded by this mythology. Unfortunately, Winchester Castle was in a state of disrepair, so Elizabeth stayed at the nearby priory.

Priory of St Swithun, Winchester

Elizabeth was given the prior's Great Hall to serve for her chamber. A series of ordinances had been set down to dictate how the queen's chamber was to be arranged. Elizabeth's chamber was to be hung with rich cloth of arras covering the sides, roofs, and all but one window. The room would also contain a cloth and chair of estate, with carpet around it.

The royal bed was covered with fine linen and pillows of fustian stuffed with fine down. The headsheet was like 'cloth of gold furred with ermine'. The bed's canopy was of crimson satin embroidered with the crowns of gold, the arms of the King and Queen, and other devices. The queen was to have a mantle of 'crimson velvet, plain, furred with ermines'.

On 20 September 1486 Arthur was born. The birth of the awaited heir was greeted by celebration. Bonfires filled the streets, bells rang out and 'every true Englishman' rejoiced. Messengers were dispatched to 'all the estates and cities of the Realm with that comfortable and good tiding'. The prince would be christened in Winchester Cathedral.

Winchester Cathedral, Winchester

Winchester Cathedral was highly decorated for Arthur's christening. The porch was hung with cloth of gold and carpeted. Inside the walls were covered with hangings of cloth of arras and the chancel floor was completely draped with carpet. The font, which had been brought from Canterbury, rested on a stage of seven steps built in the middle of the church. Its inside had been lined with soft cloth. A cross overlaid with red worsted hung above it, and the font was covered by a large canopy.

The day of the christening dawned gloomy and cold. The prince, wrapped in a mantle 'of crimson cloth of gold furred with ermine', was carried in procession from the Queen's Great Chamber to the cathedral. The procession made its way to the south part of the church because the weather was too cold for the christening to be at the traditional site in the west end. The baby's grandmother, Elizabeth, awaited the infant in the church, where Bishop Alcock christened the baby. Elizabeth then carried him to the high altar and laid him down for the next part of the ceremony. The lower part of the high altar was of plate of gold garnished with stones, with a table resting above filled with jewel-encrusted gilt and silver images; a gold-plated cross hung above it. After the *Te Deum*, the Earl of Oxford took Arthur to the Bishop of Exeter for his confirmation. Afterwards the participants tread over the beautiful medieval tiles to the area behind the altar to make an offering. Here was the shrine of St Swithun, made of 'solid silver, gilt and garnished with precious stones'. After gifts were presented, Arthur was carried back to the priory for the king's and queen's blessing.

Winchester Cathedral History

For more than a millennium people have worshipped on this spot. The Normans rebuilt the Anglo-Saxon church that once stood here, moving the shrine to the new cathedral. In the fourteenth century, the West Front was rebuilt in Perpendicular Gothic. Building was started by Bishop Edyngton, but Willian Wykeham continued construction and added the entrance porches.

After the Dissolution, the priory was closed, the shrine demolished and the great treasures of the priory taken. Luckily, the church was refounded as a cathedral so it escaped complete destruction.

Visiting Winchester Cathedral Today

The cathedral is no longer covered with cloths of arras like it was during the christening, but it is still beautiful, and has several ties to the Wars of the Roses. There is much to see in the cathedral, but for our purposes, only sites related to the time period of the Yorks will be discussed in detail. Plan to spend at least an hour in the cathedral with another hour for wandering the grounds.

As you enter the nave, stand for a moment and look towards the altar. In the medieval period, there would not have been chairs and the space would have been filled with people. The large columns were part of the Perpendicular Gothic remodelling of the Norman structure. In the late nineteenth century, this nave was called 'perhaps the most beautiful Nave either in England or elsewhere'. It certainly is still impressive today.

From the nave make your way towards the font. While this is not the font Arthur was christened in, it still dates from Norman times and would have been here at the time. Continue on towards the Holy Sepulchre Chapel where you can see wall paintings dating from the twelfth century. Now make your way to the east end of the chapel. Pilgrims to the shrine of St Swithun would make their way up these stairs and onto the gorgeous medieval ceramic tiles. According to the cathedral, these tiles date from the early thirteenth century (although the brighter tiles are replacements).

Now move into the retrochoir where Bishop William Waynflete is buried. As Bishop of Winchester, Waynflete played a significant role in the Wars of the Roses. He was nominally a Lancastrian, and was one of the men sent to persuade Richard, Duke of York, not to take action at Dartford. He baptised the young Lancastrian heir, Edward, and was appointed chancellor in 1456. He eventually came to terms with the Yorkists and attended the coronation of Edward IV. Waynflete also founded Magdalen College in Oxford, which Richard III would visit on progress. His large chantry chapel is exquisite. By the nineteenth century, the head of the effigy had been so damaged that it was replaced. The effigy shows the bishop dressed in 'full pontificals of mitre, crozier, casula, stole, maniple, tunicle, rochet, alb, amice, sandals, and gloves'. An intricately carved canopy hangs above the effigy.

From here make your way to the Lady Chapel. Elizabeth of York gave an offering to the cathedral where her son had been christened, which allowed the prior to enlarge the Lady Chapel. In recognition, Elizabeth's arms and those of Arthur were mounted on shields on the walls. While the large 'Jesse Tree' stained-glass window is a recreation of an earlier window, it has a link to the queen. According to the cathedral, included among the kings is an image of Elizabeth of York, Queen Victoria and the Virgin Mary. According to the nineteenth-century handbook for the cathedral, a wall painting from 1489 once decorated the walls in the chapel.

Our next stop is the Langton Chapel. The paintwork in the chapel gives you an idea of how much of the cathedral would have looked. Thomas Langton, Bishop of Winchester, was often sent abroad on diplomatic missions by Edward IV. He was one of the men who negotiated with the King of France for the betrothal of Elizabeth of York with the Dauphin. Richard III also made use of the bishop's services, and Langton accompanied him on his first royal progress. Although he favoured Richard at Bosworth, Langton was granted a full pardon. Eventually, he was nominated to be the next Archbishop of Canterbury, but died a few days later.

Another chapel of interest is that of Cardinal Henry Beaufort, who was the half-brother of King Henry IV and the uncle of Henry V. Move on to the modern St Swithun's memorial, and make sure to see the Holy Hole, once used by pilgrims to crawl under the shrine. Before exiting the area make your way to the Great Screen. This intricately carved screen was completed by 1475. At the time of Arthur's christening, the statues would have been painted. They were removed after the Reformation and today's statues were installed during the nineteenth century. The east gable of the presbytery was done by Bishop Fox. The vault contained a series of carved and painted bosses, which included the arms of Henry VII.

For more information on visiting the cathedral, see the website at http://www.winchester-cathedral.org.uk/planning-your-visit/opening-admissions/ or call +44 (0) 1962 857200. Winchester Cathedral postcode: SO23 9LS.

Before leaving the area, be sure to walk through the cathedral close. While the Deanery is closed to the public, the priory gate still exists and may be visited. A few other remains of St Swithun's priory can also be seen in the cathedral close. Before exiting back out the priory gate, be sure to see the Pilgrims' Hall, which is believed to have the earliest known example of a hammer-beam roof.

There are several other medieval sites of interest in Winchester, including Winchester Great Hall, Wolvesey Castle and Winchester College. Getting to Winchester is easy via car, and the city operates a park-and-ride scheme. For more information on parking, see http://www.visitwinchester.co.uk/parking. Alternatively, trains leave from London Waterloo to Winchester several times a day.

Elizabeth's Coronation, London

It was not until 1487, after she had given birth to the dynastic heir, that Elizabeth was given her coronation. She and Henry travelled from Warwick, spending the feast of All Hallows at St Albans, before continuing onwards. Elizabeth and Margaret, along with several other ladies, moved on to Greenwich, while Henry went in to London.

According to Leland's *Collectanea* there were several in attendance on the queen, including the king's mother. Departing Greenwich by barge, Elizabeth's splendid procession made its way to London. As they approached the city, the mayor, sheriffs and aldermen, along with several citizens from the guilds, joined the group in their liveries on barges 'freshly furnished with banners and streamers of silk'. One particular barge, *The Bachelor's Barge,* outdid the others with its 'great red dragon spouting flames of fire into the Thames'. Other pageants were put on to please Elizabeth, and when she slowly moved up the water to the Tower, trumpets and minstrels announced her landing at Tower Wharf. Here the king welcomed her, which was a sight 'right joyous' to behold.

That night the king created new Knights of the Bath who would take part in the procession from the Tower to Westminster. The next day, Elizabeth dressed in her kirtle of white cloth of gold of damask, with a mantle furred with ermine clasped at her breast by a fastening of gold and silk lace, with gold tassels. Her long 'faire yellow hair' hung down her back and was topped with a circlet of gold, garnished with jewels. With her sister, Cecily, carrying her train she walked to her litter, which had been covered with cloth of gold of damask. Pillows cushioned with down had been similarly covered. The litter was covered with a canopy of cloth of gold supported on poles carried by Knights of the Bath.

The citizens of London would have lined the procession route as the queen passed along streets that had been cleaned and covered with gravel. Tapestries decorated the houses along the route and representatives of the guilds stood along the streets in their liveries. As she passed Cheapside, she saw 'rich clothe of gold velvet and silks' decorating the street. Goldsmiths and mercers sold their luxury wares here. This street was one of the widest and was lined with buildings three and four storeys tall. Along the route children, some dressed like angels and some like virgins, sang 'sweet songs' to her when she passed. The procession had to stop often, since the men carrying her canopy changed frequently.

The next day, Elizabeth wore a kirtle with a mantle of purple velvet furred with ermine. A circlet of gold, garnished with pearl and stones, rested on her head. Cecily once again carried her train when she entered Westminster Hall and stood under a cloth of Estate until it was time for the procession.

Ray cloth extended from the door of Westminster Hall to the cathedral. The queen exited the hall in a grand procession. The esquires went first, followed by knights, then the 'new made knights well beseen in divers silks'. Next came the barons and other estates. Heralds lined each side of the procession to make room while people pressed in close to catch a glimpse of their queen. Then followed the monks of Westminster and the King's Chapel, ahead of the abbots and bishops in their full pontifical dress. The Bishop of Norwich bore the patent, while another bishop bore the Chalice of St Edward.

Next came the Archbishop of York walking ahead of the Garter King of Arms, the Mayor of London, the Constable and the Marshall of England. The Earl of Arundel carried the rod with the dove. The Duke of Suffolk followed, bearing the sceptre. The Earl of Oxford, dressed in his Parliament robes, carried his staff of office of Great Chamberlain. The Duke of Bedford dressed in his robes of estate and carrying the crown came next.

Finally the moment came the crowd had been waiting for. Elizabeth, walking under a canopy of estate carried by barons of the Cinque Ports, and accompanied on either side by the bishops of Winchester and Ely, made her way along the cloth towards the cathedral. Cecily carried her train, and she was followed by the Duchess of Bedford and another duchess and countess, all richly attired in mantles and surcoats of scarlet. The duchesses wore circlets of gold, richly garnished with pearls and stones.

The great press of people followed behind, trying to claim the ray cloth upon which Elizabeth had walked. This led to the death of several people, likely marring the joy that Elizabeth must have been feeling when she was crowned. After her coronation, a large banquet was held in Westminster Hall to celebrate. For the next several years, Elizabeth was the beloved Queen of England.

Palace of Sheen/Palace of Richmond, Surrey

As with Greenwich, Elizabeth would know two palaces here – the palace of her youth, known by Sheen, and the palace built by her husband, known by Richmond. The palace of Sheen had been visited often by royalty over the years, with Edward III dying here. Richard II especially loved the palace, and he and his wife, Anne, visited here often. Following Anne's death, Richard II ordered the building demolished. Under Henry V and Henry VI, building commenced on another palace nearby.

The palace of Elizabeth's youth was built on a grand scale using freestone, beer stone, timber, ragstone and brick. Two large stone towers were on the east side of the palace adjoining the timber building known as Byfleet. A large brick wall enclosed a garden. The *History of the King's Works* describes a great moat, 25 feet wide and 8 feet deep, which was dug between the old site and the new buildings. A large wall was erected outside of the moat, and new chambers were constructed on the north side.

The rooms of the castle were filled with stained glass containing the king's arms and other devices. William Worcester said the castle also contained a large courtyard surrounded by chambers. Elizabeth would have visited here several times during her father's reign.

Following their marriage, Elizabeth and Henry often stayed at Sheen. During the Christmas celebration in 1497, on 'St Thomas day at night in the Christmas week about nine of the clock', a large fire broke out within either the king's or queen's lodgings and burned for several hours before being extinguished. The damage from the fire was extensive, but even though several members of the royal family were lodged here, no one was hurt. The Milanese ambassador, de Soncino, reported that the incident

> did a great deal of harm and burned the chapel except two large towers recently erected by his Majesty. The damage is estimated at over 60,000 ducats. The king does not attach much importance to the loss by this fire, seeing that it was not due to malice. He proposes to rebuild the chapel all in stone and much finer than before.

Henry V's donjon was not destroyed, although its interior seems to have been devastated. Henry began a rebuilding project, and by November 1501 had finished most of the new works, which became known as Richmond. The privy block which contained

Elizabeth's rooms was three storeys high and built of white stone. Her chambers had large bay windows which looked out over the Thames. The palace towers had turrets with pepper-pot domes, each topped with a vane of the king's arms, painted and gilded. The complex was encircled with a strong brick wall with towers of different heights standing in each corner and in the middle. The Southwest London Archaeology Unit believes that Henry's palace was also moated and built on the same ground plan as Sheen. The king's and queen's chambers were reached by a bridge over the moat from the courtyard.

Entrance to the palace was through its strong gates of double timber. Visitors entering through the inner gateway saw a large courtyard, with galleries surrounding it on each side. These galleries were well lit by many windows and led off to courtiers' chambers.

On 25 January 1502, Elizabeth's daughter, Margaret, married the King of Scotland in a proxy ceremony at Richmond, giving Henry a chance to display its 'great comodities, pleasures, and excellent goodlynes' to his Scottish guests.

As the morning of her daughter's wedding dawned, Elizabeth made her way along the paved and painted gallery to her privy closet in the chapel to observe Mass. Henry's closet was cushioned and hung with silk, and his altar was plated with relics of gold and precious stones. Elizabeth's closet, located on the right-hand side of the chapel, was similar to her husband's. The chapel itself was 'well paved, glasid, and hangyd w'cloth of Arres'. The ceiling was white washed and painted in azure, having 'between evry chek a red rose of gold or portcullis'. Each wall had niches with statues of past kings who had become saints, including St Edward and St Edmund. The choir and nave were hung with cloth of gold. After Mass, Henry, Elizabeth and many others made their way to the Queen's Great Chamber for the ceremony.

After the questioning part of the ceremony concluded, the Archbishop of Glasgow turned to Margaret and asked if she was entering the marriage of her own free will and without compulsion. Margaret answered that if 'it please my Lord and Father the King, and my Lady my mother the Queen'. Margaret then received the blessings of the king and queen before the archbishop secured the promises of King James from the Earl of Bothwell.

Margaret then spoke her vows, taking the 'said James King of

Scotland unto and for my Husband and Spouse, and all other for him forsake, during his and mine Lives naturall'. Afterwards, the trumpeters blew and the minstrels played. Elizabeth then took Margaret by the hand and they dined together as queens.

The next day a great tournament was held in honour of Margaret's marriage. Afterwards a large banquet was held in the Great Hall, which sat across the Fountain Court from the chapel. The court was paved with free stone, and in the middle of its courtyard stood a large conduit and cistern, decorated with lions, red dragons and other beasts.

As the visitors crossed the courtyard and entered the hall, they would have walked over the tile floor to stand under its timber roof, with its 'knotts craftily corven, joined, and shett toguyders with mortes, and pynned, hangyng pendaunts'. The hall was built of stone and was about 100 feet long. Its walls were decorated by rich tapestries of arras depicting scenes like the siege of Troy. Statues of former and mythical kings in gold robes and swords in their hands were placed between each of the large windows. A statue of Henry VII sat slightly higher up on the left-hand side of the hall, since he was 'as worthy that room and place with those glorious princes as any King that ever reigned in this land'.

The palace of Richmond also contained gardens which abutted the chambers on the east side. The gardens were large, containing herbs, flowers and decorative stone statues of beasts. A two-storey gallery encircled the gardens, with the upper floor enclosed so that courtiers could stroll around and admire the gardens. On the far side of the gardens was an enclosed area where visitors could play chess, dice or cards, and bowl or play tennis.

Elizabeth would spend her last Christmas at Richmond. Having lost Arthur, it was a sad Christmas for the family.

Other Yorks at Sheen

In February of 1472 a tense confrontation occurred between Richard and George at Sheen. Following the death of the Lancastrian heir at Tewkesbury, his wife, Anne Neville, was released to the custody of her brother-in-law, George, Duke of Clarence. Once Richard decided to marry Anne, George saw his chance to control the entire Neville fortune slipping away. Edward tried to restore relations between his brothers, but George angrily said that Richard could marry his sister-in-law, but would not be able to share in the inheritance.

Richard and Anne married, receiving a papal dispensation in April 1472. Edward, contrary to George's pronouncement that Richard would not share in the inheritance, did grant Richard a large portion of the Neville lands.

Visiting the Palace Site Today

Nothing remains of the palace of Sheen and all that is left to visit of the grand palace of Richmond is the main gateway. To get to Richmond from London it is easiest to take the District Line. Before leaving walk through Richmond Green to Old Palace Lane. Once you are at the river, you are standing where the palace once fronted the river. Old Palace Lane postcode: TW9 1PD.

The Funeral Procession of the Queen, London

After Elizabeth died following childbirth (see the section on Tower of London), her body lay in state at the chapel of St Peter ad Vincula. Daily Masses were sung around her body, with her sister Katherine serving as her chief mourner. Early on the morning of 22 February, following Mass, Elizabeth's coffin was placed in a chariot, covered with black velvet, with a cross of white cloth of gold atop it. The chariot was pulled by six horses trapped with 'black velvet'. An effigy was placed on the coffin of 'an image or personage like a queen, clothed in the very robes of estate of the Queen, having her very rich crown on her head, her hair about her shoulders, her sceptre in her right hand, and her fingers well garnished with gold rings and precious stones'. A gentleman usher knelt on each end of the coffin all the way to Westminster. Her funeral procession would largely follow the same route as that of her coronation.

A large group headed the procession, including the Mayor of London, the queen's chamberlain, her confessor and almoner. Walking on the left side of the procession were the choirs of King's Chapel and St Paul's, friars and 200 poor men each bearing a 'weighty torch' and dressed in mourning habits. On the right side rode the messengers, then the trumpeters and minstrels without their instruments on horseback, then groups of foreigners bearing torches, including Frenchman, Venetians and Easterlings. After these men were the gentlemen and squires, knights and chaplains. Next came the aldermen of London, then 'the great Chapleines that be of dignitye as the secretary to the king almoner the Deane of York, the archdeacon of Richmond, The Dean of Windsor and such other'. Then came the Knights of the Garter, the Chief Judges and Master of the Rolls, as well as the great lords of estate.

The Earl of Derby rode before the first horse of the queen's chariot. Two men rode the first two horses and four henchmen in black gowns rode the others. Beside each horse walked a person in a mourning hood. On each corner of the chariot was a 'white banner of our lady' denoting that Elizabeth died in childbirth. Eight ladies of honour rode behind the carriage on palfreys saddled in black velvet, with each horse being led by a man in a demi-black gown; more ladies followed in chariots. After the chariots followed the citizens of London, and then the king's servants bearing hundreds of torches.

As the procession made its way to Temple Bar, four to five thousand torches lined the streets. Thirty-seven virgins dressed in white linen and wearing circlets of green and white on their head held burning candles. As her coffin passed each church, its bells rang and the people sang. The citizens that were not in the procession lined the street, and when the queen's body reached Cheapside, thirty-seven more virgins holding candles stood along the street. Near Charing Cross, torchbearers from the crafts stood dressed in gowns and hoods in white. The procession ended in the churchyard of St Margaret's, where her coffin was removed and carried to its waiting hearse in Westminster Abbey. The nation was in mourning for their queen, said by one chronicler to be 'the most gracious and best beloved princesses in the world'.

List of Illustrations

York Family Tree © Kristie Dean
Maps © Elizabeth Milne at Lady White Art

1. Edward IV. (Courtesy of Ripon Cathedral)
2. Richard III. © The British Library on Flickr
3. Anne Neville and Richard III. (Courtesy of Yale University Art Gallery, Edwin Austin Abbey collection)
4. Elizabeth of York. From Edmund Lodge's *Portraits of Illustrious Personages*
5. Conisbrough Castle. © Sharon Bennett Connolly
6. La Tour Jeanne d'Arc, Rouen. © Kristie Dean
7. Usk Castle. © Paul Martin Remfry
8. Trim Castle, Ireland. © Kristie Dean
9. Interior, Trim Castle. © Kristie Dean
10. Coventry Chapter House Recreation. © The Continuum Group, used with permission.
11. Old St Paul's Cathedral. From Francis Bond's *Early Christian Architecture*, Creative Commons, Bhoeble
12. Worcester Cathedral. © Photograph by Kristie Dean. Reproduced by permission of the Chapter of Worcester Cathedral (U.K.)
13. Ludlow Castle. © Kristie Dean
14. Church of St Mary's and All Saints, Fotheringhay. © Kristie Dean
15. Raby Castle. © Kristie Dean
16. Church of St Mary's, Staindrop. © Kristie Dean
17. Neville Tomb, Staindrop. © Kristie Dean

18. Montgomery Castle. Cadw © Crown Copyright (2015)
19. Caister Castle. © Kristie Dean, used with permission
20. Tonbridge Castle. © Kristie Dean
21. Caister Castle. © Kristie Dean, used with permission
22. Berkhamsted Castle. © Linda Rollitt, Archivist, Berkhamsted Local History & Museum Society, and used with permission
23. Fotheringhay Castle ruins. © Kristie Dean
24. Richard III Tomb. © Will Johnston/Leicester Cathedral
25. Bosworth Battlefield Heritage Centre. © Richard Knox, used with permission
26. Cathédrale Saint-Maurice. © Kristie Dean
27. Château d'Angers. © Jan Geerling, www.microtoerisme.nl
28. Château d'Amboise. © L. de Serres
29. Château d'Amboise. Engraving by J. Androuet du Cerceau © Amboise, royal castle
30. Little Malvern Priory Church. © Kristie Dean
31. Cerne Abbey Guesthouse. © Kristie Dean, used with permission of the Fulford-Dobson family
32. Little Malvern Priory Church. © Kristie Dean
33. Pontefract Castle. © Kristie Dean, used with permission of Wakefield Council
34. Eastwell Tomb. © Kristie Dean
35. Raglan Castle. © Kristie Dean
36. Wigmore Castle. © Kristie Dean
37. Westminster Great Hall. © UK Parliament/Jessica Taylor
38. Church of St Mary's, Grafton Regis. © Kristie Dean
39. Tewkesbury Abbey. © Kristie Dean
40. Eltham Great Hall. © Kristie Dean, used with permission of Eltham Palace and Gardens, now run by English Heritage
41. Eltham Great Hall. © Kristie Dean, used with permission of Eltham Palace and Gardens, now run by English Heritage
42. Record Tower, Dublin Castle. © Kristie Dean, used with permission of Dublin Castle
43. Église de Notre Dame. © Kristie Dean
44. Tutbury Castle. © Kristie Dean, used with permission of Tutbury Castle
45. Warwick Castle. © Kristie Dean
46. Bruges Belfry. © Kristie Dean
47. Stadhuis, Damme. © Kristie Dean

Further Reading

A Collection of Ordinances and Regulations for the Government of the Royal Household (London: Society of Antiquaries, 1790)

Ashdown-Hill, J., *The Third Plantagenet: George, Duke of Clarence, Richard III's Brother* (Stroud: The History Press, 2014)

Attreed, Lorraine C., *The York House Books: 1461-1490, Volume One: House Books One and Two/Four* (Alan Sutton for Richard III and Yorkist History Trust, 1991)

Armstrong, C. A. J. (ed.), *The Usurpation of Richard III: Dominic Mancini* (Oxford: Clarendon Press, 1969)

Baldwin, David, *Elizabeth Woodville: Mother of the Princes in the Tower* (Stroud: The History Press, 2010)

Baldwin, D., *Richard III* (Stroud: Amberley, 2013)

Bruce, J. (ed.) *History of the Arrivall of Edward the Fourth in England and the Final Recovery of His Kingdom from Henry the Sixth, AD 1471* (London: Camden Society, 1838)

Bumpus, T. Francis, *The Cathedrals of England and Wales* (London: T. Werner Laurie, Ltd, 1929)

Burley, Peter, Michael Elliot and Harvey Watson, *The Battles of St Albans* (Barnsley, Pen and Sword Books, Ltd, 2007)

Butler, Lawrence, *Sandal Castle, Wakefield: The History and Archaeology of a Medieval Castle* (Wakefield Historical Publications, 1991)

Calendar of the Patent Rolls, Preserved in the Public Records Office: Edward IV, Edward V, Richard III, AD 1476-1485 (London: His Majesty's Stationery Office, 1901)

Caley, J., Sir Henry Ellis and Bulkeley Bandinel (ed.), *Monasticon*

Anglicanum: A New Edition: Volume the Sixth, Part One (London: T.G. March, 1849)

Castor, Helen, *Blood and Roses: One Family's Struggle and Triumph During the Tumultuous Wars of the Roses* (New York: HarperCollins, 2006)

Cheetham, Anthony, *The Life and Times of Richard III* (New York: Welcome Rain, 1998)

Clark, David. *Barnet-1471: Death of a Kingmaker* (Barnsley: Pen and Sword, 2007)

Colvin, H. M. (ed.), *The History of the King's Works: Volume I, The Middle Ages* (London: Her Majesty's Stationery Office, 1963)

Colvin, H. M. (ed.), *The History of the King's Works: Volume II, The Middle Ages* (London: Her Majesty's Stationery Office, 1963)

Colvin, H. M. (ed.), *The History of the King's Works: Volume III 1485-1600* (London: Her Majesty's Stationery Office, 1975)

Colvin, H. M. (ed.), *The History of the King's Works: Volume IV 1485-1600* (London: Her Majesty's Stationery Office, 1982)

Coss, Peter, *The Lady in Medieval England 1000-1500* (Stroud: Sutton Publishing, 1998)

Crawford, Anne, *The Yorkists: The History of a Dynasty* (London: Continuum, UK, 2007)

Crawford, Anne (ed.), *Letters of the Queens of England* (Stroud: Sutton Publishing, 1994)

Davies, J. (ed.), *An English Chronicle of the Reigns of Richard II, Henry IV, Henry V, and Henry VI: Written Before the Year 1471* (Oxford: Camden Society, 1856)

Davies, R. (ed.), *Extracts from the Municipal Records of the City of York, During the Reigns of Edward IV, Edward V, and Richard III: With Notes and an Appendix, Containing Some Accounts of the Celebration of Corpus Christi Festival at York* (London: J.B. Nichols and Son, 1843)

Dean, Gareth, *Medieval York* (Stroud: The History Press, 2008)

De Win, Paul, '"Danse Macabre" Around the Tomb and Bones of Margaret of York' *The Ricardian*, (Volume 15, 2005)

Dickens, A.G. (ed.), *The Courts of Europe: Politics, Patronage and Royalty, 1400-1800* (New York: Greenwich House, 1977)

Dockray, Keith and Peter Hammond, *Richard III: From*

Contemporary Chronicles, Letters and Records (Fonthill Media, 2013)

Edwards, Rhoda, *The Itinerary of King Richard III: 1483-1485* (London: Alan Sutton Publishing for The Richard III Society, 1983)

Ellis, Henry (ed.), *The New Chronicles of England and France in Two Parts: By Robert Fabyan* (London: for F. C. and J. Rivington, et al., 1811)

Ellis, Henry (ed.), *Three Books of Polydore Vergil's English History: Comprising the Reigns of Henry VI, Edward IV, and Richard III* (London: Camden Society, 1844)

Evans, Michael, *The Death of Kings: Royal Deaths in Medieval England* (New York, Hambledon Continuum, 2003)

Foard, Glenn and Anne Curry, *Bosworth 1485: A Battlefield Rediscovered* (Oxford: Oxbow Books, 2013)

Gairdner, J., *History of the Life and Reign of Richard III of England* (London: Longmans, Green and Co, 1879)

Gairdner, J. (ed.), *Letters and Papers Illustrative of the Reigns of Richard III and Henry VII: Volume 1* (London: Longman, et al., 1861)

Gairdner, J. (ed.), *The Paston Letters, A.D. 1422-1509: Volume II* (London: Chatto and Windus, 1904)

Gairdner, J. (ed.), *Three Fifteenth-Century Chronicles* (London: Camden Society, 1880)

Giles, J. (ed.), *The Chronicles of the White Rose of York* (London: James Bohn, 1864)

Gillingham, J. (ed.), *Richard III: A Medieval Kingship* (London: Collins and Brown Limited, 1993)

Goodchild, Steven, *Tewkesbury: Eclipse of the House of Lancaster – 1471* (Barnsley: Pen and Sword, 2005)

Gristwood, Sarah, *Blood Sisters: The Women Behind the Wars of the Roses* (London, HarperPress, 2012)

Hall, E., *Hall's Chronicle: The History of England During the Reign of Henry the Fourth and the Succeeding Monarchs, to the End of the Reign of Henry the Eighth* (London: Johnson, et al., 1809)

Halsted, C.A., *Richard III as Duke of Gloucester and King of England: Vol I* (London: Longman, et al., 1844)

Halsted, C.A., *Richard III as Duke of Gloucester and King of England: Vol II* (London: Longman, et al., 1844)

Hammond, P.W., Anne F. Sutton and Livia Visser-Fuchs, *The Reburial of Richard, Duke of York, 21-30 July 1476* (Richard III Society, 1996)

Harris, M.D., *The Coventry Leet Book* (London: Kegan Paul, Trench, Trübner, 1907)

Hastings, J.M., *St Stephen's Chapel* (Cambridge: Cambridge University Press, 1955)

Hawkyard, Alasdair, 'Sir John Fastolf's "Gret Mansion by Me Late Edified": Caister Castle, Norfolk'. *Of Mice and Men: Image, Belief and Regulation in Late Medieval England*. Linda Clark (ed.), (Boydell Press, 2005).

Hearne, Thomas (ed.), *The Itinerary of John Leland the Antiquary, in Nine Volumes* (Oxford: for James Fletcher and Joseph Pote, 1744)

Hicks, Michael, *The Wars of the Roses: 1455-1485* (Oxford: Osprey, 2003)

Hicks, Michael, *The Family of Richard III* (Stroud: Amberley, 2015)

Higginbotham, Susan, *The Woodvilles* (The History Press, 2012)

Hilton, Lisa, *Queens Consorts: England's Medieval Queens* (London: Weidenfeld and Nicolson, 2008)

Hindson, A.B. (ed.), *Calendar of State Papers and Manuscripts in the Archives and Collections of Milan: 1385-1618* (Great Britain: His Majesty's Stationery Office, 1912)

Hipshon, David, *Richard III* (New York: Routledge, 2011)

Holinshed, R., *Holinshed's Chronicles of England, Scotland and Ireland in Six Volumes: Vol. 3* (London, J. Johnson, et al., 1808)

Hommel, Luc, *Marguerite D'York ou La Duchesse Junon* (Librairie Hatchette, 1959)

Horrox, Rosemary and P.W. Hammond (eds.) *British Library Harleian Manuscript 433: Volume One* (Gloucester: Alan Sutton for Richard III Society, 1979)

Horrox, Rosemary and P.W. Hammond (eds.) *British Library Harleian Manuscript 433: Volume Two* (Gloucester: Alan Sutton for Richard III Society, 1980)

Hull, Lisa, *Britain's Medieval Castles* (Westport, Connecticut: Praeger, 2006)

Ingram, M., *Battle Story: Bosworth 1485* (Stroud: The History Press, 2012)

Jones, Michael and Malcolm G. Underwood, *The King's Mother: Lady Margaret Beaufort: Countess of Richmond and Derby* (Cambridge: Cambridge University Press, 1992)

Jones, Nigel, *Tower: An Epic History of the Tower of London* (London: Hutchinson, 2011)

Kelsall, Jane, *Humphrey, Duke of Gloucester, 1391-1447* (St Albans: The Fraternity of the Friends of St Albans Abbey, 2013)

Kendall, P.M. and Vincent Ilardi, *Dispatches of Milanese Ambassadors in France and Burgundy: Vol I: 1450-1460* (Athens, Ohio: Ohio University Press, 1970)

Kendall, P.M. and Vincent Ilardi, *Dispatches of Milanese Ambassadors in France and Burgundy: Vol II: 1460-1461* (Athens, Ohio: Ohio University Press, 1970)

Kendall, Paul M., *Richard the Third* (Garden City: Anchor Books, 1965)

Kendall, Paul M., *The Yorkist Age: Daily Life During the Wars of the Roses* (New York: W.W. Norton and Company, Inc., 1962)

Kingsford, C.L., *Chronicles of London* (Oxford: Clarendon Press, 1905)

Kingsford, C.L., *The Stonor Letters and Papers; ed. for the Royal Historical Society, from the Original Documents in the Public Records Office* (Ann Arbor: University of Michigan Library, 2006)

Legg, L. G. W. (ed.) *English Coronation Records* (Westminster: Archibald Constable and Company, Ltd., 1901)

Lepage, Jean-Denis G. G., *British Fortifications Through the Reign of Richard III: An Illustrated History* (London: McFarland & Company, Inc., 2012)

Letts, Malcolm Henry Ikin, Vaclav Sasek, and Gabriel Tetzel. *The Travels Of Leo Of Rozmital Through Germany, Flanders, England, France, Spain, Portugal, And Italy, 1465-1467.* (Cambridge, England: Hakluyt Society, 1957); eBook Collection (EBSCOhost). [Accessed 1 Aug. 2015]

Leyser, Henrietta, *Medieval Women: A Social History of Women in England 450-1500* (London: Weidenfeld and Nicholson, 2002)

Licence, Amy, *Anne Neville: Richard III's Tragic Queen* (Stroud: Amberley, 2013)

Licence, Amy, *Cecily Neville: Mother of Kings* (Stroud: Amberley, 2014)

Licence, Amy, *Elizabeth of York: The Forgotten Tudor Queen* (Stroud: Amberley, 2013)

Lulofs, Maaike, 'King Edward in Exile', *The Ricardian* (March 1974)

Madden, H.E. (ed.) *The Cely Papers: Selections from the Correspondence and Memoranda of the Cely Family, AD 1475-1488* (New York: Longmans, Green and Company, 1900)

McCarthy, Denis. *Dublin Castle: At the Heart of Irish History.* Government of Ireland, 2004.

More, Thomas (Lumby, J.R., ed.), *The History of King Richard III* (Cambridge: Cambridge University Press, 1883)

Morris, Marc, *Castle: A History of the Buildings that Shaped Medieval Britain* (London: Windmill Books, 2003)

Mortimer, Ian, *The Time Traveller's Guide to Medieval England: A Handbook for Visitors to the Fourteenth Century* (London: The Bodley Head, 2008)

Mount, Toni, *Everyday Life in Medieval London: From the Anglo-Saxons to the Tudors* (Stroud: Amberley Publishing, 2014)

Myers, A.R. (ed.) and David C. Douglas (General ed.), *English Historical Documents, Volume IV: 1327-1485* (New York: New York Press, 1969)

Myers, A.R. (ed.), *The Household of Edward IV* (Manchester: University of Manchester, 1959)

Newman, P.B., *Daily Life in the Middle Ages* (Jefferson, N.C.: McFarland and Company, 2001)

Nicolas, N. H. and Edward Tyrrell (eds.), *A Chronicle of London, From 1089 to 1483; Written in the Fifteenth Century* (London: Longman, et al.)

Nicolas, N. H. (ed.) *Privy Purse Expenses of Elizabeth of York: Wardrobe Accounts of Edward IV* (London: William Pickering, 1830)

Norton, Elizabeth, *Margaret Beaufort: Mother of the Tudor Dynasty* (Stroud: Amberley, 2011)

Okerlund, Arlene Naylor, *Elizabeth of York* (New York: Palgrave MacMillan, 2009)

O'Regan, Mary, 'Richard III and the Monks of Durham' *The Ricardian* (March 1978)

'Parishes: Little Malvern', in A History of the County of Worcester: Volume 3' (London, 1913), pp. 449-453 http://www.british-history.ac.uk/vch/worcs/vol3/pp449-453 [Accessed 17 July 2015]

Penn, Thomas, *Winter King: Henry VII and The Dawn of Tudor England* (New York: Simon & Schuster, 2011)

Pollard, A. J., *Richard III and the Princes in the Tower* (Godalming: Bramley Books, 1997)

Pollard, A. J., (ed.), *The North of England in the Age of Richard III* (New York: St Martin's Press, 1996)

Chipps Smith, Jeffrey, 'Portable Propaganda--Tapestries as Princely Metaphors at the Courts of Philip the Good and Charles the Bold', *Images of Rule: Issues of Interpretation* Vol. 48, No. 2 (Summer, 1989), pp. 123-129. Published by: College Art Association. http://www.jstor.org/stable/776961

Pronay, Nicholas and John Cox (eds.), *The Crowland Chronicle Continuations: 1459-1486* (London: Richard III and Yorkist History Trust, 1986)

Pryor, Francis, *Britain in the Middle Ages: An Archaeological History* (London: HarperCollins, 2006)

Reeves, Compton, *Pleasures and Pastimes in Medieval England* (Oxford: Oxford University Press, 1998)

Ross, Charles, *Edward IV* (Berkeley and Los Angeles: University of California Press, 1974)

Rosser, Gervase, *Medieval Westminster: 1200-1540* (Oxford: Clarendon Press, 1989)

Rous, J., *This Rol Was Laburd and Finished by Master John Rows of Warrewyk* (London: William Pickering, 1845)

Scoble, A.R., (ed.), *The Memoirs of Philip De Commines, Lord of Argenton: Containing the Histories of Louis XI and Charles VIII, King of France and Charles the Bold, Duke of Burgundy, Volume I* (London: Henry G. Bohn, 1855)

Scolfield, Cora L., *The Life and Reign of Edward the Fourth: King of England and of France and Lord of Ireland: Volumes One and Two* (Frank Cass and Co., Ltd., 1967)

Seward, Desmond, *The Wars of the Roses: Through the Lives of Five Men and Women of the Fifteenth Century* (New York: Penguin Books, 1995)

Schulte, Augustin Joseph. 'Churching of Women', *The Catholic Encyclopedia*, Vol. 3. (New York: Robert Appleton Company, 1908). [Accessed 9 Aug. 2015] <http://www.newadvent.org/cathen/03761a.htm>.

Steane, John, *The Archaeology of the Medieval English Monarchy* (London: B.T. Batsford, Ltd., 1993)

Sumption, Jonathan, *Pilgrimage: An Image of Mediaeval Religion* (Totown: Rowman and Littlefield, 1975)

Sutton, Anne and P.W. Hammond, *The Coronation of Richard III: The Extant Documents* (Gloucester: Alan Sutton, 1983)

Thomas, Arthur H., *The Great Chronicle of London* (Alan Sutton Publishing, 1983)

Vander Linden, Herman, *Itinéraires de Charles, Duc De Bourgogne, Marguerite D'York et Marie De Bourgogne* (1467-1477) (Brussels: Maurice Lamertin, 1936)

Weir, Alison, *Elizabeth of York: A Tudor Queen and Her World* (New York: Ballantine Books, 2013)

Weir, Alison, *The Princes in the Tower* (New York: Ballantine Books, 1992)

Weightman, Christine. *Margaret of York: Diabolical Duchess* (Stroud: Amberley, 2009)

Wilkinson, Josephine, *The Princes in the Tower* (Stroud: Amberley, 2014)

Wilkinson, Josephine, *Richard: The Young King To Be* (Stroud: Amberley Publishing, 2008)

Wolffe, Bertram, *Henry VI* (New Haven and London: Yale University Press, 1981)

Woolgar, C.M., *The Great Household in Late Medieval England* (New Haven and London: Yale University Press, 1999)